with the compliments
of the Author

ACTION IN THE LITURGY

BY THE SAME AUTHOR

PHILOSOPHICAL LIBRARY

Action in the Liturgy. 1952.
305 pp. & illustrations. $4.75.

Enchanted Island. 1952.
A rhapsody on Ischia.
200 pp. $3.00.

PANTHEON BOOKS

What is Christianity? 1953.

Art in the Early Church. 1947.
285 pp. of text & 500 illustrations. $6.50.

Religion of a Scientist. 1946.
Translations from Fechner.
281 pp. $3.50.

CHARLES SCRIBNER'S SONS

The Short Story of Jesus. 1943.
254 pp. $2.50.

OXFORD UNIVERSITY PRESS

Four volumes of Kierkegaardiana.

PRINCETON UNIVERSITY PRESS

Twelve volumes of Kierkegaardiana.

Action in the Liturgy

Essential and Unessential

by

WALTER LOWRIE

PHILOSOPHICAL LIBRARY
NEW YORK

15 E. 40TH STREET, NEW YORK

PRINTED IN THE UNITED STATES OF AMERICA

To the Memory of My Friend

ERNESTO BUONAIUTI

Professor in the University of Rome
A Brilliant Teacher of Christianity
Excommunicated by the Roman Curia
Silenced by Italian Fascism
Too Tardily Restored to His Cathedra
He Died on Easter Even
The 20th of April 1946
Having become more Catholic
The more He was Excommunicated

PREFACE

This book was finished in the spring of 1946, and since then it has not been changed. This will explain why it refers to no books published after that date—except my *Art in the Early Church,* which was in preparation at that time. The publication has been delayed for six years by several untoward circumstances, not the least of which was my preoccupation with the publication of other books and a long illness which followed that—*post hoc* and perhaps *propter hoc.* I was not impatient at this long delay, for the subject has a perennial interest, and I did not fear that somebody else might anticipate me by saying what I say before I had a chance to say it in print.

It may be doubted whether Joseph's "coat of many colors" was a thing of beauty. The Italian (and Spanish) expression, *di tutti colori* is very far from indicating praise. I have reason to fear that this book of mine, composed of addresses delivered on various occasions during the course of several years, dealing sometimes with essential things and sometimes with unessential, which were at once polemic and irenical, instructive and entertaining, may display too many violent contrasts of color. But I hear it claimed that a good thing is all the better for having many ingredients. "Not one but several quick-acting ingredients," is a phrase I hear on the radio in praise of a headache powder.

Many of these ingredients were compounded in a small volume, now included in this book, entitled *The Lord's Supper and the Liturgy,* which was published by Longmans in 1943. That was soon sold out, and I was cheered to see that the reaction was favorable, that it was read appreciatively by Presbyterians as well as by members of my own communion, by laymen as well as by clergymen, and was commended by Roman Catholics. This is not surprising, for though we are deplorably divided by what we do or leave undone in the performance of common worship, there really is not much room for disagreement about how men ought to behave in the house of God, i.e. about the rules of heavenly propriety, if such questions are candidly considered. In no other field of divinity is there so little contention as in that which is cultivated by serious students of the Liturgy. There the lion lies down with the lamb. Though I am told that nowadays nobody reads a preface, I am fain to remark here upon a fact, to which I call attention in the Bibliography at the end of this volume (where it is still more likely to be overlooked), that in the nine books I single out as the most important works on the Liturgy available in English there reigns such sweet agreement that one would hardly suspect that the authors belong to Churches so widely divided by their traditions as the Lutheran, the Reformed, the Free, the Anglican and the Roman Catholic. I was not dismayed to find also that my book was regarded as "both instructive and entertaining." It would not go far, I thought, if the instruction were accompanied by no spice.

What appears here as Chapter I reports the substance of several sermons preached in a little chapel in the Adirondacks where I have ministered off and on for fifty-six years. Chapter II contains an address delivered in 1942 at a Liturgical conference in the Diocese of New Jersey. To Part II, which contains most of the unessential ingredients, I have relegated the informal addresses made at the behest of my Bishop to a group of clergymen in the same diocese. They constituted the greater part of the volume published in 1943. That little book was barely sold out when I was called upon to lecture for a week on the same subject at the College of Preachers in Washington, and soon after to lead a Conference on the Liturgy held by the Catholic Club of New England at the Monastery of the Cowley Fathers in Cambridge. Almost the whole of Part I consists of a report of these lectures, which deal chiefly with what I call "essential action."

When I proposed to unite two books in one volume I had it in mind to add many illustrations. In fact, I have added only two, in order that the price may be kept as low as possible. For in the meantime I finished a big book on *Art in the Early Church*

(Pantheon Books, 1947) to which I can refer the readers of this small book. For although subjects like the celebration of the Eucharist and the use of ecclesiastical vestments are there treated very briefly in the text, they are amply illustrated by many of the five hundred pictures, and the index makes it possible to ferret out items in which the readers of this small book may be interested.

This is essentially an irenical book, and I observe now with dismay how polemical it may appear on the face of it. The fact that this book has had to wait so many years to find a publisher may be due to the fact that, in spite of my good intentions, I was sometimes incautious enough to tread on other people's toes. As, for example, in my disparaging remarks about the use of brass in our churches, which could not fail to annoy the purveyors of brass ornaments. The peregrinations of this book in manuscript form have been fantastic. I have known nothing like it in a rather wide experience of running from Pilate to Herod. I wonder now how I could have been so naive as to believe that this book, because of its peaceable intentions, would be acceptable to a Roman Catholic publisher like Sheed and Ward, or to the Westminster Press, which is the Presbyterian publishing house, or to the High Anglican house of Morehouse-Gorham. They all rejected it. Yet I dare to affirm, as Kierkegaard once did, that "I am only infinitely polemical"—not polemical against this or that person or communion. I am not willing to admit that satire is incompatible with edification, or that unessentials are always unimportant. How earnestly St. Paul pleaded for a ritual custom peculiar to Christianity, which required that men should pray with the head uncovered, and women with the head veiled. This seems a trivial matter, and the arguments St. Paul advanced are hard to understand; yet the divergent custom he condemned was condemned absolutely when in conclusion he said, "But if any man is disposed to be contentious, we have no such custom, neither have the Churches of God" (1 Cor. 11:16). Today, when the Churches of God are deplorably divided, and hardly any ritual custom can claim to be universal, the only possibility of union or reunion lies in the peaceable disposition *to act always in accordance with a maxim fit at all times to be law universal in the house of God*—especially with regard to such things as we regard as indifferent or unessential. This is what I mean by being a Catholic.

There was a good deal of repetition, of course, in the addresses I made on the same subject before different audiences. Many of them I have expunged, and for the rest I make no apology, for I know how necessary it is to reiterate precepts which are likely to be ignored however strongly they are emphasized.

I venture to hope that this little book, which because of its many ingredients I cannot fashion into a work of art, may by reason of its very blemishes prove endearing to some. But in such a book as this I can take no pride. Never before have I felt so keenly the pathos of Paul Válery's remark: *On ne finit jamais une œuvre—on l'abandonne.* Walter Lowrie

Princeton, April 26, 1946

NOTE

The date of the Preface apprises the reader that this book was completed six years before its publication (for reasons so fabulous that they will hardly be credited), and this explains why more recent books have not been noticed here, even in the Bibliography. I take (or create) this occasion to mention some of them with commendation.

First of all, I would say of *The Living Liturgy* by Professor J. Massey Shepherd, Jr. (New York, Oxford University Press, 1946), that being a collection of occasional utterances meant for popular consumption, it is so much like this book of mine that the two could not be published at the same time, and Professor Shepherd forestalled me. By emphasizing this likeness I do not mean to praise Shepherd's book faintly, for I account it better than mine, because it is written in a more sprightly style, and is likely to be more popular, because it is slighter in bulk and even with the addition of a subsequent book, *"At All Times and in All Places,"* is hardly half the size.

On the other hand, *The Shape of the Liturgy* (London, Dacre

Press, 1945) by Dom Gregory Dix is not only a better book than mine but a bigger one—more than twice as big. It is commonly said that this is an erudite book. It is all of that. But I would say of it rather that it is a very wise book. In my eyes, this book is so much better than mine that it quenched my zeal for publishing a book which might seem superfluous. Yet perhaps because it is not so obviously erudite, is smaller in size and more popular in form it may have a *raison d'être.*

The latest work on this subject is *The Christian Sacrifice,* by Professor W. Norman Pittenger, New York, Oxford University Press, 1951. Alas, this book belies the boast I made in the Preface that the Liturgy is a pacific field where "sweet agreement" reigns. For Pittenger's book is not in any proper sense of the word an historical study: it is thoroughly dogmatic, in my opinion narrowly dogmatic, and therefore is so incongruous with this book of mine that there is no place where it would be appropriate to deal with it, and because I cannot well ignore such a book I have had to make an extra place, an appendix, where I endeavor to refute it. But upon my book it has left an impression. For it challenged my assumption that the meaning of the Eucharist is sufficiently explained by the action of the Liturgy and provoked me to insert in Chapter IX some fourteen pages giving an account of the many rich meanings associated with this sacrament by the Fathers of the second century—an historical account which is very far from being dogmatic. Fr. Dix (on p. 6 of *The Shape of the Liturgy*) finds "many meanings" in the Eucharist and gives an account of them in Chapter IX, declaring at the beginning of this chapter that "communion is the deepest meaning of the rite." On the other hand, Pittenger, although on p. viii he professes to rely upon Dix's book, regards sacrifice as the deepest meaning of this rite, gives scant attention to other meanings, and hardly regards the Holy Communion as a sacrament.

It has been suggested that in a book which employs so many technical words the glossary might be printed at the beginning; but it will suffice, I think, if the reader is here apprised that there is a glossary at the end.

Walter Lowrie

CONTENTS

Part I.

ESSENTIAL ACTION IN THE LITURGY

Part II.

IMPORTANT NON-ESSENTIALS

ILLUSTRATIONS
(To be found at the end of the book)

Part I

Essential Action in the Liturgy

PRAYERS IN THE SACRISTY

BEFORE AND AFTER THE HOLY COMMUNION

O GOD, who in the person of thy dear Son has given us the true Bread from heaven, that a man may eat thereof and not die; Grant that we may so partake of the Sacrament of the Body and Blood of our Saviour Christ, that we may also be partakers of his resurrection, and inheritors of thine everlasting kingdom; Through the same Jesus Christ our Lord. *Amen.*

BLESSED be thou, O God, who hast deigned to feed us with the true manna which cometh down out of heaven; Evermore, we beseech thee, give us this Bread, the viaticum of our earthly journey, till we reach the kingdom where we shall neither hunger nor thirst any more; Through Jesus Christ our Lord. *Amen.*

CHAPTER ONE

THE LORD'S SUPPER IN THE NEW TESTAMENT

I am not proposing here to formulate a doctrine of the Eucharist, but would merely call attention to the historical data which are the stuff out of which a doctrine must be made, if it is to be a Christian doctrine. I have of course in mind the high estimation in which the Eucharist was held in the early Catholic Church from the second century on; but that presents a subject far too large for this little book, and I have referred to it only occasionally, to throw light backward upon the earliest conceptions. The data furnished by the New Testament, when they are viewed in this light, suffice to prove that Jesus and his Apostles understood the Sacrament sacramentally. But the Reformed branch of Protestantism, which derives from Zwingli and Calvin, formed so rational a notion of the Christian religion that it had no place in its philosophy for sacraments, which are superrational, as indeed all religion is; and because it arbitrarily refused to interpret the New Testament in the light of early Catholic thought and practice, the data furnished by the New Testament itself appeared so paradoxical that they had to be ignored.

1. THE FEEDING OF THE MULTITUDE

Neither in Catholic nor in Protestant circles has attention commonly been directed to the feeding of the multitude in the wilderness, which St. John regards as the origin of the Eucharist. This has been discounted as a harmless little invention of his. It is clear that he had a compelling reason for suppressing the

Last Supper, and therefore for tracing the Eucharist to this earlier beginning, because he was intent upon representing that Jesus died at the moment when the Paschal lamb was sacrificed, and therefore could not have eaten the Passover with his Apostles. But it is not probable that he invented the association of the Eucharist with the feeding of the multitude. It is certain that this notion was very widely entertained in the early Church. For in the earliest pictorial art in the Roman catacombs, which are far away from Ephesus, the Eucharist is commonly represented, not by a picture of Christ and his Apostles seated at table in the upper room, but by groups of Christians which by the presence of baskets of bread and the two fish are clearly associated with the multitude in the wilderness. It is well known that the fish by itself sufficed as a symbol, and that it was further endeared to the Church by the discovery that the Greek word for fish, ΙΧΘΥΣ, was an acrostic for Jesus Christ God's Son Saviour (ΙΗΣΟΥΣ ΧΡΙΣΤΟΣ ΘΕΟΥ ΥΙΟΣ ΣΩΤΗΡ). It is evident that the primary thought was not the acrostic, which must have required time and reflection, but the recognition that the feeding of the multitude was much more than a miracle, was in fact a sacrament, which Jesus imparted to the disciples who were zealous enough to follow him to Bethsaida when he was on the point of leaving them for good. It was a pledge which was comforting to him, and no less effective for the fact that the multitude did not fully understand it, a pledge that those who were his guests at this symbolical banquet would sit down with the Son of Man at the celestial banquet in the Kingdom of God. Because the people could not understand all that Jesus meant, it is evident that he regarded it as a sacrament in the strictest sense, a sacrament which was effective *ex opere operato,* that is, not merely as an intelligible symbol, and not merely in the measure in which it was intellectually understood.

This connection, therefore, to which St. John calls attention is important because it determines the nature of a sacrament. The most specific proof that it was not his invention is furnished by the fact that the symbol of the fish appears in a fully developed form in the Crypt of Lucina (in the Catacomb of Calixtus), which is ascribed to the first decade of the second century, and is thus earlier than any literary allusion to the Fourth Gospel, earlier perhaps than the date when that Gospel was written.

The fact that under this symbol the Eucharist was very frequently depicted in the catacombs shows that it was regarded as a pledge of Eternal Life, just as St. John regarded it in the sixth chapter of his Gospel. It was this which made it appropriate for the adornment of Christian cemeteries, and made it natural also for Christians to celebrate the Eucharist there, not as a sacrifice offered in suffrage of the departed, but as an act of communion with the living dead. In the *Cappella greca* (Catacomb of Sta. Priscilla) there is a fresco, as early as the one mentioned above, which represents a family group of seven persons, men and women, celebrating the Lord's Supper in this very place. It depicts with extraordinary vividness the act of breaking the loaf, and the character of the sacrament is further defined by the two symbolic fish.

In a little book I have just finished, on "The Short Story of Jesus," I described quite fully, as I cannot do here, the historical situation which defines the feeding of the multitude as an eschatological sacrament; and I sought to show that only as sacraments are regarded with a view to "the last things" are they entirely free from the equivocation which threatens to overthrow the nature of a sacrament, either by treating it as the self-same thing which is promised, or by conceiving of it as an ineffectual symbol. The eschatological reference was preserved essentially even when the apocalyptic picture was discarded and the expectation of the coming of the Kingdom of God became less vivid. According to the Synoptic Gospels, Jesus himself used Eternal Life as an equivalent for the Kingdom of God. The apocalyptic picture was preserved essentially only so long as the Eucharist was consciously oriented towards the future, as it was, for example in the exclamation, *Maranatha* (O Lord, come!), which we find in the earliest liturgical document, contained in the "Teaching of the Twelve Apostles," and in St. Ignatius' description of this sacrament as "the elixir of eternal life" or "the antidote of death." Even St. John, who was inclined to suppress the more definite expressions of eschatology, associated with the Eucharist the hope of the *resurrection* of the dead. The association of Eternal Life with the Eucharist was the primary significance it had for early Catholicism, and we cannot now afford to ignore it. It is ominous that in our liturgy the only definite reference to the last things is the brief phrase, "until he come," which we take from St. Paul.

Of course the Fish, as it was understood in the Church, was much more than a reminiscence of the feeding of the multitude, and meant also much more than a pledge of life after death; for it meant that Christians partake of Christ himself as their celestial food, their "supersensual" bread, to use the word the Latin version uses in the fourth petition of the Lord's Prayer. This "much more" is expressed emphatically in the long discourse which, according to the Fourth Gospel, followed the feeding of the multitude; for there St. John uses the words "flesh and blood," and thereby betrays the fact that the explanation of the Eucharist must be sought in the Last Supper, where the words, "my body," "my blood," were first pronounced. In the wilderness there was no wine to serve as the symbol of Christ's blood, and the fresco above mentioned in the Crypt of Lucina was likewise drawing from the account of the Lord's Supper when it represented flasks of wine shimmering through the baskets of bread.

The Catholic liturgies may be justified in discarding any reference to the banquet in the wilderness, except the phrase which describes Christ as "looking up to heaven" when he broke and blessed the bread, a phrase which none of the accounts of the Last Supper contain, although it is a reasonable assumption that this heavenly glance was characteristic of Jesus and explains in part why his way of breaking the bread was so memorable that the risen Lord "was known in the breaking of bread," and why the phrase *fractio panis,* though it describes a common act, was never used except to denote the Eucharist.

Of course the similarity of Christ's action in the wilderness and at the Last Supper is too striking to be ignored. And it is interesting to note that the various accounts we have of each of these events alternate in the same way between the use of the word "blest" and its equivalent "gave thanks." This surely should make it clear to everyone that the Church in using the word "blessing" merely put in a Hebrew form the thought which was more naturally expressed by the word "thanksgiving." The Jews "blest" God for their daily bread, and thereby, as they conceived it, the food was sanctified. The formula was, not "Bless, O God, this food," but "Blessed be thou, O God." Accordingly, the Greek-speaking Christians, when they spoke of "giving thanks," also conceived that thereby the food was sanctified—thanksgivingized or eucharisticized is an expression used by Justin Martyr. St. Paul (Rom. 14:6) represents that even food which might be ceremonially unclean is sanctified by the prayer of thanksgiving. Much misapprehension of the Eucharist, and much of our dissension about it, might be avoided if all were to accept the self-evident proposition that the prayer by which Jesus consecrated the sacrament in the wilderness and at the Last Supper was the ordinary prayer of thanksgiving at meals, which therefore did not have the express intention of transmuting the bread and wine into something different, but of consecrating it as an efficacious sacrament. A necessary inference is that the early Catholic Church, intending to do what the Lord did, conceived that the Sacrament was consecrated by the Eucharistic prayer as a whole.

The story of the Lord's first appearance to Peter and the other disciples in Galilee, which we now find at the end of the Fourth Gospel, contains an evident allusion to the feeding of the multitude, and hence to the Eucharist, when it relates (Jn. 21:13) that Jesus "taketh the bread and giveth them, and the fish likewise." The story of the two disciples at Emmaus who recognized the Lord by his way of breaking the loaf and giving thanks, is also of course an allusion to the Eucharist, but it might have been a reminder of many a meal they had shared with Jesus. The mention of the fish in the other instance is under the circumstances so natural that it cannot very plausibly be regarded as an idiosyncrasy of St. John. It is evident that this story, which was tardily added to the Fourth Gospel, is much more in keeping with the Synoptic tradition, and by some it is regarded as the missing conclusion of St. Mark's Gospel.

2. THE LAST SUPPER

The Catholic liturgies are undoubtedly right in treating the Last Supper as the occasion when Jesus instituted what the Church called the Lord's Supper. St. Paul (1 Cor. 11:23–26) refers expressly to that supper as the norm of the Eucharist. It was then that the sacrament celebrated in the wilderness received a new and profounder meaning. But as the liturgies were never scrupulous about reciting exactly any one of the four accounts of the Last Supper, it is evident that they did not regard the exact words as necessary for the effective consecration of the sacrament.

Of all the accounts of the Last Supper, that of St. Mark is the most instructive and the most primitive, owing to the fact that St. Paul's account, though it is earlier, was influenced by the current liturgical practice. Inasmuch as St. Paul was proposing a norm for the celebration of the Eucharist in the Church, it was natural for him to report our Lord's words in the form in which the Church actually repeated them, to make it clear that the body and blood which the communicants received were given *for them* personally, and it was natural to assume that what the Church did as a matter of course Christ had expressly commanded his disciples to do. Mark's account is evidently more primitive when he reports that Jesus said simply (but under the circumstances how eloquently!), "This is my body," and that of the cup he said, "This is my blood of the covenant, which is shed for many." In our liturgy we rightly say "for you," but we do not neglect the "many." This word was very important to Jesus, for he could not be satisfied to think that his life was given only for the twelve men who sat with him at the table. To his great and endless comfort he had found this word in Isaiah (53:11, 12): God's righteous servant was by his knowledge to justify *many* and to bear the sins of *many.* This was an answer to the query, "Are there few that be saved?" He had this prophecy in mind when he said (Mk. 10:45), "The Son of Man came to give his life a ransom for many." Because of these associations the word "many" is rightly included in our liturgy, and we may be glad to have this express indication of the sacrificial background of the Eucharist.

Another singularity in St. Mark's account is the surprising statement that only *after* they had all drunk of the cup did Jesus tell his disciples what it meant. We might say in St. Paul's phrase that they drank the wine "without discerning" the Lord's blood. But as it was in the wilderness, so it was in this instance: the sacrament was effective even though they did not understand it. But more astonishing is the inference we must draw from this: that the words, "This is my blood" (and, by parity of reasoning, "This is my body") were not the formula which consecrated the first Eucharist, seeing that the wine was drunk before these words were pronounced, and that consequently they cannot well be regarded as essential for the consecration of subsequent Eucharists.

There may have been a special reason for not declaring the significance of the cup *before* the disciples had drunk of it; for the meaning Jesus attached to it was *blood*—and blood was tabu. It was prohibited to all men, for it was proscribed in the law announced to Noah (Gen. 9:4); and no scruple was so deeply ingrained in the Jewish mind as was the prohibition to eat flesh in which the blood remained. Eating *kosher* means substantially this. The Law explained that the *life* of the animal was in the blood. *That* therefore must be returned to God as a libation, lest the life of another creature be devoured by man. We can understand therefore the report of St. John that "many of the disciples said, This is a hard saying—who can hear it?" But we can understand too that when this scruple was overcome, the disciples would find inexpressible comfort in the thought that they were partaking not of Christ's body only, but of his *life*. This, I suppose, is what Dom Damasus Winzen meant when at our Liturgical Conference of the past summer in the Diocese of New Jersey, he remarked cursorily that the Liturgical Reform in the Church of Rome had enriched the conception of the Eucharist by requiring men to dwell upon the Old Testament meaning of such words as "blood." Yet I hear that among our clergy there are finely fibered souls who shrink from this word and would eliminate it from the Liturgy as an offense to refined sensibilities. We who take comfort in the thought of sharing the life of Christ must be reluctant to discard this word, and dubious about the Roman custom of denying the cup to the laity—even if there are practical reasons for it, which are now felt in Protestant circles. Yet rather than offer the people unfermented grape juice and abolish the common cup as the symbol of fellowship, I should prefer to interpret, rather disingenuously, St. Paul's words, "as often as ye eat this bread *or* drink this cup," as a warrant for communicating the people in one kind.

3. TRADITION OF THE UPPER ROOM

We have seen in §1 that St. John suppressed the Synoptic tradition of the Last Supper in the "upper room" because this story suggested too evidently that Jesus had lived to eat the Passover with his disciples, and collided therefore with his favorite notion that "the Lamb of God which taketh away the sin of the world" (Jn. 1:29) was put to death before the Passover meal, at the hour when the paschal lamb was sacrificed. But the Synoptic tradition of the Last Supper, together with other stories about the "upper room," was too vivid to be ignored. It was confirmed by St. Paul (1 Cor. 11:23-26), and St. John himself inadvertently substantiates it by the stories he related at the end of his Gospel (20:19-29) about the appearances of the risen Lord. These stories, if they have any historical foundation, must have been derived from the tradition current in Jerusalem. There the "large upper room" was regarded as a sacred spot, not only because of the celebration of the Last Supper, but also because it was the first meeting place of the Church, especially for the celebration of the Lord's Supper, and, according to the tradition preserved by St. John, it was the place where Christ twice appeared to his disciples. The Church of Zion, in which the upper room was incorporated after the days of Constantine, preserved also the tradition that here occurred the manifestation of Christ as Spirit on the Day of Pentecost.

So soon as we recognize that these stories which are told by St. John referred originally to the "upper room," we perceive that they are relevant to the Eucharist and were used by him to substantiate the doctrine of the real presence of Christ in the Sacrament.

Inasmuch as the special significance of these Johannine stories has not often been observed, and as the intended implications are not obvious to readers who are unacquainted with the early traditions, I point them out here.

"When it was evening on that day," the very day of the Resurrection, the first day of the week, i.e. Sunday, the Lord's Day, the day on which ever afterwards the Church celebrated the Lord's Supper as its principal and peculiar act of worship, and even on the first Easter evening could celebrate it in the faith that the Lord was risen, because early in the morning of that same day Mary Magdalene, Simon Peter, and the "other disciple," had beheld the empty tomb and "believed," Mary having also a baffling but convincing vision of the Lord, whom she hailed as "Rabboni" (Jn. 20:1-18), when the doors were shut "for fear of the Jews," and not for other reason only, but as the church doors were always shut against the outside world when the Church was assembled, not with a missionary aim, but to enjoy the peculiar privilege of the people of God—just as today the Mass of the Faithful in some of the Eastern Liturgies begins with the announcement of the deacon, "the doors! the doors! recognize one another. Let none but the faithful remain."

On this occasion the disciples had gathered together for just such a fellowship meal as they had often eaten with Jesus when he himself blessed the food, broke the loaf, and pronounced the greeting of peace. They met now in faith that the Lord lived, but not in the faith that he was with them. But "Jesus came and stood in the midst of them, and saith unto them, Peace be unto you, and when he had said this he showed them his hands and his side." Thus the real presence of Christ in the Eucharist is attested—just as the discourse reported in Jn. 6:48-56 attests the reality of the "flesh and blood," *flesh* being so crude a word that even the disciples were repelled, and many are repelled today, if they have not learned what Oskar Goldberg means by *Die Wirklichkeit der Hebräer*. "He breathed on them and saith unto them, Receive ye the Holy Spirit." The Lord's breath (*pneuma*) is the Spirit which conveys power.

The same experience was repeated "after eight days," i.e. on the next Lord's Day, when "doubting" Thomas was present. It is not to be supposed that Thomas separated himself from the other Apostles and from the Church by doubting the Lord's resurrection and his divinity, for in that case he would not have been with them at the sacred supper. Like the other Apostles in the first instance, he doubted the real presence of Christ in the Sacrament. Of this he was given then an even more crass demonstration, being told to thrust his finger into the nail holes in the Lord's hands and his hand into the wound in his side, and at once he identified the apparition by exclaiming, "My Lord and my God"—as Mary had identified the apparition in the garden by exclaiming, Rabboni.

This was the last materialization (*sit venia verbo*) of the risen Lord in Jerusalem. But his presence in the Eucharist was henceforth no less real for being invisible. This is the point of the saying, "Because thou hast seen me, thou hast believed: blessed are they that have not seen and yet have believed."

In this connection we must not forget that by the phrase "breaking of bread" the appearance of Jesus to the two disciples on the way to Emmaus (Lk. 24:13-35) was associated with the Eucharist, and that so also was his appearance at the sea of Tiberias (Jn. 21), where he ate with the disciples, partaking with them of a fish, which was the most abbreviated symbol of the Eucharist—as a reminiscence in the first place of the feeding of the multitude, and secondarily as the interpretation of the acrostic contained in ΙΧΘΥΣ, the Greek word for fish: Jesus Christ God's Son Saviour.

4. THE BREAKING OF BREAD

When we recognize that "the breaking of bread" was used only to indicate the Eucharist, we can find significant references to this sacrament in the Acts of the Apostles. It is significant that it was said of the multitudes which were brought into the Church on the day of Pentecost that "they continued steadfastly in the Apostles' teaching, in fellowship (or communion), in the breaking of bread, and the prayers" (Acts 2:42). It is evident that the practice of breaking bread was thoroughly established in the Church immediately after the Resurrection, and it appears from verse 46 that it was practiced daily in the homes, at a time when there was no common meeting place but the Temple. As it was commonly called the Lord's Supper, it must have been celebrated in the evening, as it was in fact for several centuries, or at least until the time when Pliny in his letter to Trajan described it as a "harmless meal" which the Christians shared in the evening. How the Lord's Supper became an early breakfast (to use the spiteful phrase invented to disparge early communions in the Church of England) is suggested by Acts 20:7 ff., which describes how at Troas the Apostle Paul talked so long that, what with the accident to Eutychus, it was nearly day when they got to the point of breaking bread. But that was an exception, and it is only significant as indicating that eventually the Eucharist was not, as we are prone to think, shifted *back* from the evening following the Lord's Day to the morning of that day, but was simply postponed from the eve of the day, which according to Jewish custom was regarded as the beginning, to an early hour the following morning, the hour on the first day of the week when the Lord rose from the dead.

I believe it was the rule in early times to celebrate the Lord's Supper more especially on the Lord's Day. In the sixth century there was no concordant rule for the whole Church. It seems likely that only in Rome was the Eucharist celebrated every day, whereas in the East it was celebrated also on Wednesdays and Fridays, in some places also on the Sabbath, and when there was the "birthday" of a martyr. It must not be supposed that in the sixth century the present Roman rule prevailed which expects every presbyter to celebrate daily the Holy Mysteries; for principally it was the bishop who celebrated, he alone among the clergy was spoken of as a priest. The early Catholic rule that *only* the bishop might celebrate had not yet been altogether forgotten, and even to this day the institution of the "stations" remains to testify to the ideal which was cherished, that the

Eucharist at which the bishop presided, now in one church, now in another, was a meeting of the whole Church. Of the divergent customs which St. Jerome noticed in his time, he says, "I neither condemn nor approve; each has reasons on its side" (*Epist. ad Pammach.* 4). But he did not contemplate the possibility that there ever might be a time or place where the Eucharist would not be celebrated on every Lord's Day as the one distinctive expression of Christian faith and worship. The effort to preserve or to restore a practice which so well deserves to be universal cannot be regarded as trivial. In the Church of Rome the "Dominical precept," i. e. the obligation to attend Mass on every Lord's Day, is not only the surest means of attaching the people to the whole Catholic tradition, but it has the immense advantage of insuring that all the people, even though they do not always communicate, are constantly exposed to the most profound religious impressions. It is only too evident today that Protestantism can give no compelling reason for going to church when sermons and prayers are all it has to offer. Our case is not much better, unless we will insist that all candidates for confirmation be instructed that the failure to assist at the Eucharist on every Lord's Day is a mortal sin, unless there is a reasonable impediment.

The custom of celebrating the Holy Communion in the evening implies that there was no obligation to fast before it. That is all the more evident at the time when it was the conclusion of a common meal or an agape. We learn from St. Paul (1 Cor. 11:20-22, 31, 34) that because the common meal was abused by selfishness and gluttony and even drunkenness, the people were urged to eat at home, *before* coming to the Lord's Supper. We must remember also that in early times the bread and wine were not distributed in minute quantities as they are with us. The early fresco in the *Cappella greca* already referred to represents that the seven persons present were about to share a large loaf, which was quite enough to break a fast.

We cannot afford to ignore the singular case of the breaking of bread which is recorded in Acts 27:33-36. This was a case of an early communion, "when the day was coming on," also a communion in one kind, and a sacrament of which St. Paul partook alone. There on a ship which seemed about to sink the Apostle solemnly celebrated the Eucharist: "When he had taken bread, he gave thanks to God in the presence of all, and he brake it, and began to eat." He did not receive the Sacrament as a viaticum when he was hopeless of saving his life, but as an encouragement to all the ship's company, and as a pledge that "there shall not a hair perish from the head of any of you." This example of the Apostle must restrain us from denouncing absolutely any exception to common custom which is prompted and justified by circumstances. In view of this example it does not seem to me intolerable to accept Harnack's interpretation of a phrase of Justin Martyr which seems to indicate that in his time, the middle of the second century, the Eucharist was not infrequently celebrated with bread and water.

But neither of these cases suggests that the Sacrament was treated as a mere symbol. To anything approaching a Zwinglian notion of the Lord's Supper, which is all but universal among American Protestants of the Reformed branch, St. Paul stands squarely opposed with his sacramental conception of the Sacrament. Not only is it "a communion of the body and blood of Christ" (1 Cor. 10:16), which makes the Church one body, but to partake of it unworthily is to be "guilty of the body and blood of the Lord," and one who does not "discern the Lord's body," i. e. fails to discriminate it from ordinary food, "eats and drinks condemnation to himself." St. Paul conceived the consequences of this much more materially than we are inclined to do, when he attributed to this abuse of the Sacrament the sickness of many and the death of some.

5. THE SACRIFICE

When we speak of the Eucharist as a sacrifice we must speak with great circumspection. To affirm bluntly that it is a sacrifice may not be much wiser than to deny it.

We had best begin by considering some of the sacrificial aspects of the Eucharist which are accidental rather than essential. And I would remark at the outset that to associate the idea of Christian priesthood exclusively with the sacrifice of the

Eucharist is clearly not Scriptural. The priesthood of all believers is surely not adequately exemplified by "assisting" at the Mass, even when the people are encouraged to take a more active part in it than they commonly do. And as for the Christian ministry, the only place where St. Paul regards it as a sacerdotal ministry is Romans 16:15, where he had in mind the sublime function of preaching the Gospel: "ministering as a priest (*ierougounta*) the Gospel of God."

I have remarked elsewhere in this book that when we translate the word *koinonia* sometimes as "communion" and sometimes as "fellowship" we obscure the sacramental significance of Christian giving or sharing, and that we have completely lost the sacrificial meaning of it when we translate it by "contribution" or "distribution." Christian giving is an act of communion, a practical expression of the communion we enjoy in the Eucharist. For this reason it properly has its place in the Liturgy, and the very name offertory indicates that it has the character of sacrifice. The poor are the altar of the Church, was the dictum of early Catholicism. St. Paul also regarded all such expressions of communion or fellowship as "offerings" (Acts 24:17), and that he used this word in a definitely sacrificial sense is shown by the phrase he employed in thanking the Christians in Philippi for the gifts they had sent to him (Phil. 4:18): "an odor of a sweet smell, a sacrifice acceptable, well-pleasing to God." We must remember that the word communion as it was used of the Sacrament had ultimately a sacrificial reference, as we see by the analogy St. Paul draws between this and the "communion" the Jews had, and even the heathen had, in their sacrifices (1 Cor. 10:16-21). But hardly is there any religious practice which has not as its remote background a sacrificial idea. The common blessing at meals, which Jesus pronounced at the Last Supper, can be traced to an ancient sacrificial custom, to which allusion is made in 1 Samuel 9:13: "For the people will not eat until he [Samuel] come, because he doth bless the sacrifice." Our Lord's saying (Mt. 5:23, 24), "If thou art offering thy gift at the altar, and there rememberest that thy brother hath aught against thee, leave there thy gift before the altar, and go by thy way; first be reconciled to thy brother, and then come and offer thy gift," was uttered with a view to the ritual of the Temple, but when it was read in the Gospel it had a pungent application to Christian practice, and it might well be used as an offertory sentence.

We see how natural it was, how inevitable it was, and how reasonable, that this whole range of sacrificial ideas should cluster about the sacrifice of Christ, and therefore become associated with the Liturgy. In the Old Testament we see that the advance from the cruder practice of animal sacrifice was not made by discarding the sacrificial idea but by sublimating it—as in the saying, "The sacrifices of God are a broken spirit."

In the "Teaching of the Twelve Apostles," about the end of the first century, the Eucharist is called, "your sacrifice." More than a century later, by St. Cyprian of Carthage, the word sacrifice was for the first time definitely associated with the body and blood of Christ which were offered in the Eucharist. This may be justified by St. Paul's saying, "Christ our Passover is sacrificed for us," but this hardly justifies us in treating the Eucharist as a *repetition* of Christ's sacrifice, and in view of the scandalous traffic in masses which grew up in the Middle Ages, we cannot wonder that all the Protestant leaders, Lutherans no less than Calvinists, took a short cut to reform by discarding every notion of sacrifice which had become associated with the Liturgy. For this reason Luther discarded the whole of the Canon, except the words of institution; and the Church of England not only followed him in this but put into the small vestige of the Canon which remained the strongest possible repudiation of the Roman notion of the sacrifice of the Mass. We still have these words in the American Liturgy: "Who made there (by his one oblation of himself once offered) a full, perfect, and sufficient sacrifice, oblation and satisfaction for the sins of the whole world." I cannot regret that we have these strong words in our liturgy, for they are true. The Epistle to the Hebrews (10:12, 14) affirms that Christ "offered one sacrifice for sins for ever," and that "he did this once for all." St. Peter also affirms (1 Pet. 3:18) that "he suffered once." We cannot doubt that St. Paul shared this faith—and yet he was inconsistent enough to think that other sacrifices were needed, to adjure his fellow-Christians to present their bodies a "living sacrifice," and in the end he was inconsistent enough to present his body a *dead* sacrifice. Contemplating his approaching martyrdom he was bold enough to say (Col. 1:24), "I fill up on my part that which was lacking in the afflictions of Christ," and to the Philippians (2:17), "If I be poured out as a libation upon the sacrifice and service (liturgy) of your faith."

Is it not evident that in speaking about the Eucharist as a sacrifice we must be very circumspect? We must be at least as circumspect as Roman scholars are inclined to be today. I reflect the well-considered opinion of one of them when I protest against the notion that it is the human priest who offers Christ at the altar. "Christ," said he, "is never to be treated as an *object*: the *Kyrios*, the Lord of glory, is always the *subject*, the active agent, whether it be in the Eucharist or in any other activity of the Church. It is he who gives himself, whether as sacrament or as sacrifice."

CHAPTER TWO

ESSENTIAL ASPECTS OF THE LITURGY

This chapter covers briefly the same ground I must traverse more slowly in the next thirteen chapters, to the end of Part I. The ground could not well be different, for in both cases it is the Liturgy we are dealing with, and that prescribes a definite order. The difference is that here I dwell upon "aspects" of the Liturgy, and there upon "action"—"essential aspects" and "essential action." The same ground is traversed again in Part II; but because the action contemplated there is only ritual action or ceremonial, I have emphatically described it as "unessential."

1. DOMUS ECCLESIAE

It is perhaps a truism that the form of church edifice, the so-called basilica, which was adopted by the Christians as soon as they were free to erect buildings appropriate to their cult, was precisely adapted to house the Church in the performance of its most distinctive act of worship, the celebration of the Eucharist. It was not like the pagan temples in front of which the people stood to behold a priest perform a sacrifice in their behalf. It has been said cleverly that it was a peristyle temple turned outside in. And yet it was not simply an auditorium (a *schola*), although on account of its flat ceiling it was a good auditorium, and the bishop's chair in the middle of the apse was in a position where he could be seen and heard. Neither was it a *triclinium* (dining hall), for though the faithful "came together into one place" to partake of the Lord's Supper, it was a symbolical meal, and when they received the Sacrament they heard also God's

Word read and preached, and they joined in the prayers of thanksgiving and supplication. Accordingly, the Holy Table, though inconsiderable in size, was the most observable feature of this house of the Church, and it stood in the most important position, either on the chord of the apse or in front of that, so that the people did in fact surround it, not indiscriminately, however, as the pagans commonly surrounded their altars, but in such a way as to distinguish diversities of administration (to use St. Paul's phrase), singling out for special honor those who were accounted worthy of occupying "the chief seats" at table, that is, the whole group of office-bearers, who therefore might be described as "chief-seaters," as they were called invidiously by Hermas, or, more commonly, as "those about the altar." Because this discrimination of rank in the Church was the Christian tradition the Emperor Constantine did not succeed in permanently putting over his half-pagan preference for churches built on a central plan with the altar in the middle.

But if it is a truism that the people surrounded the Holy Table, it cannot be said that we have been alert to draw the obvious inference from the well known form of the church edifice and the position of its altar, and to argue backward with the aim of discovering the essential character of the Christian cult and the Christian ministry, which are clearly expressed by this arrangement.

The most illuminating name bestowed in ancient times upon the church building was *domus ecclesiae,* the house of the Church, or perhaps it would be better translated by the home of the Church, for in the basilica the Church was obviously at home and perfectly expressed its true nature. I lay the more stress upon this name because not long ago I heard a visiting speaker affirm to the Trenton Clericus that the church edifice was properly called "the house of bread" to indicate that it was designed expressly for the reservation and adoration of the Blessed Sacrament. Now it may be true that Bethlehem means house of bread, but it is quite as likely that it means house of war—and whatever it means, it is perfectly certain that it never was used as a name for the church. On the other hand, what I have to say here is summarily expressed by the ancient name *domus ecclesiae*. Let us call this house, if you will, a temple—not by any means with the thought of attaching to it a pagan significance, but in view of the ambiguity of all of our modern tongues, which have only one word for both Church and church, i. e. for the congregation of God's people and for the building which houses it. Our temples then are built expressly to enshrine—what? The *Ecclesia*, the mystical body of Christ, his Church. The proponents of Liturgical Reform in the Church of Rome lay the utmost emphasis upon this description of the Church, insisting that it implies hearty participation of the people in the action of the Mass, and also in the Catholic action which must be performed outside the temple after the people have been dismissed with the *Ite, missa est*.

I do not know if in all of Christian art there is to be found a more vivid representation of the hearty participation of the people in the action of the Mass than you may see in the ivory relief of the eleventh century which Dean Ladd used as the frontispiece of his little book, *Prayer Book Interleaves*. But, unforunately Dr. Ladd misconceived the meaning of this picture. I have reproduced it in my recent book on early Christian art, Plate 128. The people united heartily but silently in the prayer of the priest, and were vocal only when in "the dialogue of the Mass" it was their place to respond. In the Church of Rome the reformers of today have put themselves to prodigious pains to prompt the people to take their part in the dialogue. We, because we recite the Liturgy in the vernacular, have fortunately no need to instruct the people how to make the responses, but only to prompt them to do this more heartily, more intelligently, and, when the occasion calls for it, to do it musically. There is nothing I propose to say here which would not be appropriate as instruction for the people, for I say nothing that sounds erudite—and, after all, the people are not always less intelligent than their priests.

From what I have already said it will be obvious why the Liturgical Reform has made much of the proper position of the altar and the propriety of having the priest face the people. Because this position is maintained in all the early basilicas in Rome it cannot seem to Roman Catholics revolutionary. And yet even for them it is not a reform which is easily accomplished, and though it is the first item in the program of the reformers, it may be the last to be put generally into execution. It is still more difficult for us, and although perhaps it is still more necessary with a view to an ecumenical understanding, I am not pressing here this practical reform, but am only indicating what is the right position, for the sake of a right understanding of the communal character of the Liturgy. Without taking the trouble to move the altar away from the wall, the people may be led to recognize that ideally they are gathered about the Lord's Table. Perhaps only when we unite with Presbyterians can this and other desirable reforms be brought about.

2. INTROIBO

I speak first of a feature of the Mass which is not found in our Prayer Book, though we often use it, and use it unfortunately as if it were not properly a part of the Mass but a preparation for it, the *private* preparation of the celebrant and the server. So it was regarded in the Roman Church at the time of the Protestant Reformation, and for this reason it was excluded from our Prayer Book. Private prayers, it was thought quite rightly, had best be said in the sacristy. Conversely, everything that is said and done at the altar in view of the people implies the participation of the congregation. It is true that this introduction is not a very ancient feature of the Liturgy. An introduction involving confession and absolution could not have been used so long as the distinction was plainly marked between the *Missa Catechumenorum* and the *Missa Fidelium.* Outsiders who had not yet resolved to be baptized might well be permitted to hear the reading and the preaching of God's word, but they could not be expected to unite in the prayers and to recite the Creed, still less to make confession of their sins and expect absolution. When this distinction was practically abolished by the fact that everybody in Christendom was baptized, nothing could be more natural and nothing more appropriate than to begin the Mass with a humble approach and a confession of sin, such as we use at the beginning of Morning and Evening

Prayer, with the just apprehension that we need to prepare not only for the reception of the Sacrament, but need to prepare by prayer for communicating worthily in the prayers of the Church. If the Confession were made at this point by the whole congregation, it would not need to be repeated before the Prayer of Consecration, as in our liturgy, or before the Communion, as they do in Rome.

A casual remark made by Oscar Wilde in his *De Profundis* points in the right direction. "The server at the Mass," he said, "is the last vestige of the Greek chorus." The Greek chorus expressed audibly and vividly the feeling of the audience appropriate to each development of the drama. In that sense it represented the audience. But the server represents the congregation in a far deeper sense, and the congregation must never be regarded as an audience—not even when it is hearing a sermon. The server represents the congregation more obviously when, as is so common in the Church of Rome, he is dressed like the people and not vested like a little clergyman, a *cherichetto*, as they call the altar boys in Italy. But this remark of Oscar Wilde's merely points in the right direction. The Roman rubrics point further in the same direction when they prescribe that at least all who are about the altar must take part audibly in the introductory dialogue. It is even required expressly that the Pope, if he be present, shall audibly make the Confession with the server, and of course apply to himself the prayer for pardon made by the celebrant. Indeed the celebrant expressly asks the congregation, *fratres,* to pray for him, and the Liturgical Reform will be satisfied with nothing less than the audible participation of the whole congregation in this introductory dialogue.

I have dwelt upon this point at some length because this is the one place where we deny to the people an opportunity of participating actively in the Mass, indeed withhold from them even the knowledge of what is going on; and perhaps there is no other point where it is so necessary to insist upon the participation of the people. If they begin here to participate, they will recognize that they have a part in the whole action. It is obvious enough that when the people participate in it there is no feature of the Liturgy which is more evangelical.

But as an introduction to the Liturgy I very much prefer the very much shortened form of Morning Prayer we are now permitted to use—Venite, a short selection from the Psalter, an Old Testament lesson and a canticle. It takes not much more time, it encourages the participation of the people, and is welcome to those who are rightly devoted to Morning Prayer. Most important of all, it associates with the Liturgy the Scripture which Jesus knew and in which he found a prophecy of the Gospel. I am astonished that few have taken advantage of this recent permission which I promptly welcomed with enthusiasm. This perhaps is due to the fact that this introduction has not been made a part of the Liturgy, is supposed to be said in the choir, not at the altar, and may require the celebrant to wear other vestments. Another revision, even if it were only a revision of the rubric, might contrive to unite with the Liturgy more closely a Psalm, an Old Testament lesson and the *Te Deum* or another canticle.

3. MISSA CATECHUMENORUM

The Mass of the Catechumens, as already I have had occasion to remark, is in our liturgy and in the Roman Mass no longer plainly distinguished from the Mass of the Faithful. This distinction was blurred, even in the Eastern Liturgies, when everybody was baptized. Nevertheless there is a difference, and we must have it in mind if we would understand the relation of the several parts of the Liturgy to the whole. But this distinction is not disparaging to the first part of the Mass, which consists principally of the Scripture lessons and the sermon, for the Word of God is not less important than the Sacrament. It would be odious to contrast them. At least from the beginning of the second century the Eucharist was not ordinarily celebrated without the office of instruction. This part, if it includes a sermon, may be longer than all the rest, yet I can deal with it here very briefly because there is hardly room for misapprehension about the significance of the several parts and their relevance to the whole.

It cannot be regarded as an imperfection of our Liturgy that it solemnly introduces the Summary of the Commandments and thus justifies the humble petition, *Kyrie, eleison,* which in the Roman Mass is obviously appropriate after the confession of sin. But it is a great misfortune that our Reformers transferred the *Gloria in excelsis* from this which is its proper place and put it after the Communion, where it is so generally felt to be out of place that it is commonly omitted. I venture to say "its proper place" because a respectable commission of our National Church, the members of which are above any suspicion of partisanship, has lately recommended that it be placed after the *Kyrie.* Lacking the *Gloria* here, we are left with an abrupt transition from the *Kyrie* to the Collect, and this gap is not adequately bridged by the recent permission to use at this place the traditional greeting, The Lord be with you. The *Gloria,* in the place where it is properly used, serves as a *scala paradisi,* a ladder upon which we climb up from the disconsolate apprehension of our impotence, which is voiced in the *Kyrie,* to the lofty plane where we can hear and believe the incredible Gospel of God. But this is a ladder so curiously fashioned that while one can ascend on it, one cannot descend. At the place where we have elected to use it, we propose to climb down from the paradise of Communion to the practical concerns of everyday life; but when we begin to sing the *Gloria,* our foot is upon the lowest round of the ladder, and we find that we are climbing up again from the apprehension of God as Creator to faith in him as the incarnate Redeemer. In order to climb down, we should have to sing this hymn backward.

It is devoutly to be wished that the Old Testament Scriptures might be read along with the Epistles and the Gospels; for that was the early Catholic practice, and indeed our rubrics now make this possible in case Morning Prayer has not been said by the whole congregation as a preparation for the Liturgy. I wonder that few take advantage of this possibility. However, we properly accord to the Gospel, as a report of the very words of Jesus, the highest honor, though the Apostolic Epistles sometimes contain more Gospel than the passage selected from the report of the Evangelists. We *stand* to hear the Gospel, and thereby display more reverence for it than the early Church could do when all the people stood all the time. Unfortunately the gospeler shows scant reverence for this book when he reads it with his back to the people—or with the Gospel in his hands turns for a moment to the altar, as though to do reverence to *that* at the moment when the holiest thing in the temple is the book of the Gospels. It would be more Evangelical as well as more Catholic if to exalt the Gospel an ancient ceremonial were used and a minister were to hold up the book before the gospeler—or the more ancient ceremonial of mounting the steps (*gradus*) of an ambone erected face to face with the people. But whether such things are done or not, the people are now permitted (if their pastor permits them) to acclaim the Gospel with an appropriate hymn, the gradual.

Although the Creed (of course the Nicene Creed) is properly placed by the Eastern Liturgies in the Mass of the Faithful, it cannot be said that it comes inappropriately after the Gospel, as a summary expression of our faith. It is important too that it should come before the sermon, as an assurance, though a somewhat dubious one, that the preacher will conform to it. In this place it sheds additional luster upon the Gospel.

But in no way is the Gospel so much exalted as when the preacher uses it as his text and preaches it truly. It is no accident that in every liturgy the sermon follows the Gospel. In this, or in the Gospel proclaimed in the Epistle of the day, enough texts can surely be found which are appropriate to the season. The preacher is not expected to say anything that happens to come into his head. Alas, I should say rather, not *permitted*—and if we have to expect him to say what he pleases, and the choir-master to do as he pleases, we may as well say good-night to any essential significance in the Liturgy. Albert Schweitzer remarked that the sayings of Jesus are lying about like duds, like the unexploded shells which strewed the fields of Europe after the first world war; we have made them apparently harmless, yet they are still capable of exploding—to our consternation, but also to our great and endless comfort. It is the business of the preacher to explode them.

We are now permitted to say a bidding prayer *before* the sermon. The fact that nobody does it may be taken to imply that this place is inappropriate—or perhaps that the so-called Bidding Prayer is inappropriate in any place. I am minded to say that a prayer is more appropriate *after* the sermon. If a sermon does not dispose us to pray and to work, it had better not be delivered. Moreover, I venture to express the opinion that the Bidding Prayer is not a prayer. Evidently it is no more than a piece of instruction, a little lecture to ignorant people about prayer. That is precisely what it was intended to be. The early Lutheran agenda contained little else but this sort of instruction, and the Calvinistic Directory of Worship is the only prayer book which contains nothing but rubrics.

I should hesitate to interject this negative criticism if I had not something positive to suggest. But that we have in the *Synapte* of the Eastern Liturgies. That is a definite invitation to pray, and it grants time to the people to unite silently in making the supplications which are suggested by the deacon. Since we have no deacons, this invitation may be pronounced by anybody and might well be pronounced from the pulpit after the sermon. No one will doubt that the preacher is at liberty to invite the people to pray, and the formula, "Let us pray" for this and that, may be used for any intercessions which time and circumstance suggest. I would say emphatically that this sort of prayer is not antiquated. Today it is commonly used in Protestant circles, especially at missionary meetings, and it is strange that only Catholics have neglected a custom which may be traced to the second century. Such an invitation to prayer is now sanctioned by the rubric which says, "Here the priest may ask the secret intercessions of the congregation" etc. It is true that "here" means just before the Prayer for the Whole State of Christ's Church; but surely it is not only I who have felt that this is a very awkward place for it, seeing that no prayer is actually made at that time and the "intentions" proposed are maybe so different from the prayer which follows that it might seem as if the people were encouraged to make their private prayers while the priest is making his. It is not less awkward, though for a different reason, when special prayers are interjected at this place and are uttered vocally, not secretly as the rubric prescribes. Doubtless there ought to be flexibility enough in the Liturgy to allow for special supplications, but clearly the place for this is after the sermon.

4. MISSA FIDELIUM

The Offertory

However vague the line which marks the beginning of the Mass of the Faithful, it must be drawn *before* the Offertory; for this is the first act of oblation and sacrifice wherewith we respond to the supreme sacrifice of Christ which is commemorated in the Eucharist. Essentially none but the faithful may venture to make offerings to God. If the act of carrying the alms to the altar is viewed in the light of sacrificial symbolism, the pomp we associate with it is not misplaced. The reformers in the Church of Rome are eager to revert to what they recognize as an early practice. And the fact that our gifts are not made in kind but in money does not detract from the solemnity. The gifts which St. Paul was so eager to collect from the Gentile Christians in behalf of the poor saints at Jerusalem were also in money, but he calls them a "grace," and he calls them a fellowship or communion (not "contribution," as King James' Version coldly translates the word). The gifts this Apostle received in Rome for his own needs from the Church in Philippi were partly in money, and he calls them "an odor of a sweet smell, a sacrifice acceptable, well-pleasing to God." Fortunately we have among our Offertory Sentences the saying, "To do good and to communicate forget not, for with such sacrifices God is well pleased"—but unfortunately we have translated the significant *koinonia* by the heartless word "distribute." The Offertory expresses the thought of sacrifice to God in the form of communion with the brotherhood. At the same time the elements of bread and wine are offered as an act of fellowship or communion. Because we are instructed to "present" and "offer" at this time both the alms and the oblations, no sentence is so appropriate (*pace* Dr. Ladd!) as "All things come of thee, O Lord." In the following prayer we do not offer them again but only pray God to receive them, and therefore there is room to doubt whether the priest must leave the alms upon the altar.

Prayer for the Whole State of Christ's Church

This is a great prayer—it might be better, but surely it could not be put in a more appropriate place. Its relevance is therefore so obvious that I need say no more about it.

Confession and Absolution

Nor need I say much about the Confession and Absolution. If they are not said at the beginning of the service, no better place than this could be found for them—though perhaps as good a place would be before the prayer for the Church. The Comfortable Words are not superfluous after an absolution, especially when it is not a particular absolution; for there is nothing so incredible in our religion as that God will forgive sins. Therefore we need to hear the most authentic assurance.

The Preface

You will observe that I am in a hurry when I pass so quickly over two important parts of the Liturgy. My minutes are numbered. But my motto is *Festina lente,* I would make haste slowly, dwelling deliberately upon the points which need elucidation. And here we have come to such a place.

The Preface begins with the festal exhortation, *Sursum corda.* That might appropriately be preceded by the common salutation, "The Lord be with you." But above all we need to note that the Preface is the beginning of the great Eucharistic Prayer —it is the preface *of* it, not a preface *to* it.

I have for fifty years meditated upon the Liturgy, being so much older than you to whom I am speaking, and I speak with some confidence when I essay to define the significance of the Preface, although I am aware that the view I am about to present is not a commonplace. Though it is an illuminating view, it has perhaps more truth than evidence on its side, seeing that the distinctive character of the Preface has been in some measure obscured even in the Eastern Liturgies, and in the Western Rite has been totally obscured by the introduction of Proper

Prefaces, which, referring as they do to the events commemorated by the greater festivals of the Church year, give thanks (very properly in this sense) for God's signal works of grace in the redemption of mankind through Jesus Christ. But when we turn back to the earliest complete liturgy which we possess, that of the Eighth Book of "The Apostolic Constitutions," written in the fourth century, we see that the Preface originally made no mention of Christ or of the works of God performed through Him. It was a thanksgiving for God's merciful providence, and though it goes beyond this, it goes no further than the mighty works God wrought for his people before the coming of Christ. It fitly ends therefore with the *Tersanctus*, a hymn in praise of the Creator.

Thus until the fourth century at least the Preface was understood to be the blessing or thanksgiving for the elements of bread and wine, the common provision of God's bounty. That is to say, for all its elaborate eloquence, it points back to the common blessing at meals, already elaborated in the *Didache*, which Jesus pronounced at the Last Supper and at the feeding of the multitude.

Although the distinctive character of the Preface has been obscured by the introduction of Proper Prefaces (a proof that by the eighth century the Church was no longer conscious of the true nature of the Preface), yet we must have this in mind if we would understand the Liturgy, for it has left traces which otherwise we could not account for.

It explains in particular why the *Benedictus qui venit* is appropriate precisely at this point—not as a negligible addition to the *Tersanctus* (as the organist commonly takes it to be), but as an appropriate transition to a new and greater theme of thanksgiving, the redemption of man through Jesus Christ. The *Tersanctus* is a hymn to the Creator, the *Benedictus* acclaims the Redeemer.

Perhaps if this had been well understood, there might not have been so much opposition to the effort to restore the *Benedictus* to our liturgy. This effort was lamely supported by the plea that the *Benedictus* heralds the moment when Christ is about to appear bodily upon the altar under the hand of the priest. It means, as you see, far more than that, and to me at least it is precious as an expression of a more ancient implication of the Lord's Supper, the eschatological implication, of which there is left to us now only a negligible reminder in the phrase, "until he come," but which in the *Didache* rings out clearly in the *Maranatha,* "Lord, come!"

It seems to me very evident that, if any part of the Liturgy is to be sung by the celebrant and the people, it should be first of all the Preface, beginning with the *Sursum corda* and ending with the *Benedictus.*

Why not the subsequent prayer too, the Eucharist most properly so called, for that attains a sublimer note of praise? Yes, but it introduces a deeper pathos. It is not lyrical like the praise of the Creator. It does not begin with the Incarnation, as the Syrian Liturgies do, it does not recite the idyllic events which occurred beside the Galilean lake, does not even refer to the feeding of the multitude, to which St. John traces the origin of this sacrament, but it begins austerely with "the night in which he was betrayed." No man has yet written music appropriate to this pathos. It is obvious that here the celebrant must speak in a quieter tone—though by this I do not mean to imply that he should utter his prayer *secrete,* as though the people had no part in it. That custom was suggested by a very different line of thought, being the last vestige which remains in the Western Church of the attempt to interpret the Lord's Supper in terms of the pagan mystery cults. No, this prayer should be uttered distinctly, but in a quiet voice. The people must hear it and appropriate it as their prayer. That this is the sacrifice of the people as well as of the priest is the plain implication of the Roman Mass, when the priest, turning to the people, says, *Orate, fratres, ut meum et vostrum sacrificium acceptabile fiat.* "My sacrifice and yours"—that doubtless prompted the choice of the title *Orate, fratres* for the magazine which is the organ in America for Liturgical Reform. However, since this prayer attains towards the end a more confident tone, and we no longer are prompted to ask, "Is it I?" there is no reason why the celebrant might not sing the whole doxology with which it concludes: "by whom, and with whom, in the unity of the Holy

Ghost, all honor and glory be unto thee, O Father Almighty, world without end." That would be more solemn than the *per omnia, saecula saeculorum,* which the Roman priest sings, perhaps only to apprise the people that the prayer is ended and it is time for the Amen.

The Confusion Occasioned by the Proper Prefaces

The confusion occasioned by the introduction of Proper Prefaces is so great that it requires a prodigious effort to clarify the situation. The Gallican preference for having a different liturgy for every festival did not in the first instance occasion the confusion I have in mind, for, whatever form these liturgies took, the Eucharistic Prayer was evidently a unit. But it came about when this tendency was severely curbed by the Church of Rome, which, though it allowed for eleven Proper Prefaces, would tolerate no change in the second part of the prayer, and by calling it solemnly the Canon separated it formally from the Preface. But far more serious was the mechanical separation which was created in the Missal by the necessity of putting the Proper Prefaces somewhere between the Preface and the Canon. If in spite of this the Roman liturgists are able to perceive that the prayer is essentially one, this is possible only in the light of the Eastern Liturgies, which have no Proper Prefaces and clearly include the Preface in the *Anaphora.* The English Reformers had no inkling of the unity of this prayer, and, finding here a conspicuous gap in the Missal, they thought it a convenient place to put the Prayer of Humble Access—or anything that might occur to them.

The Essential Character of the Canon

We have reason to be grateful that we did not inherit from the Church of England its mutilated Canon. If our Canon were not on the whole so adequate, I would hardly have the heart to talk about the Liturgy. But here I must be brief, and therefore I shall confine myself to the aspects which most need illumination, with a view more especially to illustrating the wholeness of this prayer. I stress the fact that from the *Sursum corda* to the Amen it is one prayer, and predominantly a prayer of thanksgiving. I express my own conviction when I say that in conformity with the Apostolic and early Catholic view the Eucharist is consecrated (or "eucharisticized," as Justin Martyr says) by the prayer of thanksgiving as a whole, just as common food is hallowed by the blessing at meals. This implies that the Sacrament is not consecrated specifically by the Words of Institution, nor by the Invocation. To my mind therefore the appropriate moment for the Elevation would be after the Lord's Prayer, where we find it in the Eastern Liturgies. However, I have no intention of introducing here any question of ritual. I have said perhaps too much about such things in other places.

With a view to making more evident the wholeness of this prayer, I call attention to the fact that the description of what Jesus did at the Last Supper is not here, as it is in the Calvinistic Churches, recited as a warrant for celebrating this Sacrament, but that it is incorporated in a prayer, and as an *anamnesis* (grateful remembrance—*Unde et memores* is the Latin expression for it) it is appropriate in a prayer of thanksgiving which, beginning with a grateful remembrance of the wonders of God's providence, goes on to recite the miracles of his grace. Of course, this prayer does not consist solely of thanksgiving. No Eucharistic prayer ever did. We needy creatures cannot properly approach God without making known to Him our wants; and if we draw near with a confident faith that He is able and willing to help, we do God more honor by our petitions than by our thanksgiving. The Hebrew acclaim Hosanna! means "Help now!" The thought is that a monarch is more sincerely flattered by petition than by praise.

Between the grateful memorials of God's abundant kindness, and the supplications which we associate with them, the Greek Liturgies establish a formal resemblance by introducing intercessions with the phrase, "Remember, O Lord"—our country, our Church, its clergy, the people, the living and the dead. Some of these intercessions we have introduced in the Prayer for the Whole State of Christ's Church; but it was a natural tendency to associate them as closely as possible with the memorial of Christ's Sacrifice, and our liturgy followed a good principle when it brought all the expressions of our sacrifice into closer relation to his.

Our Eucharistic Prayer ends properly with a doxology, and to that the people properly respond with the Amen. With that they make the whole Eucharistic Prayer their own, for this stamps it as a whole, seeing that in the course of it no other Amen occurs. This is not, of course, the only Amen in the Liturgy, but it is the great Amen—so great and significant that Justin Martyr mentioned it particularly.

The Lord's Prayer

Although not many years have elapsed since the Lord's Prayer was restored to this place in our Liturgy, where it stood in the Prayer Book of 1549, yet by use we have already become so accustomed to this blessing that we do not perhaps feel as lively a sense of gratitude as we ought. If it were not evidently appropriate in this place, we still should feel the importance of conforming to the use of all the historic liturgies of Christendom. Happily the time is far past when we feel free to scramble the Liturgy, as did the English Reformers who shuffled its constituent parts and placed them wherever their whim suggested.

Not even in the Church of Rome are students inclined to regard the Lord's Prayer as a part of the Prayer of Consecration, though this seems to have been the notion of Gregory the Great when in the sixth century he added it to the Roman Mass at the place where the Greeks used it, and in accordance with this conception of his required that the priest alone should say it, except for the last petition. We have done well in reverting in part to the Eastern practice, which permitted the people to say all but the last petition, "But deliver us from evil." Perhaps we might have done better had we followed this Eastern use entirely, leaving it to the celebrant to say the last petition and to embroider it with the Embolismus. For it appears that the addition of the last petition and the fully rounded form this prayer has in St. Matthew's Gospel was due to the liturgical use of it at a very early time, whereas the Doxology and the Amen were an addition just too late to be incorporated in the earliest texts of the Gospel.

If the Lord's Prayer is not strictly a part of the consecration, it is too closely attached to it to be regarded as a preparation for communion. It deserves the honor of being treated as an independent feature of the Liturgy.

The Prayer of Humble Access

On the other hand, the Prayer of Humble Access is plainly meant as a preparation for the Holy Communion. This intention was even clearer in the Prayer Book of 1549 where it followed the Confession and Absolution. It takes the place of the *Domine, non sum dignus* of the Roman Mass, but with us is properly expressed in the plural because the people are expected to communicate.

This is another prayer which we lately restored to its proper place, for Bishop Gardiner was disturbed by the strange scruple that it might be interpreted as an act of veneration for the Holy Sacrament, and accordingly he placed it before the Canon.

Agnus Dei

This scruple applied more obviously to the *Agnus Dei;* accordingly that was rigorously excluded, and, though it is now commonly used in the Church of England, it has not yet been restored by authority. Not so long ago it was for the last time expressly prohibited by the condemnation of the Bishop of Lincoln. The use of the *Agnus* cannot be accounted a matter of prime importance, for it was never used in the Eastern Churches, and though at the end of the sixth century it seems to have stood in the *Ordo I* of the Mass, the *Liber Pontificalis* notes that it was not till the end of the following century that Pope Sergius I ordered it to be sung by clergy and people together during the *Fractio panis.*

It may be argued that in our Church we are implicitly given liberty to use it by the rubric which follows the Prayer of Humble Access: "Here may be sung a hymn." But this only on condition that we will use it *there.* To my mind, that is the most appropriate place for it—partly because the priest is then on his knees and can remain kneeling while he says it, and chiefly because it is appropriately sung by the choir while the priest is taking the communion himself and communicating those about the altar. The distribution of the Sacrament is as a whole a continuation of the *Fractio panis.*

The Communion

It is made plain in our Liturgy that the Communion is the culmination of the Eucharist. The Eucharist has not ceased to be the Lord's Supper. Although this perception has been obscured in the Roman rite, it is one of the chief aims of the Liturgical Reform to bring it to light.

All worship, by bringing the individual consciously into the presence of God, has a tendency to isolate the worshiper. In the act of communion the members of the Church (i. e. the Congregation of God's people) are again sensibly united with one another, and when immediately afterwards they are sent forth, they go as brethren upon a social mission. Everything should be done to make this sense of solidarity real, remembering that in the New Testament "communion" and "fellowship" are the same word. This precisely is the point where the Liturgy is most vividly related to life.

The Conclusion

I have just said, and said deliberately, "when immediately afterwards they are sent forth." It seems to me a matter of course that after the Communion the priest will "take the ablutions" expeditiously, and that the people, when they have said a prayer of thanksgiving, the grace after meals, such as we have in our Liturgy, will go away to their several tasks of life. Whatever is more than this is vanity. In another place I have said perhaps too trenchantly that the formal benediction by the priest (or by the bishop) is an impertinence after the people have been blessed by the Body and Blood of the Lord. Although in the Eastern Liturgies there are many benedictions—reciprocal benedictions of priest and people—there is none so formal as ours, and the benediction at the end of the Roman Mass is a comparatively late addition. The formula which gives the name to the Mass, the *Ite, missa est,* stands as a protest against everything that has been subsequently added. In our Liturgy we had till lately the Lord's Prayer, we still have the *Gloria* and the Benediction, likely one or more post-communion collects, and often the ceremony trails off with a prayer for the receding altar-ministrants which ought to be said in the sacristy. In the Roman Mass they have not only the Benediction but the Last Gospel, and the whole thing finally peters out with a litany. To understand the primitive form of dismissal in the Roman Mass we must remember that in the early liturgies various classes of people were from time to time dismissed—hearers, penitents, catechumens—and so at the end the faithful were dismissed with a similar formula. Only this final dismissal is now retained in the Roman Mass. As the people are taught to respond with *Deo gratias,* the formula cannot be meant to be as dry as it seems. It may be interpreted, as Roman Catholics are fain to interpret it, by analogy with the dismissal our Lord often addressed to those whom he taught, whom he healed, or whom he forgave: "Go, and do thou likewise," "Take up they bed and walk," "Go, sin no more." This means liturgy and life.

5. AN EXHORTATION

In conclusion I venture to utter a word of exhortation. I said at the beginning that if there are any "musts" which apply to the proper ritual performance of the Liturgy, they can only result from a just perception of its nature. Therefore they can only be free acts. But there is one very general "must" which we cannot lightly avoid, and that is the practical necessity of attaining among ourselves some degree of uniformity in worship, especially in the celebration of the Eucharist. This again can only be a free act, but it is a duty we are not free to shun; for if we cannot worship heartily together, we are not thoroughly united. On the part of one or another who is not a middle-of-the-way Churchman this may involve a free-will sacrifice made in behalf of the brethren—"the weaker brethren," as we may like to think. That is to say, it may mean that some of us must behave perhaps a little more simply than we like, and others a little less simply.

But I am not thinking of a compromise. I am hoping rather that there might result from a thorough understanding of the Liturgy a concordant practice which, because the people actively and intelligently take part in it, would be more solemn than anything now known in Christendom. I am thinking of the trials which these times seem to hold in store for the Church, which again may become an *ecclesia pressa* as it was in the Catacombs, and perhaps again will by the lofty austerity of its worship convert the world. And I am thinking of the imperative plainly presented to us by the divisions of Christendom, and I dare to indulge the hope that our common worship, especially at the Eucharist, may be so pure, so free from anything that an outsider might regard as flummery, a *logike latreia* (a "reasonable worship," as we translate these words of St. Paul), and so genuine and hearty that, "if there come in one who is an unbeliever or uninitiated, he will fall down upon his face and worship God, declaring that God is among you indeed."

But to attain any uniformity at all we must have a desire "to do what the Church does," or, as I am accustomed to put it, we must act always upon a maxim fit at all times to be law universal in the Church of God.

CHAPTER THREE

ABOUT THE WORD ACTION

Essential and Unessential Action

Before considering the essential actions characteristic of the Liturgy we must make plain what is meant here when we speak of *action.* Some will not be ready to admit that what we here call action is properly so called. For what we have in mind here is inward action, whereas one commonly thinks of action as outward movement, which may or may not be prompted and directed by inward feeling and thought. Therefore ritual acts, which here are excluded from consideration, would be more readily regarded as action, even if they are thought to be unimportant actions. It may be that even those who use such expressions as "an act of faith," "an act of contrition," "an act of penitence," etc., have a notion that the word "action" is used here in a non-natural sense. It is indeed true that such expressions were suggested by a peculiar Latin idiom. For in Latin the notion of thanksgiving must be expressed by the phrase *gratiarum actio,* an act of thanks, the verbal form being *gratias agere,* to *do* thanks. Thus the Greek word eucharist corresponds to the Latin "act of thanks," and the "grace" at meals means simply thanksgiving. The other expressions used in religious language were formed after this analogy. But this usage, although in a measure it was fortuitous, is not thereby condemned as inept. On the contrary, it calls attention to an important truth: that no external action, however great its effects, is really significant unless it is the expression of an internal action. For this reason the inward part of action is the more essential part, which cannot be accounted either unreal or hypocritical or vain, even if it is prevented by adverse circumstances from issuing in the outward action which is its natural counterpart.

However, I have no objection if any man prefers to call such inward action "non-action," in the sense Lao-tze, as I understand him, attaches to this word; for he seems to mean precisely what I mean here. He calls attention to the fact that "non-action," if it is good, is wholly good, whereas outward action, however well it is meant, and however wisely planned, may in its consequences turn out to be bad.

For our activistic race, especially in this activistic period of history, when war involving the destruction of the whole world is unhesitatingly regarded as action, and action of the most positive sort, it is wholesome to reflect that inward action, or call it non-action, may be more real, more positive, more essential.

No one will deny that the Liturgy, which means specifically the celebration of the Lord's Supper, is action of a sort, inasmuch as it involves external expressions in word and gesture; but because these expressions are in themselves unessential, the Liturgy may perhaps be regarded, even by those who perform it, as action of an unimportant sort. But the etymology of the word liturgy suggests a much higher appraisal of the action which it implies. Webster's Dictionary gives a pretty full account of the derivation of this word. It means a work performed for the people. In Classical Greek it denoted a public work performed by a private citizen or by a magistrate for the advantage of the State. In the Septuagint, the translation of the Old Testament into Greek, it was used for the priestly performance of sacrifice in the Tabernacle or the Temple, just as we find it used in Luke 1:23 for the "ministration" in the Temple of Zacharias the father of John the Baptist. Hence it is said in Hebrews 9:21 of Moses that he "sprinkled the Tabernacle and all the vessels of the liturgy with blood." The argument here is that Christ is "a *liturgos* of the holy things and of the Tabernacle which the Lord pitched, not man" (8:16). Hence the word was applied to Christian worship in a general sense. In Romans 15:16 St. Paul says, "that I should be a *liturgos* of Christ Jesus unto the Gentiles, ministering as a priest (hierourgunta) the Gospel of God, that the presentation of the Gentiles as a sacrifice unto God might be acceptable, being sanctified by the Holy Ghost." Here almost every word has a sacrificial or sacerdotal meaning. The word has the earlier sense of a practical work of beneficence when St. Paul (Phil. 2:25, 30) says of Epaphroditus, who at the risk of his life was sent by the Christians at Philippi to carry their gifts to him when he was a prisoner in Rome, that he is "your messenger (apostle) and *liturgos* to my need, supplying what was needed to complete your liturgy towards me." But even here we must suppose that the religious and sacrificial sense was understood; for in this same passage (Phil. 2:17), where St. Paul speaks of the collection made for impoverished Christians in Jerusalem, he calls this a liturgy but connects it with worship: "For the ministration of this liturgy not only filled up the measure of the wants of the saints, but abounded through many thanksgivings unto God." Indeed in a later passage (Phil. 4:18), where he gives thanks again for the things sent him by the Church in Philippi, he says of them that they are "an odor of a sweet smell, a sacrifice well-pleasing unto God," just as in Ephesians 5:2 he spoke of Christ's death as "an offering and a sacrifice to God for a sweet-smelling savor." To prompt men to contribute to this collection (which he calls a communion or fellowship) in behalf of the saints at Jerusalem, St. Paul coined the most perfect offertory sentence: "For ye know the grace of our Lord Jesus Christ, that, though he was rich, yet for your sakes he became poor, that ye through his poverty might be rich" (2 Cor. 8:9). Here the language is not sacrificial, but the thought is.

In these instances it is evident that liturgy, though it is regarded as an instance of divine worship, means action, and that of the most practical sort, being prompted by love of the brethren and calculated to supply their material needs. In Acts 13:2 the word is certainly used of divine worship, and probably of the celebration of the Lord's Supper. In an assembly of the Church at Antioch, in which only the most distinguished members are mentioned by name, that is, the men, who were accounted prophets and teachers, including "Barnabas, and Simeon who was called Niger, and Lucius of Cyrene, and Manaen the foster brother of Herod the tetrarch, and Saul, while they were performing the liturgy and fasting, the Holy Ghost said, Separate me Barnabas and Saul for the work whereunto I have called them. Then when they had fasted and prayed and laid their hands upon them, they sent them forth." This was certainly an ordination to the Apostolate, and the "liturgy" which preceded it was presumably the Eucharist. For that was not only the preeminent act of worship in the Church, but the only distinctive act of Christian worship. The New Testament gives us no reason to suppose that there was ever a solemn assembly of the Church in which the Lord's Supper was not solemnized.

Everyone will recognize that the liturgy is an act of worship. Worship is an expression of reverence for worth. So long as the word worship was commonly used for the respect showed to human merit or worth, it was evident enough that such reverence can be expressed not by words only but by gesture, as taking off the hat, as standing in the presence of a superior, as kneeling before a sovereign, and still more perfectly by deeds. Now that we use the word only in relation to God, as "divine worship," we have an unfortunate disposition to conceive that it can be expressed only with the tongue. It is true that rational creatures find in *words* the most adequate expression for their thoughts. Yet these are not always the most natural expression for our feelings—and worship is first of all an expression of the feeling of reverence. This feeling is aptly expressed by attitude and gesture, either with or without words; and the feeling itself is inhibited if it is not thus expressed. Certainly, words which are mere words, mere vocal sounds, and not the expression of heartfelt reverence, are a poor sort of worship. In public worship too little opportunity is afforded for silent prayer (which is worship in words, though the words are unspoken), and too often men ignore or discount the importance of physical expressions of worship which, it may be, are associated with no words at all, not even unspoken words, nor with precise thoughts, but are simply an expression of reverential feeling. The sign of the cross, the bowing of the head or of the knee, or the prostration of the whole body, may or may not be accompanied by a thought which could be expressed in words; but they are none the less an expression of worship. In the Liturgy the part of the people as well as that of the priest is worship in the broad sense I have here indicated, that is to say, it is not expressed in words only. But, on the other hand, if I saw as much need of saying it, I might say even more emphatically that the Liturgy is a "rational worship" (Rom. 12:1, *logike latreia*), which is expressed not only (as St. Paul says here) by the decisive gesture of offering our bodies a living sacrifice, but finds in words an apt expression of its *ratio* or *logos*. Indeed, the whole Christian dogma is succinctly expressed in the words of the Liturgy. Words of such sacred import, therefore, must not be mumbled; they cannot be too clearly and tellingly pronounced. We are fortunate in being able to say the Liturgy in our own language, in words which, though they have been consecrated by a millennial use, are understood by all. We have no excuse for mummery, and mummery in words is an offense far more grievous than any other ritual mummery.

The inward action of the Liturgy, though it might be called non-action, does not mean inaction or quietism—no, not even if it is impeded or prevented from expressing itself in outward action. "Faith," said Luther, "is an uneasy thing"—and without faith there is no real Liturgy. The Liturgy is full of tension. It is the tension of the Holy Ghost. And even if by misadventure, by defect of opportunity, or by untoward circumstances, the arrow from the taut string does not leave the bow and fly to the mark, the tension is not in vain, if it is inwardly productive. What we call *acts* of gratitude, of faith, of contrition, of love, might also be called tensions. Such tensions are never unproductive, if they are real, although sometimes they cannot be resolved by an outward act. There is one tension which can never be resolved in this life: that is hope, or the tension of time. This tension was highly characteristic of the Liturgy as it was understood in the earliest period; but now it has dwindled to so little that almost the only trace left of it in the text of our Liturgy is the perfunctory recitation of St. Paul's words, "until he come," or, as we say, "until his coming again." Early in the second century the eschatological hope, the expectation of the kingdom of God, was gradually transformed into faith in the immortality of the soul. So St. Ignatius describes the Eucharist as "the drug of immortality," "the antidote that we may not die." Doubtless many will be astonished if they are compelled to observe how large and lofty a place is accorded to hope in the New Testament. It is significant that we do not speak of an act of hope. And yet hope is a strenuous act; it is no mere wish. In the same sense it is significant that one almost always quotes St. Peter (1 Pet. 3:15) as exhorting us to be always ready to give a reason for the *faith* that is in us, whereas in fact St. Peter says *hope*. St. Paul put hope second in the triad of Christian virtues because he accounted it greater than faith, love being put in the third place as the greatest of all. In the Epistle to the Hebrews (11:1) faith is defined in terms of hope, as "the substance of things hoped for, the evidence of things not seen." Hope represents the highest tension we can conceive of; for, as in the case of Abraham (Rom. 4:18), it may mean hoping against hope. Hope determines the total orientation of the Christian life, as an orientation away from the now and towards the time to come. Therefore, although it has no object in this world, and might therefore seem to be wholly inactive and ineffectual, it is an act which is real in the highest degree, having a definite influence upon all external actions, since it determines what they shall be and of what quality.

In the action of the Liturgy hope must be restored to its rightful place, which is second only to love. It is a delusion to suppose that communion in the Body and Blood of Christ, instead of being a foretaste, an earnest, a pledge, provides us now with all we are encouraged to hope for. No sacrament bestows upon us immediately what it implies. To ignore time and the tension of hope "overthroweth the nature of a sacrament"; for with that we regard it either as a mere symbol of what we have, or as the realization of what we are taught to hope for. That is to say, the sacraments of the Gospel can only be understood as referable to the kingdom of God, the Day of the Lord. Catholic piety has commonly favored the delusion that what the sacrament promises we can enjoy now. Loisy, though he was a heretical Catholic, expressed a common opinion when he said, "Christ promised the Kingdom—what came was the Church." St. Paul, on the contrary, depicts in the eighth chapter of his Epistle to the Romans the dolorous contrast which actually exists between "the sufferings of this present time" and "the glory which shall be revealed in us." He says there (in the 24th verse), "By hope were we saved: but hope which is seen is not hope—for who hopeth for that which he seeth? But if we hope for that which we see not, then do we with patience wait for it." Patience is therefore an essentially Christian tension. Accordingly St. Paul praises the Thessalonians (1 Thess. 1:3) for their "patience of hope"; in Romans 5:3 he explains that "tribulation worketh patience, and patience experience, and experience hope"; and finally (in Rom. 15:5) he astonishes us by speaking of God as "the God of patience," implying that God also, although He is eternal, is dealing with time. He is therefore called (in verse 13) "the God of hope."

We are impatient of having to deal with time, and therefore we have disparaged hope, which, if it is not the chief tension of the Liturgy, clearly determines the quality of the whole action.

Mystical piety in particular is an example of impatience which would eliminate time as a factor which, so far as the mystic is concerned, has already been swallowed up in life, in eternity. As applied to the Holy Communion, this means that one is not content to regard it as the *viaticum,* our temporary sustenance, on the way to the kingdom of God. And yet this is not a mean estimate of the Sacrament; and if we were to regard it as the provender for our pilgrimage, we would have a strong motive for receiving it often, and would not be discouraged by the experience that we often have need of it. St. Paul expresses the highest mystical experience by the phrase, "Christ in us." Surely the Holy Communion can impart no more than this. But even this, St. Paul says (Col. 1:27), is no more than "the *hope* of glory."

In Protestant piety the universal use of the word "commune" (instead of "communicate") betrays the fact that the Lord's Supper is regarded predominantly as an opportunity for communion with God. Communion is characteristic of the contemplative life, it is fully enjoyed only in solitude, and it may be of so passive a sort that it cannot be called action at all. But then why "come together?" We come together in order to *communicate,* that is, to share with one another the gift of God, as a fellowship, as a Church. We must not for one moment forget that in the New Testament "communion" and "fellowship" represent the same Greek word (*koinonia*). In the experience of fellowship hope is not directly involved. But nothing can be more evident than that fellowship implies action. It implies, as we shall see, every overt action which properly expresses brotherhood.

But, not to anticipate what must be said in subsequent chapters, I shall say no more here about the general notion of action in the Liturgy.

CHAPTER FOUR

THE DOMINICAL PRECEPT

CHURCH-GOING

At least by implication, the essential action of the Liturgy begins, one might say, before the beginning, with the coming together unto one place. That clearly *is* action; for maybe we come a long way, and at some inconvenience, rising at an early hour. But if we do not *come*, we cannot "do this" in remembrance of Christ, and it is obvious that for a communion we must come *together*. Alas, "you can summon spirits from the vasty deep—but will they come?"

This expresses the gravest problem of the pastor. He may be ready to feed the sheep, and even able to do it—but will they come? Those who need help most are least inclined to come. It must be confessed that the Church of Rome has in this respect a notable advantage over us; for it has the Dominical Precept, that is to say, the requirement that every Christian must hear Mass, or see it, every Lord's Day. It is called Dominical because it is the precept for the Lord's Day (*Dominica*)—and the *only* one. It might well be called Dominical for the reason that it is one of the precepts of the Lord (*Dominus*), though it is far from being the only precept. He said, "Do this in remembrance of me." To be sure, he did not say *when*. But before he was risen how could he have indicated that this was to be done on the first day of the week, the day of the Resurrection, which we therefore call the Lord's Day? However, in the earliest days of the Church the disciples had no doubt this was his meaning. Perhaps he said it to them after the Resurrection. But though he had never said it, their hearts would have prompted them to do it. At all events, this they did; and for a long time this was the only way the Lord's Day was distinguished by the Church from other days. For it must be remembered that though the Jews celebrated the Sabbath as a day of rest, there was no secular holiday on Sunday, either in Palestine or in any other part of the pagan empire of Rome. There is nothing more sure about the primitive Church than the fact that the Lord's Supper was celebrated on every Lord's Day; and by this custom the early Catholic Church was closely united with the Church of the Apostles. Inasmuch as this is still the Catholic custom, both in the East and in the West, it may be said that, in this respect at least, Catholicism is more evangelical than the Evangelicals.

I implied above, perhaps incautiously, that we lack the Dominical Precept. It is true enough that we have no such precept in our Constitution and Canons—and if we were to insert it there, it would certainly not be easy to enforce it in the face of a prevailing Protestant misunderstanding both within our Church and outside it. But as Catholics we have it; we have received it through a millennial tradition, through the New Testament, from the Lord Himself. We can enforce it upon ourselves, and we can try by sweet reasonableness to persuade others to comply with Christ's Commandment.

ESSENTIAL ACTION

Finding myself obliged some time ago to assume the duties of Student Pastor to the Episcopal youth in Princeton University, at a time when the great majority of students were enrolled in the armed forces, coming from all parts of the country, I felt more acutely than most parish priests the deplorable consequences of the fact that our people are not instructed that it is their bounden duty as Christians to fulfill the law of Christ by remembering him on the Lord's Day, and on every Lord's Day, in the Sacrament which he instituted. Although in my position I felt this more acutely than others, I know that everywhere the permanent existence of our Church, as of all Protestant Churches, is threatened by the lack of a plain rule which can be instilled into the minds of the youth and will be recognized by them as a divine commandment, the breach of which does not mean merely disloyalty to the parochial institution and to its pastor, who obviously has egoistic reasons for wishing to magnify his office, but means unfaithfulness to Christ and alienation from the life of God.

Not long ago the Roman Catholic Chaplain in this university, accosting me on the street, enquired with friendly solicitude how things were going with me. "Very badly," I replied. "But why?" "Because we have not the Dominical Precept." "Why, of course," said he, "you ought to have that!"—But this, alas, is more easily said than done, and the lack of it makes an appalling difference.

As nearly as I can reckon, there were at that time about three hundred students committed to my care. It was estimated that about one half went away every Sunday. That left one hundred and fifty. But, according to the most optimistic reckoning, there were hardly thirty, i.e., one fifth, which attended any Church. The Roman Catholic Chaplain had at that time the same number to look after. He could reckon that one hundred and fifty would be in town on any given Sunday. I asked him how many came to Mass. "Well, of course," said he, "there would be one hundred and fifty."

If we continue to confirm young people (or adults) without making it plain to them that they must fulfill the law of Christ, and that by a breach of it they are formally excluded from the Church, until they are formally reinstated as penitents, we may as well throw up the sponge. But, alas, this cannot be taught in any parish where the Eucharist is not celebrated as the principal act of worship on every Lord's Day.

Although we can call this *the* precept for the Lord's Day, seeing that it is the only precept that can be found in the Scriptures, we cannot speak of it simply as the Lord's precept, as though there were no other, as though the Law of Christ were predominantly a ritual law, as though the summary of the moral law in terms of love of one's neighbor, which St. James calls "the royal law," were not significantly called "the second commandment," and as though love of God were not emphasized as "the first." So far as we know, the Dominical Precept is the only prescription with regard to worship which can be traced to the Lord. Jesus assumed that his disciples would want to pray, and in response to their request he taught them "how." In this brief instruction, which we call the Lord's Prayer, it is implied that the disciples will want to pray with and for others. Such was the custom of the Synagogue and of the disciples of John the Baptist. But, astonishing as it may seem, Jesus nowhere exacts prayer as a duty. On the other hand, nothing could be more solemn and emphatic than his injunction with regard to the Lord's Supper, "Do this in remembrance of me." Before the Gospels were written St. Paul reported this tradition with the solemn affirmation, "I received from the Lord that which I delivered unto you."

On this point, when we take into consideration the universal practice of the Apostolic Church, the Scriptural tradition is so clear that at least two of the Protestant sects, the so-called Christians and the Brethren, have returned from the aberration of three centuries and now celebrate the Holy Communion on every Lord's Day. Their example suggests the hope that eventually some—why not all?—of the larger Communions which call themselves Evangelical may be prompted to follow a rule which is evidently more evangelical than their present practice, a rule which may well commend itself to them, not because it is Catholic, but because it is Scriptural. In performing this action they may not agree in all points with the Catholic tradition of how it is to be performed and how it is to be understood; but the principal thing is that they should *do* it. Elsewhere (in the Bibliographical Note at the end of this volume) I have remarked upon the astonishing degree of agreement which is reached by Protestants and Catholics who are well informed about the Liturgy. In view of this, how can we despair of a general agreement? For more than forty years I have been urging that Christians are not really united unless they are united in worship. It may be that in worship reunion must *begin*. Yet a mutual *recognition* of one Church by another, even though it is a formal matter, may have to precede a more essential expression of unity and lead up to it. In view of the diversity of our Eucharistic practice, that is, of our own delinquency, we do not need to wait for perfect agreement in this respect before we can recognize other Churches as

Churches, and reach a working agreement with them about the fundamental features of doctrine and Church order.

The difficulty in our own Communion is due chiefly to the old prejudice against non-communicating attendance at the Holy Eucharist. Certainly that is not ideal. In the fifth century it was already felt to be a grievous abuse, and St. Chrysostom inveighed fiercely against it. The Calvinistic Churches, in spite of Calvin's insistence upon a monthly celebration, and his preference for a weekly observance, were moved by a very reasonable consideration to observe the Lord's Supper as rarely as they did, and do. For the Holy Communion implies a coming together of the whole Church in one place; and if many do not communicate, it is as though the Church were divided, dissipated. But the dilemma which really confronts us was many years ago formulated for me very exactly by Dr. Henry Percival: either non-communicating attendance or non-communicating non-attendance. The Catholic Church never hesitated which horn of this dilemma to choose. As Catholics, therefore, we must on every Lord's Day celebrate the Holy Communion at a time when all the people *could* come together, and we must make it very evidently the most prominent feature of the celebration or sanctification of that day—whether they will hear, or whether they will forbear. Inferentially, it will be seen that this point of view is not favorable to the emphasis some would place upon the early Communion and the "Parish Breakfast" or *agape;* for it is evident that *all* the people cannot and will not come together then. It is only an emphasis upon the necessity of fasting before Communion which deflects a pastor from choosing the hour when conceivably all might come together. And the importance of this practice of "fasting" (which is Catholic but not Apostolic) must be weighed against the importance of having the whole Church together at the Eucharist. In our Church in Rome, where I ministered to Protestants of all sorts, I discovered that people are generally not so reluctant as one might expect to hear the Liturgy when they do not communicate in the Sacrament. They hear the Epistle and the Gospel, they share in the instruction of the sermon, they share many expressions of fellowship, reciting the Creed as a common expression of faith, and in the strictest sense of the word they *communicate* in the hymns, in the prayers, in the offering. They are not outsiders, even if they do not communicate in the Sacrament. Indeed the Liturgy as a whole is the most telling, the most persuasive, and the most dramatic presentation of the *kerygma*, i.e. the essential proclamation of the Gospel. If that is heard and seen by every Christian every Lord's Day, men will not easily *forget* him in whose remembrance this is done.

Now it is becoming more and more evident that this *must* be done—"lest they forget." Non-communicating non-attendance has come to mean simply non-attendance at any service in the Church.

The Protestant precept which defined how the Lord's day is to be sanctified was far more rigorous than the Catholic rule. There was a time when Protestants took no little pride in this comparison. The Westminster Shorter Catechism says: "The Sabbath is to be sanctified by a holy resting all that day, even from such worldly employments and recreations as are lawful on other days, and by spending the whole time in the public or private exercise of God's worship, except so much as may be taken up by works of necessity or mercy." I learned this in my childhood and quote it from memory. But what is left of all this? The Presbyterians may well be envious now of the simpler Catholic rule. In the course of time, people slyly discovered that there was really no historical justification for applying the Fourth Commandment to the first day of the week. And they were able to say (disingenuously) that, if it was only a question of worshiping God, they could do that under "the blue dome," in the forests and fields. They could allege also, and with more reason, that, if the sermon was the principal thing, they could get more edification by reading good books. They cannot so easily elude the Dominical Precept, which emphasizes coming together for fellowship in the Church, for communion—which does not mean individual communings with Nature or with God.

To "come together" on the Lord's Day—on every Lord's Day—in order to "do this" in remembrance of him, is indeed the very least one can do to earn the name of being a practicing Christian. But since it is obviously so little, men surely will not have the effrontery to suggest that God might put up with less. So long as they do this least thing (the Liturgy), this poignant remembrance of him will constantly remind them how little this is; and perhaps even non-communicating attendants may be led to reflect with fear and trembling whether a man can be a Christian without being a disciple, or a disciple without being a follower.

CHAPTER FIVE

PRELIMINARY ACTION

REPENTANCE, CONFESSION AND ABSOLUTION

Of all inward actions repentance is most easily recognized as a positive act, for it means a change of mind, as the word *metanoia* in the New Testament clearly indicates. No change is more radical than a change of mind, especially when it determines a man's relation to God.

But essentially this action is preliminary to the Liturgy. It must be performed *before* the act of "coming together." The warnings or "Exhortations" prescribed by the Book of Common Prayer make it plain that this is to be done, not as a part of the action of the Liturgy, but "in the mean season." It is obvious enough that the assembly for common worship is not the most apt place for us to "search and examine our consciences," "to amend our lives," and to make sure that we are "in perfect charity with all men"; and in case we have offended not only God but our neighbor, it is evident that reconciliation with him, in so far as it involves "restitution and satisfaction," cannot be accomplished in the course of the Liturgy. Christ's saying (Matt. 5:23), "*First* be reconciled to thy brother, and then come and offer thy gift," although originally it was not uttered with reference to the Lord's Supper, was certain to be remembered by the Church because it applies so pungently to this sacrament, and all the more because in the early liturgies the pax, or the Kiss of peace, took place at the Offertory.

In this saying Jesus contemplates a particular case, which is by no means rare: "if thy brother hath aught against thee." But, on the other hand, how many of his sayings are addressed to the offended person, requiring him to forgive! The Exhortation in the Book of Common Prayer expresses clearly the motive which prompts us to perform this almost impossible action: "As ye would have forgiveness of your offenses at God's hand:" and it assumes that this is to be done "in the mean season." To be sure, it is not done too late if we are first prompted and enabled to do it by the compunction we feel as we approach the Altar where the Lord's sacrifice is commemorated, and at the moment when we are expressly exhorted to "be in love and charity with our neighbors"; but we approach the Altar with the more confidence if we can regard this necessary act as already fully performed. In the Lord's Prayer (if we properly translate Mt. 6:12) we pray that God will forgive us our debts, "as we, too, *have* forgiven our debtors." This act of ours, already performed, is regarded here as a ground of confidence—though, of course, it is very far from being a measure of God's goodness to us. So in the Liturgy we might say, "we have forgiven"; but it is not then that we are most likely to perform this act, and we dare not say boastfully that we have done it, seeing that it is so necessary a part of the preparation for coming to the Lord's Supper. This is essentially a preliminary act.

And, in a sense, confession of sin unto God is preliminary, although it is seemly to make public confession in the congregation. St. James' exhortation (5:12), "Confess your sins one to another, and pray one for another, that ye may be healed," means this *at least*. Although it cannot be said that confession of sin is a necessary part of the Eucharist, yet it evidently is so appropriate that the historic liturgies offer not one occasion but many for us to acknowledge our unworthiness. Thereby we make our confession not only to God but to one another. And we need to do this, not only in order to fulfill the precept of St. James, but to make it evident that every Church of the saints is a Church of sinners. Otherwise who would have the courage, or the presumption, to join us? Only the "perfectionists," who fancy that, at least for one moment, they are without sin. I remember how deeply an American newspaper correspondent (evidently not a Catholic) was impressed when he assisted at the first Mass said by the present Pope in St. Peter's, and heard His Holiness repeat three times, *Domine, non sum dignus,* "Lord, I am not worthy."

Confession to God is, of course, the essential part of this act; but the practice of psychotherapy demonstrates that the counterpart, confession to our fellow-men, is important, if not equally important. It is astonishing how far confession itself avails to "quiet the conscience," to relieve the oppression of guilt. Kant's ultra-Protestant ideal that every man should be his own confessor is not only cheerless but practically ineffective. The Second Exhortation in the Book of Common Prayer advises a man to "open his grief" to "a Minister of God's Word," who is supposed to give "godly counsel and advice." Only in the Visitation of the Sick is the Minister expressly charged to "assure [the penitent] of God's mercy and forgiveness." This would be a vain assurance if it were not virtually, by whatever words it is expressed, an absolution. "I absolve thee," is not the only nor the earliest form of absolution. *Pacem do* (I bestow peace), and *Communionem habeo* (I have communion [with thee]), were earlier forms, and are even more personal. For a sinner could not be better assured of his forgiveness than when a man of eminent Christian piety addresses such words to him. But this, of course, is preliminary to our coming to the Lord's Supper, although (again I say, of course) an absolution expressed in more general terms may be repeated in the Liturgy as a collective assurance of pardon. In this case it is properly expressed in a conditional form, or as a prayer for pardon. The Freudian practitioner, not being able to avail himself of the tonic of absolution, has no other resource but to extenuate guilt by ignoring sin, that is, by denying God.

Repentance and silent confession to God may appear to be less active than the act of confession to another man and his absolution; and yet these latter acts are not effective at all without the former. This is a consideration which illuminates clearly the concept of essential action.

Of all these actions we have to speak here because they are implied in the action of the Liturgy. But if they are to be expressed in the Liturgy, the question arises, Where? In a way, this is like asking, Where is the seat of the soul in the human body? A sense of penitence, of sins confessed, and of sins forgiven, is a feeling which should pervade the Liturgy. And in fact it does. But if it is asked whether these things ought to be expressed particularly in one definite place, and *where,* it may not be easy to agree upon an answer. We cannot appeal to early tradition, because the early liturgies, including the Roman, had no place for a formal confession and absolution—although it might be said that in the dialogue between priest and people many occasions for this were offered. "Peace be with you," is a benediction, and every benediction is an absolution. In our Liturgy we have had since the Reformation a special place for Confession and Absolution; but it has not always been the same place. This too is a prominent feature in all the Lutheran and Reformed *agenda.*

If the action of the Liturgy is thought of as a *whole,* the most appropriate place for Confession and Absolution would evidently be at the beginning or before the beginning of the Liturgy. There it is we find this feature in the Roman Mass of today, beginning with the *Introibo.* But because it is there treated as a dialogue between the priest and the server, as an act which concerns them alone and might as well be performed in the sacristy, it is repeated before the Communion, for the benefit of those who are about to communicate. This is an indication that the Roman Church, viewing the Liturgy as a whole, does not commonly regard the Communion as essentially the climax. So long as the Sacrifice, or the act of transubstantiation, is regarded as the climax, the Communion, as an addendum, seems to need a separate introduction. What *we* ought to do (supposing we were allowed and encouraged to do what is not now prescribed) depends upon our notion of the Liturgy, upon whether we have or have not a perception of its wholeness.

I speak of one and another action which is involved in the Liturgy, and therefore of actions in the plural. It is only thus we can discuss discretely the action of the Liturgy. But I do not wish to distract attention from the wholeness of the action, which in fact is the theme announced in the title of this book.

CHAPTER SIX

THE *ECCLESIA*

THE AGENT IN THE LITURGY

When we think of the Liturgy as action, it is of the utmost importance to understand at the outset who is the agent. It is the priest, many will say. But this is a slovenly answer, which is suggested not so much by the ambition of priests to lord it over God's heritage as by the slothfulness of the people, who, even when they insist upon the priesthood of all believers, are prone to be inactive and let somebody else, be he called minister or priest, act for them. It cannot be said that this is the answer of the Roman Church, for it is belied by the invitation to prayer which precedes the Preface of the Mass: *Orate, fratres, ut meum ac vestrum sacrificium acceptabile fiat apud Deum omnipotentum*—Let us pray, brethren, that my sacrifice and yours may be acceptable to Almighty God.

Indeed, no one will affirm that in the Liturgy the priest acts by himself, independently of God; but neither does he act apart from the people. The laity not only have their particular part in the Liturgy, but whatever the priest does he does as their representative. Laity is not a word which can rightly be used disparagingly, at least in the Church. For it means the *people,* which in the Church is not regarded as the *plebs* but as "the people of God," in the sublime sense in which it was applied by the Old Testament to Israel. The word clergy (the *lot* of God's inheritance) implies a distinction—not, however, a distinction *from* but *in* the people of God. If the priest does not remain in this sense a layman, he has no place in the Church and no part in the Liturgy.

The right answer is that the action of the Liturgy is performed in and for and by the Church.

But this answer is not intelligible unless we have a right notion of what the Church is. It is not an easy notion to grasp, because it is a spiritual notion, and we are prone to think in mechanical terms, which involve the concept of extension in space, a concept which is appropriate only when we are dealing with matter—in fact with dead matter, for to living matter, to plants and animals which are alive, the categories we most naturally use do not perfectly apply. I subscribe here to the well known thesis of Henri Bergson.

Last September, when I was asked to lead a Liturgical Conference sponsored by the Catholic Club of New England, I was delighted to see that one of the topics in the proposed agenda was, "The Parish as a Cell in the Body of Christ." For the conception of the Church as the Body of Christ is essential to a right understanding of it, and the notion of the cell, whether we think of it biologically or sociologically, is a modern notion which comes opportunely to our assistance.

I am not eager to exalt the *parish* as such, nor to make the notion of it more concrete and separate than it aleady is, even in lands where it is not a geographical expression. But when the Church is regarded as the Body of Christ, we have, at the very least, a biological concept which obviously cannot be handled by mechanical categories.

It would be well if we spoke more frequently of the Church as the Body of Christ, for by that we are reminded of the proper meaning of membership. In our language, unfortunately, the word "member" is so commonly used in a trivial sense to denote a unit (*socius, sodalis*) of any secular society or club that we do not easily associate with it a deeper meaning when we speak of membership in the Church. Indeed, our common use of this word reinforces a natural tendency to think of the Church as like any other human society or club, and to account ourselves "members" of it only in the same sense in which we speak of being members of a club in which we are legally enrolled and to which we pay our dues, or of a political party for which we cast our votes. With that we totally ignore the analogy which

St. Paul emphasizes in Rom. 12:4, 5: "As we have many members in one body, and all the members have not the same function, so we many are one body in Christ, and severally members which supplement one another." Or, to quote only a few verses from 1 Cor. 12:12-31, the passage in which St. Paul draws out this analogy in detail: "For as the body is one and hath many members [i. e. organs and limbs], and all the members of the body, though they are many, are one body, so also is Christ" one body with members. "For in one Spirit we were all baptized into one Body. Now ye are the Body of Christ, and severally members thereof."

This is the same analogy wise patriots employed to put a stop to the dissension between the plebs and the patricians in the early days of the Roman Republic. But with St. Paul this was not a mere figure of speech; for Christ, being the indwelling life or entelechy in the Church, makes it indeed one Body, determining the function of each several member and the direction, aim, or *telos,* of the whole. The Church therefore is a *whole* in a sense in which no material thing is, nor any society which is merely a human organization. Its wholeness is that of a living body. A living body, whether of an animal or a plant, because it is composed of many members, having divers functions, may seem to be less whole than a crystal, which is made up of identical parts. But in reality it is more thoroughly a whole. The diamond-cutter can divide a big stone into many little diamonds; but a living body cannot be divided in the same way, not even ideally.

I welcome the use of the word "cell" which was proposed for this conference, because this too is a biological term. The cell of the plant was discovered only a hundred years ago, and before long it was recognized as the building material of all living tissue. The mechanical trend of the human intellect has led some scientists to ignore the living wholeness of the plant or animal and to treat the cells as if they were undifferentiated monads into which the body could be intelligibly resolved—just as we are prone to do with respect to the members of the Church. But of the cells it is no less true than of the organs and limbs—sight, hearing, smell, hands and feet—that they perform definite and different functions. In the plant it is perfectly evident that the cells of the root, the stem, the leaves and the flower, similar as they are, perform different and highly specialized functions; and although in most animal organisms this is not so plain to the eye, every histologist knows that here the differences are even greater. If St. Paul had known of the cell, he likely would have used it as an analogy; but doubtless he would have applied it, as he did the analogy of the members, to the individuals who compose the Church. As we have many cells in one body, and all cells have not the same function, so we many are one body in Christ.

Nevertheless, the analogy of the cell can profitably be applied to groups in the social structure, in the sense in which it is used now of the smaller Soviet groups. If it is applied to the parish, it instructs us that the function of the parish is to "bore from within," but that it functions for the sake of the whole. As applied to any Christian group, it draws attention to the fact that the whole exists ideally in every one of its parts, inasmuch as every cell is in spirit and organization identical with every other and with the whole.

In the second century, the first stadium of Catholic development, this was very evident in every Christian community, which we would call a parish or local Church. For so long as in every city there was only one congregation, it possessed the organization of the whole Church: bishop, presbyters and deacons. So each Church (we would say parish) was a cell of the Body, and, in a sense as obvious as it was real, this was *the* Church, the whole Church. It is likely that in Rome, even in the earliest times, there was not *only* one congregation. But the situation there, as time went on and the Church increased in numbers, is peculiarly instructive; for by various fictions the notion was zealously maintained that there was but one Church in Rome, the Bishop being actually present in each basilica or *titulus* in turn, and ideally in them all, even though his seat was empty, and two presbyters presided as though he sat between them.

The Church is a body, it is the Body of Christ; consequently, though the Spirit of Christ is invisible, the Church is never in the strictest sense invisible, it is not a mere ideal or a generalization, for apart from men it does not exist at all. But wherever it exists, it is whole, the whole Church.

This is the point where every biological analogy, be it of the body, or of the members, or of the cells, breaks down completely. For the Church, in spite of the fact that it is composed of men, is not a biological entity, it is a spiritual entity. The Church is not informed or inspired by an individual soul but by the universal Spirit. Therefore it cannot be pinned down to a particular place, as every other body can. It is now here, now there, wherever the Spirit of Christ finds men who are faithful.

The saying attributed to Jesus in Matt. 18:20, "Where two or three are gathered together in my name, there am I in the midst of them," is definitive for the idea of the Church which prevailed in the earliest times. The first clause suggested a proverb which was current in the second century: *Ubi tres ibi ecclesia.* Tertullian quoted it three times. In the early years of the second century St. Ignatius (in the first instance we have the word catholic as a qualification of the Church, *Ad Smyr.* 8:2) dwelt rather upon the second clause when he said, "Wherever Jesus Christ is, there is the universal Church." This affirms that the Church wholly is wherever Christ is. Indeed, what can be more *whole* than a body of Christians, however few they may be, if only Christ is in the midst of them? But the practical question arises, Where is Christ? How can we know that He is here or there? To this St. Ignatius gave a practical answer which roughly corresponded with the actual situation in his day, when the Gnostic heresies were drawing disciples away from the fold one by one, but could not commonly seduce the shepherds. He affirmed roundly that one may safely assume that Christ is "wherever the bishop is, with the presbyters and deacons." This perhaps was true enough at that time, but it did not long remain a safe assumption. For the time came when the bishop and all his clergy went over into heresy. And we may say that at no time would it be reasonable to assume that where the signs of Christ's presence were evident there was no Church, because the customary organs were lacking. For where Christ is, there is the Church—and cannot Christ create the organs? It not only is permissible to recognize as the Church every body in which Christ is known to be, but it is obligatory. Otherwise we stultify the notion of the church.*

In his little book on *The Christian Ecclesia* Dr. Hort gave a full account of the use of the word Church in the New Testament, which I summarize here more briefly than I did in a book written twenty years ago.

That there is some discrepancy between our idea of the Church and that which prevailed in the earliest times we are compelled to recognize when we observe that the terms we most naturally use are not found at all in the New Testament. Nothing comes more naturally to us than to speak of *a* Church. Perhaps we might prefer to write the word without a capital. For this phrase implies that the particular church we have in mind is only a part of a larger whole, which we regard as the summation of all the individual churches. But in the New Testament no such expression is to be found. We find only "the Church." This implies that any Church, if it deserves the name, is the Church universal. We have difficulty with this notion because we think of universality in terms of special extension, although this evidently does not apply to spiritual phenomena. The New Testament applies to the Church no other adjectives but whole and glorious. So far as I can recall, the early Catholic age used only such adjectives as true, holy, catholic, ecumenical and apostolic, avoiding any terms which could be taken to imply that the Church anywhere is merely a local Church.

Likewise we find it natural to speak of the Roman Church, the Ephesian Church, etc.; and when we observe that such an expression, which defines and limits the Church geographically, is foreign to the New Testament, we would be inclined to correct

* In my book on *Problems of Church Unity,* chapter II, pp. 11-39, I made as clear as I could twenty years ago the early Christian idea of the Church. I can make it no clearer now, although perhaps I might make it more persuasive. It is not an easy idea to grasp; but certainly it is a lofty idea; no *higher* idea of the Church has ever been entertained. Perhaps the more or less mechanical or legalistic idea which ultimately prevailed was handier; but that it was not more practical is proved by the consideration that it has accounted for some of the divisions in the Church, and still more for the persistence of them.

it by saying, the Church of Rome, etc. But this expression, too, it foreign to the New Testament. The New Testament says, "the Church *in* Rome," etc. By way of exception the Church is twice spoken of as "the Church of the Thessalonians," and once as "the Church of the Laodiceans." Six times, when reference is made to a plurality of Churches in a large region, St. Paul uses a territorial expression: "the Churches of Judaea" (Gal. 1:22), "of Asia" (1 Cor. 16:19), "of Galatia" (1 Cor. 16:1; Gal. 1:2), "of Macedonia" (2 Cor. 8:1), and, more generally, "of the Gentiles" (Rom. 16:4). "In these collective instances," says Hort, "the simple and convenient genitive could lead to no misunderstanding."

It is significant that, although in his Epistles to the Ephesians and the Colossians St. Paul thought of the whole multitude of Christians throughout the world as constituting the Body of Christ (which here is evidently much more than a metaphor), he could say without any sense of inconsistency to the Church in Corinth, "You are the Body of Christ." For where Christ is, though there be but two or three disciples, there is the Catholic Church, the Body of Christ.

But how about the use of the plural?* This seems to favor our common view that a local Church is only a fractional part of the whole. It does in fact express the understanding that the Church might be here and there at the same time. But the argument which we might be disposed to found upon this becomes even in our eyes a *reductio ad absurdum* when we take into consideration an expression which is totally strange to us, namely, "the Church in the house."† Here the lofty name of the Church is applied to a group of disciples who were accustomed to meet, perhaps with no definite organization, in one or another private house. Although they did not comprise all the Christians in that place, they were not regarded as a fraction.

We learn incidentally from St. Paul (2 Cor. 3:1) that when the disciples went from place to place they were expected to carry

* We find the word churches, for example, in 1 Thess. 2:14; Rom. 16:16; 1 Cor. 7:17; 11:16; and generally throughout this Epistle (except in the first verse); and in Rev. 2:7 and similar passages.

† Rom. 16:5; 1 Cor. 16:19; Col. 4:15; Philemon 2; cf. Rom. 16:14, 15.

"a letter of commendation" to the Church or Churches whither they might come. That was a very natural precaution. But it would be over-hasty to conclude that this must mean precisely what it means with us, that they would be received into the "membership" of another parish. No, it simply meant that they needed to be *recognized* as genuine disciples, who already were members of the Body of Christ, and therefore were members of every Church, wherever they happened to be. It is characteristic of the whole thought of the early Church that recognition of membership in the Church was all that was needed. This was needed even for teachers and prophets. St. Paul needed no letter of commendation only because he was well known in the Church which he had founded. And, according to the very idea of the Church, it is just as true today that the recognition of genuine Christian character, and, it may be, a specific gift as a teacher, ought to assure to every disciple a welcome in every Church.

Although I have said so much here about the Church, I have hardly said more than enough to justify the affirmation that in the action of the Liturgy it is the Church which is the agent—and to guard against the presumptuous notion that any human society as such, or any man as the representative of such a society, is the sole agent, as though the action of the Liturgy could be performed apart from Christ.

The Church is thoroughly Christocentric; for Christ is in the midst of it, and the Church is his Body. Even more evidently the Liturgy is Christocentric, even though it is the rule that the prayers are addressed to God the Father. Indeed this rule is justified by the fact that Christ is the *subject* of the Liturgy; that is, he is not a passive object, but is preeminently the agent. This is the emphatic affirmation of one of the Benedictine fathers who is a prominent exponent of Liturgical Reform. We need to heed it. For we are not entirely immune to the mad delusion which conceives that the Creator might be created by his creatures, justifying Robert Browning's characterization of St. Praxed's as a church in which one can "see God made and eaten all day long." It is Christ who in the Eucharist gives himself to his people as the Bread of life; it is he who makes the sacrifice of himself. The Church is the agent—but not the Church apart from Christ. Man's part in the action of the Liturgy is small, and for the most part it is representative: he who acts on behalf of the people is not so much *their* representative as Christ's, for the *liturgos* acts really in Christ's stead, *vice Christi vere fungitur*, as said St. Cyprian (Epist. 63).

CHAPTER SEVEN

DOMUS ECCLESIAE

A PLACE FOR THE LITURGY

It was affirmed in the preceding chapter that the Liturgy is "in and for and by the Church." When we say "in the Church" we do in a sense determine its place, yet not locally, as we have seen; for it may still be asked, Where is the Church? The ubication of the Church is defined by the *ubi* of Christ. Where Christ is, there is the Church. As a body, composed of men and women, it must be, if only temporarily, in a definite place—"in Rome," in the house of Nymphas (Col. 4:15), etc.—and therefore it needs a house, a habitation, a home, although it may get along without a roof (Acts 16:13, 16).

The Church in the wilderness, that is, the people of Israel, had the Tabernacle, which went where it went, and a "rock," which, as St. Paul said (1 Cor. 10:4), "followed them" and gave them drink; and wheresoever they were God gave them manna from heaven. We must remember that by St. Paul and St. John (Jn. 6:31-33) such thoughts were expressly associated with the Eucharist. They were types of it. We must remember, too, that Jesus also fed his followers in the wilderness, when "He took the loaves, and, having given thanks, He broke them, and gave to his disciples" (Mk. 8:6). St. John regarded this as the first Eucharist. So the Church can make itself everywhere at home. St. Paul "broke bread" on a ship which seemed ready to sink, where there were no Christians to communicate with him (Acts. 27:35). But naturally the Church seeks a house, as Jesus did when he repaired with his disciples to the upper room to celebrate the

Last Supper. And as soon as it could the Church found an earthly home, a place for worship.

What are we to call this house of the Church? Alas, we have only an equivocal name for it—the same word church, only with the difference, which is not very striking to the eye and not at all obvious to the ear, that it is written without a capital letter. We can properly speak of *a* church, because it denominates a material entity which may be one of many. It seems probable that the English word church, as well as the Scottish kirk and the German *Kirche,* was applied originally to the material edifice rather than to the people of God. For it is plausibly derived from the Greek *kyriaka,* an adjective corresponding to the title Lord which was applied to everything that was regarded as God's possession, held in trust by the Church. This notion of God's property gave rise in Roman Law to the totally new concepts of trusteeship and the corporation sole. The Romance languages have unfortunately the same defect as ours: they have only one word (*église, chiesa, iglesia*) to denote the people of God (the *ecclesia*) and the building which houses it. So likewise have the Greeks and Russians. But the word denotes primarily the people of God, and only secondarily the building. To escape from this equivocation, which tends to materialize the idea of the Church by fixing attention upon the edifice, the Puritans preferred to use the term meeting-house. We have seen that this preference was preposterous, in the sense of putting the cart before the horse. It is more deplorable that the word meeting-house was used intentionally to divest the church edifice of every numinous association. For by "meeting-house" the Puritans did not mean the place where the Church meets God, but where the people meet one another. They would not, like Moses (Gen. 3:5), put off their shoes from off their feet because this is holy ground, and the Quakers would not even put off their hats from off their heads. Yet every meeting for prayer is a meeting with God, and the Lord's Supper is the most preeminent instance of it. By its constant repetition it hallows the house of God more really than a spot of ground in Syria was hallowed by Jacob's dream, which prompted him to exclaim, "How dreadful is this place! This is none other but the house of God, and this is the gate of heaven" (Gen. 28:17). The Puritans, who were so adept in exploiting the Old Testament in their own interest, failed to observe that the "tent of meeting" (Ex. 29:42-44) was so called because it was there Moses met with God, and that the assembly which they called the Church deserves that name only because it is a meeting with God. The house in which the Church constantly meets acquires necessarily, unless we do violence to our natural feelings, a character of holiness, of numinous awe.

Obviously, in its earliest stadium the Church could not often acquire a permanent abode. But that it had a disposition to seek it is proved by the fact it found such a home earlier than might be expected. For it is certain that while the Church was still a prohibited society it began to build churches; and it is significant that the churches which were built in Rome immediately after the Peace of Constantine, and which still exist, were so commonly built upon sites already consecrated by Christian worship that we can count upon finding beneath them the walls of the house in which the Church had been a guest. It is therefore a seductive theory, and one by which I was for a while seduced, that the form of the church (the so-called basilica) when it emerged into the light of history was determined by the customary use of the atrium of a private dwelling. This theory might account for the fact that the Christian temple is, as has been aptly said, like a pagan temple turned outside in, i.e. with its colonnades inside it. But this is sufficiently accounted for by the consideration that the Christians assembled within the temple, instead of standing in front of it as the pagans did. According to the pagan notion the temple was the house of the god—and, notoriously, that was also the Hebrew notion: the Hebrew people stood in front of the Tabernacle and entered only into the court of the Temple. When we speak of the church as the house of God we do not understand it in the same sense. And the theory I have mentioned, however seductive it is, does not account for the semicircular apse, which was an almost universal feature of the early churches, and yet was not characteristic of the Roman or Greek house. There seems now some reason to suppose that the apse was suggested by the buildings used for the mystic cults which in some ways were analogous enough to the Christian societies to provoke frequent comparison. They had, at all events, this in common, that they were conscious of performing a cult. It is true that the semicircular apse was also a prominent feature of the halls of justice and political administration which were called by the Greek name *basilica* (i.e. royal) because they served the interest of the sovereign people. In this sense the name was not only tolerated but popular, in spite of the prejudice the Romans felt against the oriental title of king (*basileus*). The Christians, too, liked this name and appropriated it to their churches—not because they resembled the Roman basilicas, but because (like *kyriaka*) this name indicated that the house was appropriated to the service of the divine King. As for the notion that the early churches were built like the Roman basilicas, it is enough to observe that, though this is true of St. Peter's in Rome when it was built a second time in the sixteenth century on the plan of the Basilica of Maxentius, it was very evidently not true of the church built by Constantine in the fourth century. It was only because of a formal resemblance that the apsidal platform was often called the tribune. We shall see that the Christian basilica is entirely *sui generis.*

The most appropriate name ever used for the Christian edifice was *domus ecclesiae,* the house (or we might say, the home) of the Church. It was the Church which consecrated the house; and this house was so characteristic an expression of the needs of Christian worship that it was evidently designed to fit it—as thoroughly as the shell fits the snail. This, of course, is not to affirm that it was in the least degree independent of the prevailing fashion, which was determined in the first instance by the Classical styles of architecture, by the materials available, and by the building techniques which were currently used. The gradual changes which came about in the house of the Church (the transition from the Classical to the Romanesque, to the Gothic, to the Renaissance styles) were due in large part to developments in building techniques, which in turn were dependent upon the rise and fall of the economic level; but they reflect also a change in the conception of the action of the Liturgy. Yet it may be said that at each stage the house fitted the Liturgy; and as the Liturgy itself was not essentially changed, neither was the plan of the house.

The form of the house defines the character of Christian worship. Although more than two centuries elapsed between the days of the Apostles and the earliest churches we know, yet the fact that spontaneously throughout the whole Empire they were built everywhere upon the same plan gives us reason to assume that the cult which was universal in the fourth century was not essentially different from that of a much earlier time. This assumption is strongly supported by the accounts we have of the Liturgy at the beginning of the second century. During the whole course of Church history the form of the church has not been essentially changed, except by the deep monastic choir, which was characteristic of the late Middle Ages, chiefly in Northern Europe, and by the Spanish fashion, beginning with the Renaissance, which expropriated a great part of the nave for the choir of the cathedral canons.

It must be evident why I have dwelt so long upon the *place* of the Liturgy; for the character of this place defines for us the essential action of the Liturgy.

Although it is true that the Liturgy, at least from the time of Justin Martyr in the middle of the second century, always included Scripture lessons and a sermon, yet the house of the Church was not built as an auditorium—as many churches are today by Christian denominations which do not often celebrate the Lord's Supper. On the other hand, we must remark that it was suitable enough for hearing and seeing everything that was done by the *ecclesia.* The Greek iconostasis, designed to hide the sacred mysteries from the people, is due to a perversion, which for a while prompted the use of curtains even in the West. The normal basilica was nevertheless a good auditorium because it had a flat ceiling, and the bishop could be heard and seen by all when he spoke from his seat in the apse or stood behind the Holy Table. Visibility and audibility always remain, though they are often ignored, important requisites for the house of the Church.

Although the house was evidently designed for the celebration of the Lord's Supper, yet it was not built as a *triclinium* (dining room), because the "Supper" was a symbolical meal which did not require the participants to recline at tables. The one table was enough, the Holy Table.

We ought to use more frequently than we do the word Holy Table, which is preferred by the Book of Common Prayer. For the word table indicates what our altar primarily is. St. Paul (do not forget that he was a Catholic) compares the altar of the Church with the pagan altars; but to make the analogy clear he calls them both "tables" (1 Cor. 10:21). That, in fact, is what the pagan altar was: it was a table from which the gods were fed, and the people along with them. It reveals a strange misapprehension to say of the Holy Table when it is thrust up against the wall like a shelf that it is built "altarwise"; for pagan altars were never built that way, they always stood free, as did the altars of Israel also, so that the worshipers might surround them. The Christian altar was in the midst of the congregation, yet not in the center of the room, as it was in the Greek proscenium where the chorus danced around it. It is true that Constantine built several churches on a central plan, which would require the Altar to be in the center. He was doubtless influenced by pagan notions, and therefore the precedent he set was not often followed. For the central plan, though it was appropriate for a baptistery or for a tomb, was not suitable for the Liturgy. There was a reason for placing the Holy Table near the end of a long rectangular room. The people of God, though ideally they surrounded the Table, did not do so indiscriminately. No doubt in the earliest time all the disciples sat at a common table. Indeed a family group celebrating the Holy Communion in memory of their dead is so represented in an early picture of the Roman catacombs. Ordinarily the principal men—apostles, prophets, teachers, and, when they were lacking, a bishop with the presbyters—would sit, of course, at the head of the table, and whosoever presided was understood to sit in Christ's place and expected to do what he did at the Last Supper. And when because of the growth of the Church it was no longer possible for all to sit, the chief personages would, of course, continue to do so—and thus nothing remained of the table but, as we might say, the upper end. That was sufficient for a symbolical feast. And no need was felt of enlarging the table to correspond with the size of the building. It was enough that its importance was indicated by the position in front of the apse, to which the eye was led by all the prominent lines of the building. At a later time (we hardly know how early) it was indicated also by the ciborium or baldachin, which might correspond in size to the building.

As I have said, the people did not gather around the Altar indiscriminately. It was of course the clergy who enjoyed the privilege of sitting or standing behind the Altar, facing the people, who would approach it more closely at the *fractio panis* in order to communicate. It is thus that the clergy, the more prominent members of the Body, were distinguished from the people, and in no other way were they so ostensibly distinguished. This was the "place" to which St. Clement of Rome plead to have those Corinthian presbyters restored who, being deprived of their place, were practically deposed from their office. Hermas denounced the pretensions of what he called "the chief-seaters." At the beginning of the second century it was ordinarily the bishop who presided, with the presbyters seated on either side of him, and the deacons standing. Whosoever presided occupied evidently the place of Christ. This is the reason why St. Ignatius compared the bishop with Christ and the presbyters with the Apostles. The thought of "succession" was not involved in this analogy. In our day, when it is generally a presbyter who presides at the Eucharist, this analogy applies to him too.

Such was the arrangement of the *domus ecclesiae* until well into the Middle Ages, and such it still is in all the most ancient churches, notably in the basilicas of Rome. No wonder Liturgical Reform stresses the importance of restoring the Altar to its proper place, in order that the action of the Liturgy, especially the reciprocal action of priest and people, may be rightly understood. Yet what is first in intention may be last in execution. We may have to be content with regarding the Altar *as if* it were in the midst. This reform can be accomplished more easily by the Roman Catholics than by us, because, after all, it represents the custom of the Papal basilicas, and also perhaps because the people, being accustomed to the side-altars which are commonly very approachable, are ready to treat the great Altar with more familiarity than we do. Yet it is difficult for them too, since at the Papal altars the celebrant does not any longer face the people openly, being hidden by the crucifix and the candlesticks with which a late medieval fashion encumbered the Altar. This is one of the changes our churches underwent by reason of an altered understanding (not to say misunderstanding) of the action of the Liturgy; and we who have inherited these changes are constantly under a temptation to adopt the understanding of the Liturgy which they express, i.e. to conceive that the priest acts instead of the people, rather than with them and on their behalf. In the Roman Church the Reformers have accomplished this much, that in many places the bishop prohibits the construction of new churches unless the high altar is at such a distance from the wall that the celebrant might stand behind it if he would.

In this respect we are not likely to get so far. For our bishops have no such authority, and the people are not so well instructed about the character of the Liturgy that they could wish to carry out such a reform. Moreover there is a material difficulty; for this change involves a great alteration in the sanctuary, and perhaps in the choir. But in other respects it might be said that what the Roman reformers aim at was accomplished for us in large part by the Protestant Reformation, which in this case was evidently not a revolution but a recall to ancient practice. Because in the Liturgy we use the vernacular, the people do not need much persuasion to join in the dialogue of the Mass: they already do it, if not musically or even heartily, at least audibly. Far more important is the fact that we need not be reminded that Communion is the culmination of the Liturgy. The Liturgy of the Book of Common Prayer was formulated with the express intention of making this truth clear. Too clear, one might be inclined to say; for the English book had the intention of suppressing other aspects of the essential action of the Liturgy, especially sacrifice. And although this defect has been repaired in the American book, and in the "Deposited Book" of the Church of England, there remains with us a wide-spread prejudice against non-communicating attendance, which reflects the notion that in the Liturgy there is no essential action except the Communion. This can be understood as a revulsion against the prevalent Roman view that there is no essential action except the Sacrifice. That view was fostered by the custom of saying many, many Masses at which no one communicated but the celebrant. Vice versa, the people are encouraged to gather in the church to communicate in the reserved Sacrament which is administered *before* the Mass. This is evidently a misunderstanding; and the notion that the Liturgy culminates in the Sacrifice is belied as often as we speak of the Table of the Lord, or of the Lord's Supper, or of the Holy Communion, or indeed of the Eucharist. Only the neutral word mass is compatible with this view, and hence this is the word most commonly used.

I hope it is evident at this point, and at all events it will be evident later, that this description of the *domus ecclesiae* is by no means irrelevant to our theme, which is essential action in the Liturgy.

CHAPTER EIGHT

SCRIPTURE AND SERMON

THE DIDACTIC PART OF THE LITURGY

The part of the Liturgy devoted to instruction is perhaps the part in which action is most obvious—at least on the part of the clergy, who have the duty of preaching the sermon. The delivery of the sermon is action of the most obvious sort, and the preparation of it, though it is action of a different sort, is evidently no less important. But the public reading of the Holy Scriptures (which surely are not less edifying than the sermon) implies action which is quite as real, being more directly the action of God through his Word. And the priest too, if he is accustomed to pray, "Lord, purify my heart that I may worthily announce thy Gospel," must be aware that he has a part in this sublime action.

On the other hand, it may be thought that the people who listen to the Scriptures and the sermon have a purely passive part to play. But if, instead of saying of the people that they listen, we should say that they *hear* the Word of God, theirs will not seem to be an inactive role. For the Scriptures both of the Old and of the New Testament commonly speak of an inner hearing which results in obedience. Hence St. Paul says (Rom. 10:17), "Faith cometh by hearing, and hearing by the Word of God." Hearing therefore means at least a resolution to obey—and what a decisive action in the heart of man is implied by this resolution! The sermon, if it is, as it ought to be, an obviously personal application of God's Word, may provoke the same decision; and a sermon which has not the aim, directly or indirectly, of bringing men to the decision that they will strive to obey God in all their actions, or of confirming them in this resolution, does not deserve to be called a sermon. The word "didactic" therefore does not adequately describe this part of the Liturgy. Yet it must be that too; the people will always need instruction, and they need in particular to be instructed about the Liturgy.

This part therefore cannot be regarded as preliminary to the Liturgy. It is an integral part of it; but it is the first part, the part which prepares for the reception of the Sacrament; and it may be used, as traditionally it was regarded, as the missionary part, appropriate to those who are not yet Christians, to catechumens, to penitents, and to all who for any reason are not in full communion with the Church.

The reading of the Scripture is an essential part of the action of the Liturgy, and the sermon is too, even though it is often omitted. I do not mean to say that without them the Liturgy would be vain and the Eucharist invalid; for when I speak here and in other cases of "essential action" the meaning is that such action properly belongs to the Liturgy, and that something very important is lost if this is lacking. The Creed, for example, though it was introduced late into the Liturgy, was aptly introduced, for it provides the people with an opportunity to express their faith in the doctrine of the Scriptures which have just been read.

Normally the sermon as well as the Scripture lessons belong in the Liturgy. This fact is obscured when many masses are said every day and many times a day where there is no audience at all or a very scanty one. It would of course be vain to preach the Word of God if there is no one to hear. But we must not forget that the normal Sunday Eucharist includes the sermon. It was so from the earliest times. St. Paul's sermon at Troas, where he "prolonged his speech until midnight" (Acts 20:7), before they "broke bread" in the early hours of the first day of the week, was doubtless abnormally long, but this instance suggests that the sermon was a normal part of the Sunday Eucharist, as it certainly was a century later when Justin Martyr (in his *First Apology*, c. 67) described for outsiders the general character of Christian worship: "And on the day named after the Sun all who live in the cities and the surrounding country gather together in one place, and the memorials of the Apostles [i.e. the Gospels, the Acts and the Epistles] or the writings of the Prophets [including of course the Law] are read as long as time permits; then, when the reader has ceased, the president [i.e. the bishop] utters a discourse instructing the people to imitate these good examples." We see here that the instruction was hortatory and practical, and that it was based on the Scriptures which had just been read. This indicates the proper position for the sermon, immediately after the reading of the Scriptures, where in fact we have it in the Liturgy, though at Morning and Evening Prayer do not think of following this good example. We are apprised too by this passage of the propriety of including in the Liturgy, not only Gospels and Epistles, but also passages from "the Prophets." The lack of this was not felt so long as Morning Prayer commonly preceded the Sunday Eucharist; and now, if we do not say Morning Prayer, we are permitted here in America to read an Old Testament Lesson—not, however, *in* the Liturgy, but just before it. Really the oracles of God given in the Old Testament belong *in* the Liturgy, not only because they are generally instructive and edifying, but because they may be instructive about the Liturgy itself. Only a couple of months ago Dom Damasus Winzen delivered in New York, at no less conspicuous a place than the Barbizon-Plaza, four lectures on "The Old Testament—Our Guide to the Mass." We are in danger of falling behind in the procession of Liturgical Reform.

In the time of Justin Martyr, when apostles, prophets and teachers were no more, and when the presbyters were not yet supposed to be able to preach, only the bishops were available as preachers. According to the Pastoral Epistles, the bishop was expected to be "apt to teach" (1 Tim. 3:2), "holding to the faithful word which is according to the teaching, that he may be able both to exhort in the sound doctrine, and to convince the gainsayers" (Tit. 1:9). That was not expecting very much from the bishops, who, it must be remembered, had no formal theological training, and for the most part were obliged to earn their own living. Every parish priest today would seem to be better prepared to preach a learned and perhaps even an oratorical sermon. No more was required then of the bishop than the Roman Church requires now of every priest, that he be able to "explain the Gospel." The second century, one might say, registered the low watermark of Christian preaching; and yet such simple sermons converted the world. This was the beginning of all good preaching. The great bishops of the fifth century preached homilies. If such were the character of sermons today, though they were ever so simple, there would be no plea made for a "moratorium on preaching."

One might think that for us there can be no great need of emphasizing the importance of the sermon in the Liturgy, seeing that the Book of Common Prayer assigns it a place here—and *only* here. "Here followeth the Sermon," seems to be mandatory, and I suppose it was meant to be. For when this rubric was written no one expected that there would often be celebrations of the Eucharist when there was no audience. Reasonably enough, we do not now observe this rule strictly; and very reasonably, too, we do not confine the sermon to the Liturgy. We make a place for it *after* Morning and Evening Prayer. That is unfortunate because it puts the sermon after the prayers, whereas in the Liturgy it is aptly assigned to a place before the prayers. And unfortunately our book—perhaps because it is a prayer book—makes no provision for a sermon without prayers. It need not be without prayer, of course, but it might be held apart from a long service of worship which necessarily curtails the length of the sermon, which, if it is expressly intended for instruction, should have at least as much time allotted to it as the conventional fifty minutes of an academic lecture. But that is not ordinarily possible in the Liturgy.

In the Liturgy the position of the sermon is significant. It implies that the sermon has an appropriate place in the Eucharist, serving not only to incite the people to such action as is becoming to Christians outside the church, but to enhance their devotion in prayer and their understanding of the action they are performing in the Liturgy.

Although the Eucharist is a sacrament, that is, a mystery (as originally it was called), and therefore surpasses all understanding and has an effect which is incommensurate with our intellectual grasp of it (and in this sense is *ex opere operato*),* yet as a Christian sacrament it has a spiritual operation and does not work in a purely material way, like a drug, or like the food which nourishes our bodies. The Eucharist is (to use St. Paul's phrase in Rom. 12:1) "a reasonable service," meaning a cult in which reason has its part. Hence instruction has its place within the Liturgy and is an essential part of the whole action.

But whether within the Liturgy or outside it, the sermon must not be treated as an inferior part of Christian worship. Those who think meanly of this part of the liturgical action will perform it badly—perhaps only because they perform it badly they think meanly of it. St. Peter exhorts us (1 Pet. 4:11), "If any man speak, let him speak as it were oracles of God." Indeed, unless the words of the preacher are "lively oracles," there is not much use in uttering them. Luther laid equal emphasis upon the Word and the Sacraments—and that is good Catholicism.

Wherever and whenever the Church was great the sermon has been held in the highest esteem; and in the early age the gift of teaching was accounted the highest gift (*charisma*) after charity (1 Cor. 14:1, 39). Nowadays we are likely to forget that when the minister of the Gospel was first regarded as a priest it was precisely because he was a *minister of the Gospel,* one who "handled the Word of God." St. Paul instituted this comparison with the Old Testament priesthood when he said (1 Cor. 9:13,14), "Know ye not that they which minister about sacred things eat of the things of the Temple, they which wait upon the Altar? Even so did the Lord ordain that they which proclaim the Gospel should live by the Gospel." And about the end of the first century the *Didache* prescribed that "all the first fruits shall be given to the prophets, for they are your high priests." It was not till later

* Fie upon me! I have before now been criticized, and rightly, for using this term. It was roguish of me, if not impish, to use it in this connection, knowing what *opus operatum* originally meant in Roman philosophy (Plutarch). I have no good right to use it even as a pugnacious protest against the notion that the efficacy of a sacrament depends upon man's understanding of the *modus operandi.* It might be used to denote the fact that bread in itself is so constituted that it can nourish the human body. But even this efficacy I should prefer to ascribe, if only remotely, to an *operatio dei;* and certainly it is to this I would ascribe, directly and wholly, the efficacy of a sacrament.

that the dignity of priesthood devolved upon the bishop; and until well along in the Middle Ages, after the presbyters had for many centuries been the ordinary celebrants of the Eucharist, were they commonly given the title of priest (*sacerdos*). This sounds rather ironical, seeing that our English word priest is derived from presbyter. Tertullian, however, called the presbyters priests and distinguished the bishop as the *summus sacerdos.*

CHAPTER NINE

THE OFFERTORY

MATERIAL ACTION SPIRITUALIZED

No one can fail to see that the Offertory is action; but perhaps to finely fibered souls such action as this, action so material, may seem incongruous with a spiritual worship. In early times the offerings were more crassly material than they are now, for they were gifts in kind, including the food for the common meal, the *agape,* and to serve the wants of all who looked to the Church for support. There was nothing abhorrent in this, like the blood of bullocks and calves which were offered in the Temple. Jesus, as soon as He saw this worship, knew that it was dated, and put on end to it forever. The Christians could justly boast that theirs was an "unbloody sacrifice." They offered only the fruits of the earth, including the bread and the wine which were the symbols of Christ's presence.

But can even the fruits of the earth be an integral part of a spiritual worship? The early Church had no doubt of it, for it did not think of spirit as opposed to matter. The contempt of matter which characterized the Gnostic sects was not shared by the Catholic Church, which believed in God as the Creator. Moreover, the Incarnation was for the Church the preeminent instance of the congruity of matter—a human body—with the divine Spirit; and, in a way, the Incarnation was repeated when bread and wine were spiritualized in the Eucharist. Reflecting especially upon the bread and wine which we call specifically the "oblations," several early Christian writers saw in the Offertory an essential action which illuminates the character of the whole Liturgy.

Having here reached a point where it is possible to survey the action of the Liturgy as a whole, I must quote a couple of these passages and comment upon them. I cannot here be as concise as elsewhere I have endeavored to be in order to keep this book as small as I would like. What I say here is substantially what I said twenty years ago in *Problems of Church Unity.*

At a very early age, and presumably from the beginning, the Church was able to see an instructive parallel between the work of creation and the work of redemption. Justin Martyr (*First Apol.* c. 67) sees in the Eucharist the exaltation of both of these things, the material creation and the spiritual re-creation. "On Sunday we all hold a meeting in common, since it is the first day, in which God transformed the darkness and dead matter to create the cosmos, and Jesus Christ our Saviour on the same day rose from the dead." He implies (c. 13) that at every meal the Christians gave thanks for the gifts they received as instances of God's goodness as Creator, and for the gift also of Christ as the Redeemer, although doubtless he had especially in view, not the little eucharist for daily bread, but the great Eucharist for the bread of life, when he asserted that the Christians, not being atheists, as was vulgarly believed, praise the Creator for all the good things they receive, "employing pomps and hymns to express their gratitude for the incorruptibility they expect to attain through faith in Christ." This double remembrance or memorial (*anamnesis*) of God's goodness as Creator and Redeemer, which is profoundly characteritsic of the action of the Liturgy, is mentioned again in the *Dialogue,* where it is said (c. 117) that prayers and thanksgivings are the only sacrifices perfect and well-pleasing to God, and that these alone are offered by Christians in the commemoration effected by their "solid and liquid food" (i.e. bread and wine), whereby the sufferings endured for us by the Son of God are brought to mind; and also when he speaks (c. 41) of "the bread of the Eucharist, the celebration of which our Lord Jesus Christ ordained in remembrance of the sufferings he endured, that *at the same time* we might give thanks to God for the creation of the world with all that therein is for the sake of man, and for delivering us from the evil in which we lay." At about the end of the second century this same thought was more fully developed by Irenaeus, who says (*Adv. Haer.* IV, 18), "For we offer unto him the things that are his, proclaiming appropriately the communion and oneness of flesh and spirit. For that which on earth is bread, when it has received the invocation of God is no longer common bread but Eucharist, consisting of two things, at once earthly and heavenly. So also our bodies, when they have received the Eucharist, are no longer corruptible, having the hope of the resurrection."

Whenever I have spoken or written about the Eucharist I have constantly had in mind a precious book which in some respects is the best we have on this subject: *Der christliche Gemeindegottesdienst im apostolischen und alt-katholischen Zeitalter* (Christian Common Worship in Apostolic and Early-Catholic Times), by Theodosius Harnack, published at Erlangen in 1854, when the author was Professor of Theology in the university of that name. I think of it as a little book, but actually it contains 524 closely printed pages. I acquired this book when I went to Germany as a student in 1893, and the following year I attended at Berlin a seminary on this subject which was conducted by Adolf Harnack and was struck by the fact that he followed closely the path his father had marked out. I took occasion to ask him if he agreed entirely with his father's books. He said, "I might add something to it, but I would subtract nothing from it."

In spite of such high commendation, I have not seen this book mentioned in English, although I have read, I think, everything of importance that has been written about the Eucharist.

Perhaps I have been inhibited from talking about the doctrine of the Holy Communion by the consideration that so much has been said vainly, and for the most part contentiously, about the sacrament which was instituted to express Christian love and unity; but perhaps also by the reflection that the form and shape of the Liturgy is the most adequate definition of the Sacrament. For in this case the form and the essence are not distinguishable. It might be said therefore that I have already defined the Sacrament implicitly. And now when I essay to say in words what it essentially is, I prefer to use terms which are found in the earliest

Christian records; and I hope to avoid suspicion of sectarian bias when I follow the lead of a Lutheran who was a scholar as well as an ardent Christian. So from this book I here translate a few paragraphs (pp. 298-302) in which Th. Harnack summarizes the lessons he learned from Justin Martyr and Irenaeus, eminent representatives of the Church in the second century. I translate these paragraphs literally, except for a Latin quotation from Irenaeus, which I put into English, and a few Greek words which I transliterate.

> Comparing now what we have just learned from Irenaeus with what we learned from Justin, it will be seen that both our early-catholic fathers agree perfectly in what they say about the Eucharist, except that Irenaeus, fortunately for us, explains and completes what Justin said less distinctly or only by implication. Both describe the action of the Liturgy as consisting of two intimately related acts: (1) a general ascription of praise to God for the work of creation, represented by the creatures of bread and wine, which were aptly chosen by Christ as the vehicles for this Sacrament; and (2) the specific act of eucharist and consecration, consisting of the thanksgiving, with express reference to the words of institution (the "word of God" as Justin calls it), a word which was developed into a petition (*epiclasis* or *eclasis*) for the sending down of the Holy Spirit with the intent of making the earthly gifts vehicles of Christ's body and blood, sanctifying them as the means of securing the promised creative grace, and sanctifying also the partakers that they may be worthy and blessed recipients of the sacramental food—this being the sole and only end to which the whole action was directed, the moment towards which it hastened as its final and proper goal.
>
> The relation of these two acts to one another is clear enough, for there is obviously a progress, a climactic progress, from the general to the particular, from the theme of creation to that of redemption, an ascent from praise to thanksgiving, and from thanksgiving to petition—though it was not on this scheme the prayer was intent, but on the right attitude of the heart to God (Ps. 51:19, "Then shalt thou delight in the sacrifices of righteousness"; Isa. 57:15, "I dwell in the high and holy place, with him also who is of a contrite and humble spirit"). But Irenaeus

defines the relationship more definitely: he sees in these two acts a demonstration, not of community and fellowship only, but also of union, God placing Himself in union through the Lord's Supper, not only with the creaturely elements of bread and wine, but also with the faithful recipients of the Sacrament. So he says in a passage which already has been cited in part and now shall be quoted in full (*Adv. Haer.* iv, 18, 5): 'We offer unto Him what are His, aptly proclaiming the communion and unity of the flesh and the spirit. For the bread when it has received the *epiclasis* of God is no longer common bread but eucharist, consisting of two things, the earthly and the heavenly; so also our bodies, receiving the Eucharist, are no longer corruptible, having the hope of the resurrection.'

Here we have in a nutshell the progress of the liturgical action as a whole: the offering and the proclamation, then the invocation and consecration, and finally the reception of the Sacrament with the blessing which accompanies it. However, the statement which especially interests us at this point is the first, where Irenaeus, if we understand his view in relation to the context, says in effect, We offer unto God what is His, when, in distinction from the Gnostics, we believe and teach that there is a communion, indeed a oneness (*henosis*) as between the bodily and the spiritual, the earthly and the heavenly, the human and the divine. For not only is there by virtue of the creation a general communion between God and all His creatures, but also for our salvation the eternal Logos has come into union with the creature by taking upon him our flesh. Upon this double basis rests the Eucharistic oblation (*prosphora*), testifying to the intimate relation which subsists between creation and redemption. The communion (*koinonia*) assumes this and proclaims it in the prayer of praise, while the thanksgiving along with the petition which follows proclaims the oneness. In this petition, the *epiclasis*, faith in the fact of the Incarnation and in the creative 'word' of the Lord's institution asks for and confidently expects the oneness of the body and blood of Christ with the bread and wine set apart for sacramental consumption; and in turn it expects through this that oneness of Christ with the partakers of the Sacrament, in which not only their souls are united with Him, but their bodies too are assured of sharing His incorruptibility (*aphtharsia*) and of their future resurrection (*anastasis*).

Thus it is that in the celebration of the Eucharist the congregation finds itself transported into the midst of God's great acts: the acts of creation and those of redemption, the acts already performed as well as those that are promised, those that are performed for us as well as those performed upon us and in us—all have for the congregation assembled in worship their center and point of meeting in the Eucharist, which on the one hand makes the effect of them possible and actual, and on the other hand takes them for granted and relies upon the future fulfillment of the promises. And here these acts are not only taught but actually recognized and accomplished, and at the same time actually felt and experienced. For this holy action is likewise actually an effect of the incarnate Logos in the Church, and is an actual confession of faith on the part of the congregation in the communion (*koinonia*) and oneness (*henosis*) of heaven and earth, of God and man, of which we have here the earnest and pledge, which already is accomplished in the incarnate Logos and in those that are his. In fact the whole Christian view of the world and of history is mirrored as at a focus in this simple action as the faith of the early Church conceived it.

Although here the Church is intent only upon its own edification, yet in fact it is seen to exclude from its midst every sort of dualistic or pantheistic notion. For what it professes in the Sacrament is not division or tension between the heavenly and the earthly, nor the absorption of both in an indifferent unity, but a *koinonia* which, while preserving the distinctions, implies a *henosis* of such a sort that it is the truth and actuality of *koinonia*. And this the Church expresses on an ascending scale in the liturgy of the Last Supper, being led to this, not by philosophic reflection, but simply by following the sequence of God's acts.

For in the prayer of praise, beginning with the *koinonia* of God with all His creatures, as manifested in the creation, the Church presents to Him the elements of bread and wine as the first fruits, chosen as representative of the whole creation; and in lifting them up the people also lift up their hearts in thanksgiving for the personal oneness revealed in Christ, believing in His institution and making petition for the accomplishment of the sacramental oneness with him of the creaturely elements—doing all this, however, to the end that by partaking of these sacramental elements the believers may be partakers of the mystical oneness with Christ, both spiritually and bodily, this being the aim of the whole transaction, and therewith they await expectantly the complete and transfigured oneness which is reserved for the future, of which they have in the reception of the sacrament the sure pledge and earnest. So for them, as Irenaeus has indicated, the Eucharist is a meal of faith, love and hope, a factual testimony to the creation and redemption of the whole world of nature and of spirit in Christ, and to the sanctification and perfection of believers through sacramental union with Him who is their human-divine Head and Lord.

Perhaps the first thing that will strike the reader in this passage is Harnack's conception of the Eucharist as "action" and as a commemoration of "the great acts of God." Both of these conceptions have been so recently acquired by modern scholars that they have not yet become common property. Yet they were familiar to the early Church, when men had not had time to forget that the Lord's Supper was to be *done,* according to the Lord's command, "*Do* this." The art of the early Church, even more than the literature, bears witness to the common understanding that God has revealed himself more clearly, and "spoken" more emphatically, in his acts than by his words. And this not only in the greater acts—the Creation, Incarnation and Redemption, Christ's nativity, his sacrifice, his death, his resurrection, and the coming of the Holy Spirit, the great acts which are commemorated in the Catholic Creeds—but in the many acts of deliverance which are recorded in the Scriptures to the great and endless comfort of those who live in Christ and those who die in him, and for this reason were commonly depicted in the sepulchres and in the churches. "My Father worketh hitherto, and I work," is the Johannine expression of the Christian faith in God who does things and "with whom all things are possible." The predominant interest in God's acts is "mirrored as at a focal point" in the Liturgy. But all this was forgotten by the theologians when they converted theology into a philosophy, into a theory of conceptual and static relationships, a logical system in which nothing could happen and in which God himself could bring nothing new to pass. Adolf Harnack, the celebrated historian, did not apprehend that Christianity is historical in so full a sense that it is constituted, not by ideas about God, but by what God has done, what he is now doing, and what he has promised to do—historical in so broad a sense that it comprises a future event, the *Parousia,* which, in accordance with Christ's word, "until I come," is commemorated in the Eucharist. Only a short while ago when Tennyson sang,

> And so the Word had flesh and wrought
> With human hands the creed of creeds,
> In lowliness of perfect deeds,
> More true than all poetic thought,

the theologians had hardly begun to remember that God's deeds are more true than theological thought, and that the action of the Liturgy defines more effectively than words (though words are an essential part of it) what Christianity is and ever must be. Because Th. Harnack had this perception, his book is ultra-modern, although it was written a century ago. The Eucharist, because it is historical in this superlative sense, commemorating what was and what is and what is to come, was in olden times intimately associated with the hope of eternity; and now, because it is commonly regarded as the commemoration of one solitary event in the past, men hardly know what to make of it. For, even apart from this institution, mankind is not likely to forget the life and death of Jesus. Jesus is remembered with honor in the Koran; and, if Islam outlasts Christianity, many a Moslem will call his son Isa after the Saviour of the world. What we are only too prone to forget is the fact that we are immortal, and we need the weekly Eucharist to remind us of it.

Some may wonder at the sharp distinction Harnack makes between praise and thanksgiving, and still more that he reckons petition higher than either. It must be admitted that in the Roman Mass these distinctions were obscured by the intrusion of the so-called Proper Prefaces before the end of what Cyprian properly called the Preface which concludes with the *Sanctus,* a hymn of glorification, addressed to the Creator of all things as a fit conclusion to a prayer which was devoted exclusively to the praise of creation and providence—up to the moment when Hosanna! heralds the coming of the Saviour. The Proper Prefaces were introduced during the Dark Ages, and consequently all the Anglican Forms of the Liturgy inherit this defect. The prayer which follows the *Sanctus* is still, as it was originally, a thanksgiving to God for His works of redemption, concluding with a petition for the consecration of the bread and wine and of those who are about to partake of them. Even in the Greek liturgies of the fifth century, such as those ascribed to St. James and to St. Chrysostom, the distinction I dwell upon here is blurred, yet it is clear enough to confirm the presumption that it once was recognized universally, as it certainly was in the fourth century liturgy found in the seventh book of the Apostolic Constitutions.

We are not accustomed to think of petition as higher than praise, although praise is a mode of prayer which we rarely practice. Praise is conspicuous, however, in the Psalter, some of our modern hymns strike this note, and we have a pure example in the *Gloria in Excelsis Deo,* which is the most ancient hymn we use and testifies to an earlier fashion of which the hymns in the Apocalypse are an example.

But at this point we may pause to reflect that, if praise is the mode of prayer most pleasing to God, the Moslems have an advantage over us, for the glorification of God is the only sort of prayer they ever make. Mohammed, having learned from such Christians as he encountered in Arabia the doctrine of predestination, logically deduced from it a doctrine of fatalism, and therefore did not encourage or even permit his followers to address any petitions whatever to God, or to thank him inadvertently for general or special favors they could not reasonably ascribe to divine love. Islam means submission, and the only prayer a Moslem can make is a glorification of God's name. This consideration should lead us to reflect how different is the attitude Jesus taught men to assume towards the heavenly Father. Thanksgiving, the expression of a grateful heart, because it is personal, may well be more pleasing to God than the loudest glorification of his name. It has been said cynically that "gratitude is a lively expectation of favors to come"; but this is not so disparaging to man as it sounds. For, especially in relation to God, the receipt of favors properly encourages a man to expect still more—to expect of God's omnipotent love even so much as forgiveness of sin and sanctification and eternal life. We are acquainted with men who, under the incubus of materialistic determinism, think it vain and improper to ask anything of God, decry all prayers of petition, and find themselves painfully inhibited when their heart moves them to give thanks. But to God the Father even importunate petitions may be welcome, because they indicate a trusting heart and a lively faith that he can and will save to the uttermost those who cry unto him through Christ Jesus the Lord. In Jesus' parable in the Temple the Pharisee could only give thanks, and only the publican could pray, "God have mercy!" So it is that the cry Hosanna! though it is only a petition and means simply "Help now!" was accounted equivalent to Hallelujah!—Praise be to Jah! (Jehovah). An earthly potentate is pleased to hear a petition which proves that men believe he is able and willing to help. The Lord's Prayer was only petition till the Church added a doxology. Jesus taught men to ask of their heavenly Father what might be needed for the support of their earthly life, since even an earthly father whose son asks bread will not give him a stone; and to ask most of all for the Holy Spirit. This is the principal petition of the Eucharistic prayer, and it may well be the prayer most pleasing to God.

However, according to Justin and Irenaeus, it was not alone the petition for the Holy Spirit (*epiclesis*) which consecrated the Eucharistic bread. Both attribute this virtue to the prayer of thanksgiving as a whole, Justin calling the consecrated bread and wine "eucharisticized food" (*Apol.* 66), an extravagant expression equivalent to thanksgivingized, while Irenaeus called them simply eucharist (*eucharistia*). This is on a line with what is said in 1 Tim. 4:4, 5 about food which was accounted ceremonially "unclean": "For everything created by God is good, and nothing is to be rejected if it is received with thanksgiving; for then it is consecrated by the word of God and by prayer."

Yet with all this we have not yet begun to deal with the doctrine of the Holy Communion. We get to that only when we reflect upon the meaning Irenaeus attached to *koinonia*, a word we have been accustomed to translate by communion or fellowship. This Greek word (if we include the verb and the adjective derived from it) occurs 50 times in the New Testament, and we use 12 different English words to translate it—all of them aptly used, except the detestable "contribution" and "distribution," which ignore the intimate sympathy the word properly suggests. The most literal translation is "communion," and the most endearing is "fellowship"; but neither is adequate, and therefore many feel impelled to say "communion *and* fellowship." Yet even this is not enough and does not suit in all connections. The Revised Standard Version has introduced a new word, "share," and employs it 16 times very appropriately, but with questionable taste it has dropped the word "communion" even in such a passage as 1 Cor. 10-16, using "participation" instead. In itself participation is a good word, and (including with it the verbal forms "partake" and "take part in") it is used appropriately 16 times, and another new word, "partner" (or "partnership") is used 5 times.

But does not this great variety suggest that we have not yet hit upon the deepest meaning of the Greek word, that all the possibilities have not been exhausted, and that we might do well to heed the suggestion of Irenaeus, who explained *koinonia* as "oneness"? Presumably Irenaeus knew Greek better than any one in our day. He came to Gaul from Asia Minor, bringing with him the traditions of the venerable Churches which treasured the memory of St. John; he became Bishop of Lyon, and by Th. Zahn he is exalted as "the first Christian theologian."

I make this eulogy of Irenaeus for the sake of recommending his word "oneness," which was heartily welcomed by Th. Harnack. It is evident that "oneness" is more appropriate than fellowship to indicate the union of the Father and the Son, and also to describe what happened when the Logos "became flesh" (to use St. John's phrase), or when God "became man" (to use the expression adopted by the Council of Nice more than a century after the death of Irenaeus). These are instances in which the word *koinonia* was never used, because it was inadequate. Neither was it adequate to express the relation between Christ and the sacramental elements, which was rather a relation of identity, Jesus having assured his disciples that in partaking of the bread and wine they partook of him—partook of his life, as St. John put it. Because of this union with him the disciples had *koinonia* with one another. This is the relationship to which *koinonia* was first and most appropriately applied. It indicated a oneness so heartfelt that in very early days it was exhibited practically in the ephemeral experiment with communism recorded in Acts 4:32: "Now the company of those who believed were of one heart and soul, and no one said that any of the things he possessed was his own, but they had everything in common (*koina*)." This was a form of oneness which did not survive the first brief experiment; but the spirit of it was expressed later by "communicating to the necessities of the saints." St. Paul affirms this oneness when he says (1 Cor. 10:17), "Since there is one loaf, we who are many are one body, for we all partake of the one loaf." It hardly needs to be remarked that the "one body" implies oneness with Christ.

Irenaeus, combatting the Gnostic heresies, extends the word "oneness" to include the relation of God to his creation. This thought is suggested and also justified by the oblations (consisting in his time of much more than the bread and wine used for sacramental consumption), which were presented to God with the declaration, "We give Thee what is Thine." The affirmation of the oneness of God with his creation was a formidable confutation of Gnosticism. In the presence of pantheistic heresies such a word might have seemed dangerous. But it was not with false doctrine of this sort Irenaeus had to deal, and Harnack remarks justly that the oneness he had in mind did not abolish individual distinctions or merge them in an indifferent unity.

Perhaps no other word but oneness can be used to express an analogy between all the relationships which are suggested by the Eucharist and which make it an epitome of Christian doctrine, indeed of the whole world-view which, as Harnack says, is mirrored as at a focal point in the celebration of the Holy Communion.

Doctrinally the two most important points in Irenaeus' account of the Eucharist are: (1) It is to be understood, not merely as a memorial of Christ's death, but as a memorial of the Incarnation, which is the analogy that explains the Sacrament. Rather than call it a "repetition" of Christ's sacrifice, we might call it the repetition of his becoming flesh. (2) It bears witness to the oneness of God and his creation.

As for the second point, it would be foolish to find fault with Irenaeus in particular for expressing a view which prevailed in his time and for a couple of centuries later. Because of this trait the doctrine of the Apostolic and Sub-Apostolic Fathers has often been decried as a falling away for the Apostles—though it would be hard to prove that it is unscriptural. But this is an outstanding feature of the view which Professor Alexander V. G. Allen lauded nearly seventy years ago in his *Continuity of Christian Thought* —showing by the choice of this title how unwilling he was to admit that the Christian thought he discovered in the early Church had for fourteen centuries been suppressed by an unconscious Manichean tendency in the theology of St. Augustine. Rather than reproach St. Irenaeus, one might with some show of reason denounce Harnack, Allen and me for embracing in our several generations an orthodoxy so ancient that it is now regarded as heresy. Th. Harnack was in some measure prepared to welcome such a doctrine because he was a Lutheran born in Moscow, that is, at the heart of Holy Russia, Allen because he was an Anglican enamored of the perennial Christian philosophy which emerged afresh through Frederick Dennison Maurice, Charles Kingsley and Phillips Brooks—and I because of my revolt against Calvinism. With a lopsided Augustinianism, that is, with Calvinistic orthodoxy, old or new, this ancient Christian worldview cannot be made to agree.

What first attracted Karl Barth to Kierkegaard and held him for a while was the affirmation of "an infinite qualitative difference between God and man." At first he had no suspicion how dialectical this affirmation was; and as soon as he recognized that this "spiritual ancestor" in his practical religious life stood for "immediacy after reflection," which is the dialectical opposite to infinite separation and remoteness, he uttered that sonorous NEIN with which he repudiated Kierkegaard along with Brunner, sitting beside a window of the Pension Hasseler on the

Pincian Hill from which he had a view across the Campus Martius of the Vatican Palace and Basilica of St. Peter and could point thither when he wrote, "If I were to follow them, I might as well go over there." In this apprehension Barth was almost right.

No one who has read Chapter III of the *Fragments*, especially pp. 35 f. about the Absolute Paradox, can doubt that Kierkegaard was keenly aware of the dialectical character of the affirmation that God is "the Unknown," "the absolutely Different." He would not even try to resolve this paradox, although by the tension it created he was profoundly tormented. He exalted to the highest place "the religion of transcendence" ("religiousness B") and rightly accounted it distinctive of Christianity; but he would not allow that it superseded "the religion of Immanence" ("religiousness A"). In fact, all his Edifying Discourses, even those which eventually he ventured to call "Religious" or even "Christian," exemplified, as he himself said, not the religion of transcendence, but the religion of immanence. And it was not as an accommodation to the weakness of others he wrote in this mode, for he himself lived in it, and repeatedly he reproached himself for this. He often declared (thereby leading many astray) that he was not a Christian in the stricter sense, whereas the pseudonym Anti-Climacus, the consistent exponent of Religiousness B, was a Christian in such a superlative degree that it appeared to him dreadful. It is touching to see that the real Kierkegaard in his talks with God ignored the infinite qualitative difference and spoke with the familiarity a child would show in addressing his father. The word father would be badly chosen to denote an infinite qualitative difference or an unapproachable remoteness. To him the unknown God was so well known by this analogy (*analogia entis*) that he could say in his Journal (XI2 A 98), "God has only one passion—to love and wish to be loved." But I need not multiply instances to prove what is so obvious in most of Kierkegaard's writings, especially in the Journals.

The dialectical character of the "infinite qualitative difference" and all that goes with this has been commonly ignored, and because of this misunderstanding, most of the Lutherans in Denmark, indeed throughout Scandinavia, though they are proud to claim kinship with Kierkegaard, are not disposed to accept from him the religious guidance which in other lands Catholics, Protestants, Buddhists and even infidels have been glad to receive. But even in these United States of America, because of this same misunderstanding, Kierkegaard encounters antipathy as well as sympathy, and it may be because of a misapprehension that the Neo-Orthodox find him so much to their liking. They mean to exalt God by putting him at an unapproachable distance. But so too did the Gnostics when they declined to regard the good God as the creator of this miserable and naughty world. We can well imagine that Irenaeus, engaged in a life and death struggle with Gnostic heresies, would have regarded as treasonable an utterance which affirmed the infinite qualitative difference between God and man. The Gnostics very inconsistently—inadvertently, we might say—imitated the Catholic Church so far as to celebrate the Eucharist, even to the point of using the *epiclesis* in their liturgies; but since they denied the Incarnation, they could not attach to this sacrament the sense of oneness it properly suggested at every level. The Calvinistic Churches also celebrate the Holy Communion, but they observe it rarely, it would seem grudgingly, and only as a concession to a tradition which even in the New Testament is too imposing to be ignored—except by the Quakers. But commonly they understand it, not after the analogy of the Incarnation, but simply as an edifying memorial of the sacrificial death of Christ, and without any association with the hope of eternal life. Regarded in this way, the Eucharist would be especially appropriate on Good Friday, the only day on which the Catholic Church does not celebrate it, and it would have no obvious relevance to Christmas and Easter and the Lord's Day, when the Church requires its performance most particularly.

When speaking of the doctrine of the Holy Communion as it was understood in the time of Irenaeus, it is not necessary to speculate about the physical conditions which might be supposed to correspond with the oneness of Christ's body and blood with the bread and wine; for in such a question the early Church showed no interest. This is a question for faith, not for philosophy or science. And today it would be futile in the highest degree to discuss the doctrine of transubstantiation as it was formulated in the Middle Ages and presumably confirmed by the miracle of Bolsena so dear to St. Thomas that he wrote the office for the feast of Corpus Domini and composed the hymns for it. For today no one, even in the Church of Rome, seriously entertains a philosophy which justifies the notion that a substance can be separated from its "accidents."

This broad survey of the action of the Liturgy serves at this point to emphasize the significance of the Offertory. Evidently it is not, as many may be inclined to think, an element essentially extraneous to our spiritual worship, which for rather shabby economic reasons has been introduced into the Liturgy. No, it is an integral part of the Liturgy, and the offering we make here is a sacrifice. The word offering, of course, is equivalent to sacrifice. Offertory (*offertorium*) means the *place* for sacrifice. The gifts we make here are the only reminder we have left of the common meal which originally preceded the Eucharist. From the earliest times the Church regarded the gifts as offered to God, hence as a sacrifice. The Liturgical Reformers in the Roman Church are doing what they can to restore the Offertory.

I shall not say much here about the broader idea of sacrifice, because in a subsequent chapter we shall have to consider the exalted idea of it which was exemplified by the death of Christ. In view of that preeminent sacrifice it may seem presumptuous to dignify by the same name our gifts in money or in kind, even though we "give until it hurts." And yet St. Paul did in fact compare such dissimilar sacrifices when he was urging the Corinthians to contribute to the collection for the poor saints at Jerusalem, coining the most touching and effective offertory sentence when he said (2 Cor. 8:9), "For ye know the grace of our Lord Jesus Christ, that, though he was rich, yet for your sakes he became poor, that ye through his poverty might become rich." This lofty conception of the gifts of the Church as sacrifices in imitation of Christ would hardly have been so common as it was if they had not been usually offered at the altar which was associated with the sublimer sacrifice represented by the Incarnation of the Son of God and his death upon the cross.

But now, even if one is reconciled to the inclusion of material gifts in a spiritual liturgy, and may even think it poetical to offer unto God the fruits of the earth, one may feel that it is repugnant to offer *money*, as we commonly do. Incidentally it may be observed that of all material things the most abstract is money. It may mean anything. It is simply a conventional token, a general claim upon goods and services. To one who by "spiritual" means immaterial, money might seem almost spiritual. But it is more to the point to remember that from the very beginning money was offered in the Church as a sacrifice to God. It was money which Ananias and Sapphira laid at the Apostles' feet; and the sin of holding back part of the price of their field was so heinous because their offering was made not unto men but unto God. The aid which the Philippians sent to St. Paul when he was a prisoner in Rome must have consisted chiefly of money, yet he regarded it (Phil. 4:18) as "an odor of a sweet smell, a sacrifice acceptable, well pleasing to God." These phrases are the more significant because it was almost in the same terms he spoke of the sacrifice of Christ (Ephes. 5:2). The collection for the poor in Jerusalem was made exclusively in money, yet St. Paul described it as a "grace" (like the grace displayed by the Lord Jesus Christ) and as a "communion" or fellowship (Rom. 15:26; 2 Cor. 8:4). Of the Philippians said St. Paul (Phil. 4:15) that in the beginning of his apostolic ministry "no Church had communion (fellowship) with me in the matter of giving and receiving but ye only"; and having this aid, he declined to receive support from the Church in Corinth.

Remembering that *koinonia* means communion or fellowship—rather that it means both at once and is not perfectly understood when we translate it by either word alone—we can perceive the profound religious significance of the Offertory. Although the sublimest experience of communion, as the culminating action of the Liturgy, comes last of all, it casts its shadow before it, and in the Offertory, as a practical expression of Christian fellowship, we have an adumbration of communion in the Body and Blood of Christ. This does not represent community of goods, like the experiment reported in the Acts of the Apostles, but it is a communion. It is an expression in the Liturgy itself of the fellowship which should prevail in all situations. Therefore

Heb. 13:16, if it were correctly translated, would be very appropriate as an Offertory Sentence: "To do good and to communicate forget not, for with such sacrifices God is well pleased." Such practical communion means "doing good" to others; and hence it is appropriate as a part of the action of the Liturgy. We shall have occasion later to consider what it implies outside the Liturgy. So understood, this action can hardly be performed with too much pomp and solemnity; and of course the alms as well as the oblations ought to be offered unto God by an obvious gesture. What are alms (*eleemosyna*) but an evidence of human mercy (*misericordia*), which is a faint reflection of the divine mercy?

Gifts which are thus offered become God's property—not the property of the Church regarded as a merely human society which might claim the right to dispose of its funds as the majority thinks best. No, the property held by the Church, being God's property, is held in trust and must be used only according to his will. Therefore it cannot be held or administered rightly except by men who as ministers of the Word may be supposed to know the will of God. Accordingly, as we have seen, it was prescribed in the *Didache* that "all the first fruits shall be given to the prophets." They did not thereby become the property of these "high priests," but were distributed by them in accordance with God's will, and principally to the poor. In early times it was proverbial that "the poor are the altar of the Church."*

* The "prophets" who are mentioned in the *Didache,* and are there confused or rather identified with certain so-called "apostles," were evidently itinerant evangelists of a sort, who, though they were received in the Churches with honor, were regarded with some suspicion. For the Church had reason to fear "false prophets." Therefore, unless these men desired to settle permanently in a community, they were not allowed to stay "more than one day, or at the most two," and when they departed they might take nothing with them but the bread which would suffice till they came to another lodging. They were expected to live "according to the rule (*dogma*) of the Gospel," that is to say, without worldly cares or possessions, like the Apostles when they were sent on their mission in Galilee (Mk. 6:8-10). "If he asks for money, he is a false prophet," it was said. They were required to exemplify "the ways of the Lord," and verse 11 (which probably is an echo of Ephes. 5:32) implies that they must be unmarried: "Every prophet who proves to be genuine, acting in accordance with the cosmic mystery of the Church, yet not teaching others

Tertullian (*Apol.* c. 39) says that the contributions made by the Christians are not used for feasts and drinking parties (as in the pagan guilds) but for feeding and burying the poor. And in the passage cited above in which Justin Martyr describes the Liturgy he says of the Offertory, "They that are willing and well-to-do give what they think fit, and the collection is deposited with the president [i.e. the bishop], and he succors the orphans and widows, and those who through sickness or any other cause are in want, those who are in prison, and the strangers sojourning among us—in a word, he becomes the caretaker of all who are needy."

Although this was written only about half a century later than the *Didache,* it shows that in the meantime the bishop had acquired all the honor and authority which had been accorded to the "prophet." It shows too that this authority accrued to him because he was "president" at the Eucharist—not because (as Hatch and Harnack contended) his functions were first of all economic. During the first centuries the Church had no need of a purely economic supervision; for it did not hoard money but lived from hand to mouth, its only capital being the readiness of its members to contribute.

A short while ago, when celebrations of the Holy Communion were infrequent, it was customary for us to devote the "communion alms" to the poor. Today this would be a very uneconomical practice, seeing that almost everything given to the Church is now presented upon the Altar as a part of the action of the Liturgy, and most of it is needed for the support of the clergy of various ranks, including sacristans and organists and singers. Neither in early times were all the alms given to the

---

to do as he himself does, shall not be judged." These "prophets" and "apostles" were a shadowy reminiscence of the greater figures of the past and were destined to vanish soon from the ecclesiastical scene; yet on the other hand they were precursors of the itinerant monks of the Middle Ages, though without the security of a monastery to which they could return, and without the comfort the rule of the Gospel provided when they were sent out "two by two." Evidently, a ministry of this character could not last. The *Didache* gives us a snap-shot of these "prophets," taken just before their disappearance, when the honor accorded to them was about to devolve upon the local bishops.

poor. According to Eusebius (*H. E.* VI, 43), by the middle of the third century there were in Rome 155 clergy (counting only bishops, presbyters and deacons) and 1500 needy persons who were supported by the Church. This was no novelty, for from the earliest age some of the clergy were supported by the Church. I have already quoted St. Paul's saying in 1 Cor. 9:14: "The Lord ordained that they which proclaim the Gospel should live by the Gospel." He had in mind Jesus' saying (Mt. 10:10), that "the laborer is worthy of his hire." It was as preachers of the Gospel the ministry might claim such support, and of course the Apostles above all. Hence St. Paul says (1 Cor. 9:6, 11) of himself and Barnabas, "Have we not a right to forbear working? . . . . If we have sowed unto you spiritual things, is it a great matter that we should reap your carnal things?" In the next verse he implies that others besides the Apostles "partake of this right," and presumably he is thinking of the prophets, evangelists and teachers. Yet in Corinth St. Paul did not use this right, preferring to "rob other Churches, taking wages from them, that I might minister unto you." We have seen already how the lower ministry, bishops and presbyters, were eventually accorded the same right to forbear working, or at least to receive a part of their support from the Church.

I myself have been so supported for half a century, and I like to recite among the Offertory Sentences the noble words St. Paul used to justify the clergy in receiving support from the Church. Alas, these Sentences have been left out of our new Prayer Book—presumably because the clergy were squeamish about animadverting upon the perfectly patent fact that the greater part of the alms are used for their support. Yet this participation in the gifts made at the Altar must be regarded as an honor, inasmuch as it is God's property in which we are counted worthy to share.

So it was regarded in the early Church. The word honor acquired a technical sense, equivalent to honorarium. Thus it is said in 1 Tim. 5:17, "Let the elders who preside well [I take them to be bishops] be accounted worthy of double honor." This means that they were to receive a double portion of the gifts, the widows (verse 3) being "honored" by a single portion. This use of the word honor was very frequent at least to the end of the third century. But it would seem pedantic to repeat here a note covering several pages which I published forty years ago in *The Church and its Organization* (pp. 328 ff.) to explain the use of this word.

Even without such a note this present chapter may seem too erudite for a little book which aims to be at once succinct and popular. But does it not help to illuminate the action of the Offertory? And about this the people surely ought to be enlightened, since this is preeminently their action. What could we do without the people!

And if in our day the way of raising money for the Church, the way Church property is regarded, and the way it is administered, are indicative of a bourgeois conception of Christianity, it is evident from the foregoing that they need not be. And even without such illumination of the subject, it must be evident that the methods of high-pressure salesmanship are not appropriately employed in support of the Body of Christ, however successful they may be financially. We cannot be too scrupulous in trying by every means to allay the suspicion that the Church, as the Italians say, is a *botega.*

CHAPTER TEN

THE EUCHARISTIC PRAYER

THE UTMOST WE CAN DO

When we call the Lord's Supper the Eucharist, which means simply thanksgiving, we imply that our prayer of praise and thanksgiving is the most essential part of the Liturgy, and that while this is the least we might be expected to do, it is also the utmost we can do. Although, as we have seen, this is not the only action appropriate to the Liturgy, it is by far the most important—and all the more important because in response to this little that we can do God acts to consecrate the bread and wine as the Body and Blood of Christ.

The Lord's Supper, being a sacrament, is, like Baptism, profoundly humiliating to man. Essentially, a sacrament denotes, not what *we do,* but what is done for us. In Baptism we are washed, because we are unclean; and in the Sacrament of the Altar we are fed, because we are famished. In both cases, we who are needy are saved. Our action (if in view of the Latin idiom, *gratiorum actio,* it can properly be called action) is passive action. We receive. And in receiving we admit that we are not worthy to gather up the crumbs that fall from the Lord's Table. In saying this we recall the humble expression of the pagan woman which the Lord rewarded by healing her daughter, driving out the demon which possessed her (Mk. 7:28, 29). When the Roman priest says of himself, *Domine, non sum dignus,* he recalls the humble reply of the pagan captain, "I am not worthy that thou shouldst come under my roof," which the Lord rewarded by healing his servant.

But for what we receive we are permitted to give thanks. This being the least we can do is also the utmost. God does the rest.

In view of the early and the earliest forms of the Liturgy of which we have record, nothing is more certain than that the prayer of thanksgiving as such was regarded as the prayer of consecration. But because it is difficult for us to get this notion through our heads, we are reluctant to admit the fact.

When our Lord, both at the Last Supper and in the wilderness, took bread and "blessed it," there can be no doubt that he pronounced the blessing which was customary at every meal, and this, we know, was simply a thanksgiving. Consequently, since the Church aimed to do only what Christ did (as St. Cyprian said), the great prayer in the Liturgy was merely an expansion of the "blessing" at meals. In form it was a prayer of thanksgiving to God, while in effect it was the consecration of the elements of bread and wine.

We are perplexed by the Hebrew idiom. The invariable form of the Hebrew thanksgiving was, "Blessed be God." But when in the Bible we see the phrase, "he blessed," we very naturally suppose it to mean a prayer expressly asking God to bless the food (or whatever might be the object in question), or else perhaps a more direct (not imprecatory) benediction. For that reason our "blessing" at meals is, almost universally, a prayer that God will bless this food and us—almost never does it even include a word of thanksgiving. I suspect that the "grace" or thanksgiving for the daily bread which we receive, which is an act so natural and so gracious, would not have fallen so generally into disuse, if it had not been so generally misunderstood and abused . . . as a petition for more. For, *incredible sed verum,* many when they receive the daily bread they asked for in the Lord's Prayer are too churlish to give thanks—even the few who say a prayer before meals. They may ask God to "bless this food," but they do not bless him; they may ask that God, as though he had not created this food for that very purpose, will sustain their bodies by it; they may even get so far as to ask God to *give* them grateful hearts, but almost never do they get to the point of expressing gratitude. I have before me eight forms of "grace before meat" recommended by the Presbyterian Church in the Book of Common Worship which has just been approved by the General Assembly, and I note that not one of them expresses thanks. So it was with the first edition of this book, which I criticized twenty years ago, and criticized in vain. This indicates one hundred percent of ingratitude. I see no reason to suppose that with us the percentage is very different; and I am inclined to think that, if we cannot say a more gracious "grace," it would be better to say none at all. Indeed the majority of Christians today have evidently preferred this alternative. At all events, when we are in such bewilderment about the significance of the little eucharist, it is no wonder we fail commonly to understand the meaning of the great Eucharist. And I am sure we shall not understand it feelingly until we learn again to use the grace at meals commonly and say it rightly.

The fact that "to bless" (*eulogein*) and "to give thanks" (*eucharistein*) are verbs which are used synonomously in the New Testament can easily be verified by the aid of an adequate concordance. We have two accounts of the same event, the feeding of the multitude in the wilderness; and in the first of them it is said by three Evangelists that Jesus "blessed" the bread etc. (Mt. 14:36; Mk. 6:41; Lk. 9:16), while John (6:11) says "gave thanks," as do Matthew (15:36) and Mark (8:6) in the second account. In the account of the Last Supper Matthew (26:26, 27) and Mark (14:22, 23) say of the bread that he "blessed" it, and of the cup that he "gave thanks," whereas Luke (22:17, 19, 20) says of both that he "gave thanks," as did St. Paul also in 1 Cor. 11:24. Though all were writing in Greek, they sometimes used the Jewish idiom, and sometimes the equivalent expression which would be more surely understood by the Gentiles. Yet St. Paul, though he was writing to Gentile Christians (1 Cor. 10:16) used the most striking Hebrew phrase when he said, "the cup of blessing which we bless." I have been scrupulous to indicate here the New Testament sources, because the little concordance commonly bound up with the Bible is in this instance inadequate.

We learn from Tim. 4:3-5 that the prayer of thanksgiving before meals ("Blessed be God for our daily bread," or whatever the precise formula might be) was regarded as a consecration of the food, so that even meats which were ceremonially "unclean," or indeed such as had been sacrificed to idols, were "sanctified by the word of God and by prayer" (cf. 1 Cor. 10:30). With this thought in mind St. John (6:33) used an expression which to us seems intolerable when he spoke of the bread of the Lord's Supper as "eucharisticized bread," as Justin Martyr did, too, when he was describing the Eucharist in a passage already referred to. It is exactly as if we were to say "thanksgivingized."

Having this conception in view, no one can condemn as inadequate the brief liturgy incorporated in the *Didache,* although it is hardly more than an amplified grace at meals. But this fact, if it is cordially recognized, has much broader implications. It justifies in a measure every contemporary liturgy which includes an adequate thanksgiving for God's goodness in Creation and Redemption.

Reflecting that in offering thanks to God for the blessings we have received and have still to expect we are really doing very little, it is natural for us to wish to do more—for example, to pray specifically for the consecration of the oblations, if we are not presumptuous enough to propose to consecrate them ourselves, either by word or gesture, and perhaps by virtue of some sacerdotal power (*potestas ordinis*) conferred upon us as privileged members of the Body of Christ. In fact, there is hardly a liturgy which does not contain some petition of the sort, though not always with the understanding that, like the Greek *epiclesis,* it calls down the Holy Spirit upon the oblations. This not only is natural, but humanly it may seem quite pretty, if it is not regarded as essential. For my part, I am grateful for the historic accident by which our Church in America received from the Scottish Church the Greek epiclesis; for this prayer is so natural that it may possibly become universal. But to syllogize invidiously the judgment that for the lack of this adornment the English Liturgy and the Roman are invalid . . . is comical in the highest degree.

No, rendering thanks to God is essentially all we can do. This we are bidden to do, for this is what Christ did at the Last Supper. But this being so easy a thing to do, why might not any member of the Church do it? Granted that it is a priestly act, must not the common priesthood of all believers (1 Pet. 2:5, 9) qualify every Christian to offer a prayer of thanksgiving? If it does not mean so much as that, it means nothing at all. But when we ask who may say the prayer of thanksgiving at the Lord's Table, it is like the question who may say the blessing at the family table. In the earliest recorded instance of a blessing before a meal (1 Sam. 9:15) it is said that the people would not eat till the Prophet (Samuel) had "blessed" the sacrifice, i.e. the meat provided for them. This blessing was obviously a priestly act; but so was the blessing at every meal, for we must remember that no meat was eaten which had not already been sacrificed to God. At a family meal it was naturally the father who presided and said the blessing. So it is commonly with us, though it is sometimes thought to be a pretty custom for the father to depute this office to a child. With respect to the great Eucharist of the Church it is rather a curious question than a practical one who is to pronounce the blessing (the thanksgiving prayer); for, of course, and by common consent, it is only the most highly venerated members of the community who may sit in the Lord's place and bless and break the bread as he did. And from the earliest times the place the office-bearers, especially the bishops and deacons, occupied at the Lord's Table was the most obvious distinction they enjoyed. The question who might preside and say the blessing was thus practically answered. And so it is now with us—with Christians of all denominations. At the beginning of the second century it was practically answered for St. Ignatius by the general establishment of monepiscopacy, that is, the rule that there might be but one bishop in every city (*polis*). Hence wherever this rule prevailed St. Ignatius could exhort Christians, as he did the Church in Smyrna (c. 8), to cling to the bishop as a center of unity, in order to "avoid divisions which are the beginning of evil." He said: "Let no man do anything pertaining to the Church apart from the bishop. . . . Let that be accounted a firm and sure Eucharist which is presided over by the bishop or by one to whom he has committed it. . . . It is not lawful apart from the bishop either to baptize or to hold a love-feast." This was a practical decision at that time.

But with the growth of the Church the situation changed rapidly, and before long it had become impossible for the bishop to be everywhere and to do all these things. The presbyters soon became the ordinary celebrants of the Eucharist. There has never been a time when the question whether any Christian might not be competent to say the Eucharistic prayer could have more than a theoretical interest. Yet as a theoretical question it has dogmatic importance. At the beginning of the third century Tertullian assumed that this was a position to which all would assent, when (in *De exhort. cast.* c. 7) he wrote (not arguing for this thesis but taking it as a premise for his argument): "Are not we laics also priests? . . . Therefore where there is no one to represent the ecclesiastical order, thou makest the offering and baptizest and art priest for thyself." Such a situation might occur if several godly laymen were wrecked for example, upon a desert island . . . where bread and wine were providentially available. Hence I say that the question I have raised has little practical interest—and yet the answer to it may theoretically have great importance. The query is forced upon us here by the consideration that the prayer of consecration in the Liturgy is nothing more than a prayer of thanksgiving.

I hinted above that the Eucharistic prayer comprises a double commemoration (*anamnesis*). In the first place we have the Preface, beginning with the *Sursum corda* and ending with the *Tersanctus,* which (when it is not cluttered up by the "Proper Prefaces") is devoted exclusively to the praise of the Creator for His universal goodness and for the providential guidance of his people. In the second place comes the more specifically Christian prayer, beginning with the *Benedictus* ("Blessed is he that cometh") and concluding with the Amen, giving thanks to God for our redemption by his Son. In this thanksgiving Christ's great works are recited (a summary of the Gospel), not forgetting, of course, the institution of the Sacrament. Both the praise and the thanksgiving are addressed to God the Father, because it was to him Jesus addressed the "blessing" he pronounced at the Last Supper.

In the Greek liturgies the Preface follows consistently enough the rule I have stated, although the only perfectly "pure" example is found in the fourth century liturgy of the *Apostolical Constitutions*—which perhaps for this reason we may take to be the composition of an enlightened individual, rather than a liturgy which was actually in use and had grown in response to human needs, which are not always logical.

In the second part of the Anaphora perfect consistency is nowhere to be found. We cannot reasonably expect it. It would not be human. Even in the *Didache* the Eucharistic prayer is not exclusively thanksgiving, there are petitions mingled with it. So there are also in our Liturgy. We needy creatures are fain to make our wants known unto God. Indeed, the expectation that God is able and willing to help may be regarded as a part of praise. The familiar acclaim, Hosanna! means, Help now! Especially in connection with the commemoration of Christ's great works we are moved to make petitions for those who are dear to us, the living and the dead. There is therefore no extant liturgy which exemplifies a "pure" form of thanksgiving.

Because praise implies a lyrical mood, song is nowhere so much in place as here. Hence it is appropriate that the Preface be sung. It may be observed that the Lutherans are much more scrupulous about this than we. And not only the Lutherans. Two great figures in the German Reformed Church, John Nevin and Philip Schaff, wrote about the Liturgy with greater discernment than any other Americans; and because my predecessor in Rome was a son of Dr. John Nevin he invariably sang the Preface during the thirty-seven years of his ministry in our Church of St. Paul, and made the Eucharist the principal service on every Lord's Day. I continued the practice, in spite of some malevolent criticism that I was not a good singer. But when I left Rome, both these good customs, which had been maintained for sixty years, were discontinued by four pastors who occupied that post in rapid succession.

It is not so obvious that the remainder of the Eucharistic Prayer should be sung, unless perhaps at the conclusion; for the commemoration of the suffering of Christ is not a lyric theme, and, as we have seen, petitions and intercessions are commonly included in this prayer.

We have still to consider, in another chapter, the significance of the Liturgy as a sacrifice; but viewing the Eucharistic prayer simply as an act of thanksgiving (blessing God), as we have here regarded it, not only is it what we are expressly required to do in imitation of Christ and in remembrance of him, but it is in itself an action more sublime than the thaumaturgic act some would take it to be.

Moreover, being simply a prayer of thanksgiving, it is an action which the celebrant does not perform alone, though he alone utters the prayer aloud. All the people of God are competent to join in such a prayer, and in every part of it. This, as I have already said, is the implication of the *Orate, fratres,* where the priest speaks of the Eucharist as "my sacrifice and yours." This thought, that all the people are expected to participate in the Eucharistic prayer which is uttered by the celebrant, is admirably presented to the eye by an ivory relief of the ninth century which the late Dean Ladd reproduced as the frontispiece of his little book called *Prayer Book Interleaves.* It represents the Bishop of Rome standing behind the Altar with hands spread out in the attitude of prayer. He is uttering the prayer of consecration. Behind him stand five clerics (probably deacons) wearing dalmatics. Before the Altar stand five men (as many as space allowed for), all of them clad in the planeta (chasuble), and with hands spread out in the attitude of prayer. Unfortunately, Dean Ladd, supposing that men wearing chasubles must be presbyters, understood this to mean the assisting clergy participated *audibly* in the prayer of consecration. In fact they were singing while the bishop was silent. They were singing the *Tersanctus.* Dr. Ladd was not aware that in the ninth century all men wore that dress, and he ignored a common convention of Roman art which by a few figures represented a multitude. For example, one scene on the Arch of Constantine in the Roman Forum represented the Emperor seated on the Rostrum, where he received the acclamations of the Roman populace, which was represented by a few figures clad in exiguous togas. So here the artist would represent the whole congregation actively participating in the bishop's prayer. A number of ivory carvings representing this theme have fortunately been preserved, and some of them clearly confirm the interpretation I have given. In the sixth century and later it was customary for the Roman consuls to order an ivory diptych made to commemorate the inauguration of their annual term. They depict the Consul seated upon a dais, clad in a contabulated toga heavily embroidered in gold, and holding in his hand as a token of authority . . . a handkerchief, the *mappula*. It seems likely that the bishops of Rome imitated this practice, perhaps to celebrate the inauguration of their pontificate, and they are of course represented celebrating the Mass. The picture is always a bird's-eye view, looking down obliquely through the roof of the church, as though it did not exist. Of course, the sanctuary was the focus of the picture, and in the example Dean Ladd selected there was no space left for the east wall—or the west wall, in case it was St. Peter's. But other artists, perhaps less artistically, included the walls of the church in their whole circumference, so that the whole interior is exposed to view, and we see that the few figures represent the whole congregation. This interesting ivory is well illustrated in my *Art in the Early Church*, plate 128.

CHAPTER ELEVEN

KERYGMA CHRISTI

THE PROCLAMATION OF THE GOSPEL

The proclamation of the Gospel is an important element in the action of the Liturgy, although no separate place is allotted to it. It pervades the whole Liturgy, but because of its great importance it requires a separate treatment here.

St. Paul emphasized the importance of this factor when he said, "ye do proclaim the Lord's death till he come." Jesus doubtless had his impending death in mind at the Last Supper; but he surely had much more than this in mind when he said, "Do this in remembrance of me." Indeed the Church has always remembered more. Every liturgy brings to remembrance the great deeds of the Gospel, recalling them more formally in the anamnesis, but bringing them everywhere to mind.

It is a peculiarity of the Calvinistic tradition (still maintained by Presbyterian and Reformed Churches of all sorts) that a special place is assigned for the commemoration of Christ's institution of the Sacrament, where St. Paul's directions are read as a "warrant" for doing what our Lord notoriously commanded us to do. The reading of this warrant, though it is superfluous, is not of itself a serious blemish; although, being a peculiarity which no other Churches share, it is obviously divisive. It is not conceivable that it might ever become universal; and a divisive way of celebrating the Holy Communion is deplorable. Of course, this passage, this warrant, is not a sufficient commemoration of the Gospel; and it must be remarked that Presbyterian liturgies often furnish more, and sometimes contain a more adequate anamnesis than we can boast of.

About the word Gospel something must be said here to make plain what we mean when we affirm that the *Gospel* is proclaimed in the Liturgy. This does not mean that the Gospel for the Day is read after the Epistle, and is perhaps "explained." The reading of the Gospel is indeed an important part of the Liturgy, and it is (or ought to be) introduced with great solemnity. About this I have already spoken in Chapter VI. But here we mean the whole Gospel, or rather the essential Gospel, of which the passage which happens to be read is a part, and perhaps not an essential part. It may be that in the Epistle for the Day there is more Gospel than in the portion of the Gospel which is read.

The use of the word Gospel to describe the four canonical accounts of the story of Jesus (the Gospel according to St. Matthew, etc.) has obscured the proper meaning of the word. It is obvious that not everything Jesus said—to the Pharisees, for example, and about them—is good tidings. Neither was everything that he did—the cleansing of the Temple, for example. As Jesus used the word it meant the proclamation of the coming kingdom of God. It was a promise, and therefore futuristic, even though he said that the kingdom is at hand. As the Apostles used this word it meant what Christ had done, or what the Father had done through him and for him, in sending his Son into the world and in raising him from the dead. This was the *kerygma Christi,* the proclamation of Christ. But still it was in part futuristic, for it included the hope of the resurrection. The kingdom had not yet come. We say the same thing when we say, the proclamation of the Gospel. And we can call it, as St. Paul does, "the Gospel of God."

Because, at least in the popular mind, the proper meaning of the word Gospel has been obscured, has indeed been perverted to mean everything Jesus said or did, more especially his moral and religious teaching (which liberals have presumed to call "the religion of Jesus"), it is important to see what an Apostle meant by this word—even though this requires me to quote a long passage from St. Paul's First Epistle to the Corinthians, 15:1-8:

"Now I make known unto you, brethren, the Gospel which I

proclaimed unto you, which also ye received, wherein also ye stand, by which also ye are saved. . . . For I delivered unto you first of all that which I received, how that Christ died for our sins according to the Scriptures; and that he was buried; and that he hath been raised on the third day according to the Scriptures; and that he appeared unto Cephas, then to the Twelve, then he appeared to more than five hundred brethren at once, of whom the greater part remains until now, but some have fallen asleep; then he appeared to James, then to all the Apostles, and last of all, as unto one born out of due time, he appeared to me also."

In 1 Tim. 3:16, the Gospel is called "the mystery of our religion: he who was manifested in the flesh, justified in the spirit, seen of angels, preached among the nations, believed on in the world, received up in glory." This is called (in 2 Tim. 2:8) "my Gospel," without meaning to imply that there was any other Gospel which deserved the name.

We see then that what we recite in the Nicene Creed is properly called the Gospel: "Who for us men and for our salvation came down from heaven, and was incarnate by the Holy Ghost of the Virgin Mary, and was made man; and was crucified also for us under Pontius Pilate; he suffered and was buried; and the third day he rose again according to the Scriptures, and ascended into heaven, and sitteth on the right hand of the Father; and he shall come again with glory to judge both the quick and the dead, whose kingdom shall have no end."

The Gospel includes four principal themes: the Incarnation; the Passion; the Resurrection and Ascension; and the promise that Christ will come again in judgment. All of these themes ought to be commemorated in the Liturgy; and because they are duly commemorated in more than one place, the recitation of the Creed, though it is appropriate, is not indispensable, and therefore has not always been customary.

It is a dolorous fact that the proper meaning of the word Gospel has been obscured; for because of this people have been easily seduced by the notion that they believe in the Gospel when in fact they merely believe that Jesus was a teacher who uttered incomparable words, while what is really the Gospel they contumeliously reject as "dogma." Liberalism and vague Christianity would not have scored so easy a triumph if men had commonly understood what is meant by the Gospel. Harnack's *Essense of Christianity* (to mention by way of example a book which was much lauded in its day) excluded, ironically enough, the essence of the Gospel.

Therefore it is of the greatest importance that in the Liturgy the Gospel be proclaimed. Here, of course, it is proclaimed, not to outsiders and with a missionary aim, but to believers. Rather it is the believers themselves who proclaim it as the expression of their faith; for they participate in this action.

But although this proclamation of the Gospel in the Liturgy has not expressly a missionary aim, it may have in our day, when almost everybody in Christendom is baptized, the effect of "introducing Christianity into Christendom"—to use Kierkegaard's phrase, not without sharing his recognition of the fact that this is a harder task than the conversion of pagans, who know that they are not Christians, whereas these others have first to be convinced against their will that they are not. Perhaps the Mass, as something which is seen as well as heard, may be especially apt to produce this unwelcome conviction, and may prove more persuasive than a dogmatic affirmation. This is a good reason for non-communicating attendance. I cannot think of any other part of our worship that might have the effect which St. Paul envisaged when he imagined an outsider coming into the Church and being so profoundly impressed by what he saw and heard that he would "fall upon his face and confess that God is among you indeed."

At all events, this element in the action of the Liturgy is edifying to the faithful. The worshipers (to use the expression of Jude 20) build themselves up on their most holy faith. Where the Eucharist is frequently celebrated and the Dominical precept obeyed, men can hardly fail to know what the Gospel is, even if they will not obey it.

It may seem a little thing Jesus asked when he expected his disciples to "remember" him in a cult which was to be perpetually repeated, at least on every Lord's Day. But essentially he had in view the same end that Moses had in inaugurating the sacraments of the Old Covenant: "Lest ye forget." And indeed no reminder is more effective that a constantly recurring cult. Although the ideal of the Lord's Supper is not realized when men go merely to "hear the Mass" and see it, their going is nevertheless not in vain, if they hear the proclamation of the Gospel, the *kerygma Christi,* and have seen (as St. Paul says in Gal. 3:1) "Jesus Christ openly depicted before their eyes as crucified." It is in this way that truth "can enter in by lowliest doors."

To believers this remembrance is sweet, even if it is pungent. They will be reminded in the Liturgy of many things which are not said there nor shown to them. At one time one thought will impress them, at another that. The possibilities are infinite: at one time or another the whole Gospel, every word and deed of Jesus may be set forth feelingly. Of course, there is always the pungent remembrance of the Passion.

In the Anglican Liturgy, whether in the English or the American form, Christ is plainly set forth as crucified: His death is duly emphasized both by action and by word. But it might be said that the Incarnation (although this is the doctrine upon which Anglicans are most inclined to plume themselves) is not plainly set forth in words—indeed there is no mention of it except in the Creed and in the Proper Preface for Christmas. This is a grievous omission, but it is only a verbal omission; for from the Liturgy, if it is celebrated at all, the thought of the Incarnation cannot be excluded. As we have seen, this is the presupposition of the whole action. We cannot speak of the Body and Blood of Christ without thinking of the Incarnation. St. John (6:33) expressly associates with it the Eucharistic bread when he says, "The bread of God is that which cometh down out of heaven and giveth life unto the world"; and when he uses insistently the word "flesh" (6:51-55) he has in mind the Word which became flesh.

In our Liturgy, although the Resurrection and the Ascension are commemorated in the right place, there is in no place closely connected with them an express reminder of our lively hope of everlasting life, the eschatological hope of the general resurrection at the last day, which is implied by the resurrection of

Jesus as the first fruits. We perfunctorily repeat St. Paul's words, "until he come" ("until his coming again") but the hope of that "dearly loved day" is not clearly discernible when it is lumped with "the innumerable benefits" or with "all other benefits of his passion." It is expressed too early when in the prayer for the whole state of Christ's Church we pray that "we may be partakers of thy heavenly kingdom," and too tardily in the grace after meals, where we speak of being "heirs through hope of thy everlasting kingdom," and in one of the communion sentences affirm that the Sacrament is "unto everlasting life." There is no other mention of the kingdom of God; and yet this was the central thought of the Gospel Jesus proclaimed. The Gospel is essentially a promise, good tidings of things to come, even though the Apostolic Gospel looked back upon the works of Christ which confirmed the promise. Unlike the Passover, the Sacrament of the Lord's Supper is forward-looking and has in view the Last Day, that is to say, it is eschatological. It is a remembrance of One who taught his disciples to look beyond death.

The defect which I point out in our Liturgy reflects, of course, the general abandonment of the eschatological hope which is observable during many centuries in the history of the Church, but especially during the three centuries which have elapsed since the Protestant Reformation. Now, however, many are willing to heed the dictum of Karl Barth, that "a Christianity which is not altogether and utterly eschatological has altogether and utterly nothing to do with Jesus Christ." I have said already that any view of the Lord's Supper which is not eschatological "overthroweth the nature of a sacrament," either in one way or another. But I know by experience—particularly by a recent experience with reviewers of my *Short Story of Jesus*—how desperately men will fight against, and how reluctantly they accept, an eschatological interpretation of the Gospel.

It has been remarked that the *apocalyptic* form of the eschatological hope was relinquished very early, as early as the Gospel according to St. John. I have pointed out that it was essentially discarded by Jesus. But it ought to be remarked that the hope itself was not in the least obscured by St. John when instead of "the kingdom of God" he used the term "everlasting life." Undeniably Jesus Himself used the words "life" and "everlasting life." And it should be remembered also that St. John expressed this hope especially in connection with the Sacrament of the Lord's Supper, which he describes as "the bread of life" (Jn. 6:48, 50, 51). Indeed it is evident from 6:39, 40, 44, 54 that he did not discard wholly the apocalyptic picture; for in these passages he reports, as the explanation and guarantee of "eternal life," the Lord's saying, "I will raise him up at the last day."

Apart from this range of ideas it is impossible to understand the emphatic *Maran atha* of the *Didache* or its "Hosanna to the Son of David" who was to come when this world passeth away; or St. Ignatius' estimation of the Eucharist as "the elixir of immortality" and as "the antidote of death"; or the more persistent thought that it is the viaticum, the traveler's provender, which sustains us through this earthly life on our pilgrimage to the life to come; or the fact that in the Roman catacombs, a place of burial, there are so many symbols of the Eucharist, and so many signs that this sacrament was frequently celebrated there, chiefly by family groups which gathered there to remember their dear ones, the Communion being a pledge of solidarity with them, which naturally was expressed by suffrage for their welfare, unperturbed by any dread that their souls might be in torment. When I depart, trusting in the mercies of God, I should like to be remembered by such a Mass. The impulse to do this is so natural that doubtless we would do it often, if we had a lively sense that this is the sacrament of everlasting life, and were not deterred by the strong inhibitions which have resulted from old abuses and from ancient controversy. At all events, an act of hope is essential to the action of the Liturgy, because the promise of everlasting life is an integral part of the *kerygma Christi.*

CHAPTER TWELVE

SACRIFICE

SUPERHUMAN ACTION

In a previous chapter, dealing with the practical action involved in the Offertory, I spoke of such sacrifice as is within our human competence. Prayer, too, is such a sacrifice, "a sacrifice of praise," as the Bible encourages us to regard it (Heb. 13:15). In this sense the Liturgy may be regarded as a sacrifice, since the very name of the Eucharist implies that it consists predominantly of prayers of thanksgiving, praise and adoration. Such prayer is worship in the strictest sense. Prayers of petition, though they be supplication in behalf of other men, and even though we pray for the sublimest gifts, are not so evidently a part of worship, of divine service, since we are not giving but rather expecting to receive. This, too, may be well pleasing to God as an expression of belief in his goodness and reliance upon his power; it is worship in a broader sense, but we can hardly say that it is "our bounden duty and service." Divine service, properly speaking, is an action which we perform in God's honor. It is not worship if it is performed deliberately with a view to our own interest, whether as a meritorious work or for our spritual edification. Psychologically considered, the worship of God cannot but have an uplifting reaction upon the worshiper. But prayer which consciously has this aim in view is not sacrifice. Paradoxically enough, it also fails to produce the desired effect: the worshiper is not edified or uplifted. Hence where prayer is regarded as a means of self-edification it is seldom used and is unable to hold out long. The Daily Offices and the Liturgy would never have come into being if prayer had not been regarded as homage rendered by man to God.

All will agree that in this sense the Eucharist is a sacrifice. But when we speak of the Sacrifice of the Mass, we mean something very different, and something which is not so evidently within man's competence. For we mean a propitiatory sacrifice. Christ offered such a sacrifice. Can man do it too?

Here we approach a subject which bristles with controversy today, although there was never any controversy about it until in the sixteenth century the Protestant Reformation in all its manifestations, including the Church of England, indignantly repudiated "the Sacrifice of the Mass."

In this controversy there was—and there still is—much room for misunderstanding.

Today most well-informed Catholics will admit that in time past the traffic in masses for the dead was even more scandalous than the sale of indulgences, or than the petty business of those who sold doves in the Temple, which Jesus scourged both in word and act. Against this abuse the indignation of Luther was justified, and we can understand very well how in the heat of controversy he was driven to the extreme position of denouncing every association of sacrifice with the Liturgy, even to the point of rejecting the whole Canon of the Mass except the commemoration of the institution, because it was full of allusions to sacrifice.

In this respect the influence of Luther upon the English Reformed Liturgy was tragic. For by this prejudice the English Reformers also were prompted to conclude the Canon with the words of institution. To make doubly sure that the Lord's Supper might not be contaminated by the notion that we are performing a sacrifice, they prefaced it with the strongest possible affirmation that Christ Himself upon the Cross made once for all a sacrifice which need not and cannot be repeated: "who made there (by the one oblation of himself once offered) a full, perfect, and sufficient sacrifice, oblation, and satisfaction, for the sins of the whole world." We are prohibited, therefore, from regarding the Eucharist as a repetition of the sacrifice of Christ.

For my part, I cannot wish that these words were not prescribed at the beginning of the Canon, for they are Scriptural, and they are true. It never occurs to me when I recite them that by reason of an old controversy not well understood they were placed where they are; for they seem to me perfectly in place. I do not know how others feel, but it is difficult for me to imagine that any one can recite them without complete assent and a feeling of grateful compunction. It is comforting to reflect that old wounds can be so completely healed by time. It is exceedingly necessary that they should be healed. Those who keep them open, not only exasperate the pain but hinder a good understanding which is essential to concord and unity. So long as we look each of us to our own things, and not also to the things of others (Phil. 2:3, 4), our movement is necessarily centrifugal, and that of the others is away from us. Unity can be approached only by "each counting the other better than himself." It was the sad fatality of the Western Schism that by it both Churches were narrowed. The Reformation provoked the Counter Reformation, which, though it was needed and was in many respects salutary, issued necessarily, like the Protestant Reformation, in denials and anathemas which left the Church of Rome, perhaps purer than it was before, but not so comprehensive.

Today the animosities of this controversy have been assuaged, so that we in America (and the Church of England, too, in the "Deposited Book" which the British Parliament would not legalize) have restored the truncated Canon to its proper form, introducing into it, without the slightest scruple, numerous references to the sacrifice, or sacrifices, we are performing. Now we speak of "holy gifts" which we offer, of "our sacrifice of praise and thanksgiving," of "ourselves, our souls and bodies, to be a reasonable, holy and living sacrifice," regarding finally this whole act of worship, "our bounden duty and service," as a sacrifice offered by sinful men, though they are "unworthy to offer to God any sacrifice."

St. Paul, I may remark, did not consistently affirm that the one sacrifice of Christ was sufficient in the sense that it was exclusive of other sacrifices. When he was expecting to be "offered upon the sacrifice and service (liturgy) of your faith"

(Phil. 2:17), he presumed to say (in Col. 1:24), "On my part I am filling up what was lacking in the afflictions of Christ, for his body's sake, which is the Church." In 2 Tim. 4:6 he spoke of himself as being "poured out as a drink-offering." And he who had exhorted his fellow-Christians to present their bodies as "a living sacrifice" was comforted by the thought that he was about to present his body as a dead sacrifice. The idea of sacrifice is too deeply ingrained in the New Testament to be erased from it or to be excluded from our worship.

We are justified then in regarding the Liturgy as a sacrifice. The question is, How are we to understand this?

But before considering this question we may well pause a moment to rejoice in the fact that we are now liberated from old constraints and are free again to speak of the Eucharist as the Fathers did, calling it "our sacrifice." It was a weak point in the Anglican position that it felt compelled in this one respect to ignore the testimony of the early Fathers to which it expressly appealed.

In the earliest times the Lord's Supper was interpreted in terms of a sacrificial meal; and therefore it was natural, without controversy and without scruple, to associate with it every sort of sacrifice we offer. We have seen how many sorts they were. Because the Liturgy comprises them all, it was regarded as the sacrifice *par excellence*. The *Didache* spoke of the whole Liturgy as "your sacrifice"; and so it was constantly called thereafter. So far as we know, St. Cyprian of Carthage, in the third century, was the first who spoke specifically of the Body and Blood of Christ as the sacrifice which was offered in the Eucharist.

How are we to understand that? This question is crucial in a controversy which has not yet been amicably settled. In the first place, let us reflect that, if the Body and Blood of Christ are present, even symbolically, upon the Holy Table, they cannot be thought of except as a sacrifice. This was the implication of the Last Supper, where Jesus said proleptically, "My body" and "my blood," when he had not yet been sacrificed upon the Cross. How much more clearly this was implied after his death! Does this mean that he must often be sacrificed, and therefore often die? No, we cannot say that. If this "therefore" is cogent, it is a *reductio ad absurdum.* But we must remember that Christ's major sacrifice was not his death upon the Cross, but his humiliation in becoming man (Phil. 2:5-7), becoming flesh and blood; and this he does so often as he gives himself to be the bread of life. I have insisted already that the thought of the Incarnation is vital to the Eucharist, as it is also to the conception of the Church as the Body of Christ. In this sense the fundamental sacrifice of Christ is renewed as often as the Eucharist is celebrated. God repeatedly becomes flesh. This, however, is not what Jesus had in mind when he conceived that he "must give his life a ransom for many." The Incarnation was not a visible sacrifice; for it was God's incognito—as every repetition of the Sacrament is. The visible sacrifice was Christ's death upon the Cross. Yet even this was not visibly God's sacrifice: it was the sacrifice of a man. It was not visibly a self-sacrifice. All that the eye could see was that Jesus was sacrificed. But Jesus knew that as the Son of Man (understanding this title in the highest sense) he was giving his life, was sacrificing himself. And this the disciples understood after the event. "He gave himself up for us, as an offering and a sacrifice to God" (Ephes. 5:2). But, paradoxically, this was understood to be God's sacrifice. This thought involves a complete transvaluation of the idea of sacrifice, which hitherto had been regarded, with a mounting scale of value, as something which man gives to God: a material gift, personal obedience, a contrite heart. Here it is God who is the giver, sacrifice is the expression of his love: "God commendeth his love towards us, in that, while we were yet sinners, Christ died for us" (Rom. 5:8). Consequently the Cross is the expression of the divine *agape.* This sacrifice was indeed made "once for all," and yet it is the perennial expression of God's unmotivated *agape* for sinful men. Hence St. Paul (Rom. 5:9-11) continues: "Much more then, being now justified by his blood, shall we be saved from the wrath through him. For if, while we were enemies, we were reconciled to God through the death of his Son, much more, being reconciled, shall we be saved in his life; and not only so, but we also rejoice in God through our Lord Jesus Christ, through whom we have now received the reconciliation." This great passage, with its "rejoicing" in the Cross, in the sacrifice of Christ, "now"—is it not evidently a commentary upon the Eucharist? Whenever "Jesus Christ is plainly depicted before our eyes as crucified," that is to say, so often as we "show forth his death," God commendeth his own love towards us. Yet in this completely transmuted sense of sacrifice, in which God gives and not man, we may nevertheless make bold to speak of the Eucharist as *our* sacrifice; for we *do* it, being indeed bidden to "do this." We do it, no priest does it for us, we do it collectively as the Church; but not even collectively, as the many, or as the Body of Christ, dare we presume to conceive that we, whenever we choose, are capable of offering the Son of God as a sacrifice. In the Liturgy Christ is so thoroughly the subject that he may not for a moment be treated as an object. No, he is the agent; he is not passively offered but offers himself. It could, of course, be said in a sense that Caiaphas and Pilate and the Roman soldiers "sacrificed" Jesus of Nazareth; and, alas, it can still be said, in the dreadful sense contemplated by the Epistle to the Hebrews (6:6), that we may "crucify the Son of God afresh"; but that he who was begotten, not created, by whom all things were made, might again and again be made and sacrificed by a creature, is a thought so absurd and so repugnant that no man can seriously entertain it. Therefore, when Christ is offered in the Liturgy, it is he, the great High Priest, who offers himself, as often as he gives his flesh for the life of the world, and thus again and again commends to us the *agape* of God. To express this thought I qualified the title of the present chapter by describing as "superhuman action" the sacrifice we offer. By God's grace we are capable of doing what is supernatural, but not what is superhuman.

In our Liturgy we appropriately remember "all others who shall be partakers of this Holy Communion," looking beyond the company, it may be a small one, which is actually gathered together in one place, and which, though ideally it is the whole Church, is not physically conterminous with "the blessed company of all faithful people," the "holy fellowship," which we remember in the thanksgiving after Communion. This great thought of the mystical Body of Christ is very consoling and uplifting. Yet Jesus encourages us to look even further afield when we are celebrating the Lord's Supper. In the words of institution, as they are reported by St. Paul to serve as a norm for Communion in the Church at Corinth (1 Cor. 11:24, 25), it is said that Jesus spoke of the bread as given "for you," and the implication is that "in like manner" he spoke of the cup. It is likely (though the text is uncertain) that St. Luke (22:19, 20) said the same. And indeed it is natural that in partaking of the Sacrament Christians should reflect, to their great and endless comfort, that this is for *us*, was given for *us*. That is true, even if Jesus did not say it. But if at the Last Supper, where perhaps only the Twelve were present, Jesus had said, "for *you*," it would at least have raised the doubt whether the field to which Christ's sacrifice applied might not be limited to that little company. Therefore, according to the most reliable sources (Mt. 26:28; Mk. 14:24), he said, "for *many*."

We must take time to consider deliberately the significance of this word "many," which providentially has been preserved in our Liturgy. Very rightly, we say, "for you and for many." But perhaps the addition of the second phrase was prompted rather by the scrupulous desire to conform to both traditions than by an appreciation of its significance. Rightly understood, it enlarges immeasurably the field to which Christ's sacrifice applies.

Jesus said of the cup, "This is the blood of the Covenant, which is shed for many." He had already used this enigmatic word in a prediction of his passion, just before reaching Jericho on his way to Jerusalem (Mk. 10:45): "For verily the Son of Man came not to be served but to serve, and to give his life a ransom for many." Many! A vague word. What did he mean by that? What was in his mind? (I rehearse here briefly what I have said more at length in *The Short Story of Jesus*.) We have other evidence that at this time, when Jesus had urgent reason for seeking light upon the dark path which led him to the Cross, he meditated profoundly upon the fifty-third chapter of the prophet Isaiah. There he found, not once but twice (Isa. 53:11,12), and in a context which could not but seem exceedingly significant to him, the word "many": "By his knowledge my righteous servant shall make many righteous, for he shall bear their iniquities. . . . Yet he bare the sins of many, and maketh intercession for the transgressors." To Jesus this light must have been an unspeakable comfort in view of his approaching death; and to us who view his death in retrospect it is a comfort to know that he died not only for his first disciples but for many.

Who are these "many"? Jesus could not say. He could only say, "All that the Father giveth shall come unto me, and him that cometh unto me I shall in no wise cast out" (Jn. 6:37). This expresses the thought of the divine election in the brightest and most hopeful light, although from his own experience Jesus was compelled to reflect that "many are called but few are chosen." At once it enlarges immensely the scope of Christ's sacrifice. Not only was it not limited to Israel, but it embraced "the transgressors." In the same measure the scope of the Eucharistic sacrifice is widened. It is not limited to those who partake of the Holy Communion, not limited to the pious, and not limited to the living. Although actually only those who "eat of the bread shall live for ever" (Jn. 6:51,53,54), yet it is potentially available to all, and it is offered to all in the *kerygma Christi* which is proclaimed in the Liturgy with the prophetic hope that "they shall all be taught of God" (Jn. 6:45; Isa. 54:13).

Therefore, in the act of Communion the Church is not a smug conventicle which stresses the thought that the gift is given "for us," inasmuch as in the Liturgy the Eucharistic Sacrifice is "openly depicted" for *many*. Hence we are taught to look beyond "the whole Church, the blessed company of all faithful people," the "we and all others who are partakers of this Holy Communion," and to include in our field of vision, and in our field of mission, the *many* "transgressors" for whom Christ died, for whom the Sacrifice is still available, and to whom it is still offered.

Because this Sacrifice has a scope so vast, we can understand it only as a superhuman action. The Church on earth is conscious of its association with the Church in heaven, with the spirits of just men made perfect—not only such as go from strength to strength, but such also as out of weakness are made strong. More than that, the Church exults in the thought that the worship it renders to God is consonant with the worship of "angels and archangels and all the company of heaven." In early times this experience of the heavenly hope was expressed, and at the same time made more vivid, by pictures drawn from the Apocalypse of St. John which portrayed on the east wall of the church, therefore in full view of the congregation, the sublimer worship in the New Jerusalem.

CHAPTER THIRTEEN

BREAKING OF BREAD

A SIGNIFICANT ACT

Of all the names which have been used to describe the Holy Communion, only one, "the Breaking of Bread," indicates physical action. To us who no longer have a loaf, but only wafers which are ready-made for distribution, this act seems no more than a gesture, a mere ritual gesture which is hardly perceptible. Hence we rarely use this name, and may wonder why it was the first name used in the Church (Acts 2:42, 46; 20:7) to describe the action of the Liturgy as a whole.

We have no loaf, and we have no bread properly so called. Some men feel (and I among them) that one of the obstacles to unity with the Presbyterians in our own country is the fact that they do not use wine (that is, the fermented juice of the grape) for the Eucharist. But whatever blame attaches to this must be divided between us; for we do not commonly use fermented bread—the product of fermentation in both cases being alcohol. It is perhaps more deplorable that we have no loaf, and therefore cannot see much significance in the name, Breaking of Bread. It is to be remembered that the Greek *arton* and the Latin *panis,* like the Italian *pane,* may denote the loaf. Unless we have this much instruction, we cannot see much sense in what St. Paul says in 1 Cor. 10:16, "The loaf which we break, is it not a communion [participation] of the body of Christ? seeing that we, who are many, are one loaf, one body, for we are all partakers of the same loaf"; or in the eschatological turn given to this parable in the Eucharistic prayer of the *Didache*: "Even as this Broken [i.e. the broken loaf] was scattered over the hills [as individual grains of wheat] and was gathered together and became one, so let thy Church be gathered together from the ends of the earth into thy kingdom."

But to Christ and his disciples this act must have seemed very significant. Otherwise it would not have been used to characterize the Lord's Supper as a whole, nor would the bewildered disciples at Emmaus have recognized the risen Lord in the breaking of bread (Lk. 24:35). Mgr. Wilpert published in a separate brochure an early fresco in the Roman catacombs which has an exceptional interest. He called it appropriately *Fractio panis.* It depicts a small group of people celebrating the Eucharist in memory of their dead in the family crypt; and it is painted so well that one is conscious of the exertion of the leader who employs his whole strength in breaking a loaf nearly a foot in diameter which he holds in both hands. It is one of those hard flattish loaves, so good to eat, so nourishing to the body, which may be seen in Rome today. One sees that the breaking of bread was so much more than a gesture that it can properly be called physical action. Inasmuch as only seven persons partook of this Eucharist, one may see that in early times the Holy Communion was a fairly substantial meal, quite enough to break a fast. The *Didache,* introducing the thanksgiving after Communion, says significantly, "But after they are filled, give thanks thus." Evidently, homeopathic principles had not yet been applied to the sacraments. If immersion was not accounted essential to baptism, it certainly was preferred (as it is in the *rubrics* of the Book of Common Prayer); at all events a few drops of water were not thought more efficacious than a bath; nor were the inestimable benefits of Holy Communion increased in proportion as the amount of bread was diminished.

Incidentally, this throws some light upon the practice of "fasting communion," which some people regard as an essential part of the action of the Liturgy, perhaps the most sacrificial part that they perform. People do not commonly eat immediately before a meal; and in early times the Eucharist was a fairly substantial meal, even after it had ceased to be celebrated as the conclusion of an *agape* or love-feast—at which the eating and drinking was sometimes so exorbitant that St. Paul exhorted the Corinthians

(1 Cor. 11:22, 34) to eat at home, if they were hungry, before they came to it. It is true that the later Catholic exhortation was to exactly the opposite effect. But when the Eucharist was celebrated in the morning, no one would feel the need of eating before that hour. Living for twenty-five years in Rome, I learned that in the countries encircling the Mediterranean no peasants, and not many bourgeois, take anything to eat, not so much as a cup of coffee, before noon. I was surprised to learn later that during the Middle Ages the peoples of Northern Europe took no breakfast, unless it was perhaps a mug of ale. This is very different from our custom. We must remember that fasting communion is a matter of discipline, not of doctrine. Therefore the rule may be relaxed or abandoned, if circumstances require it. It has been very upsetting to us that the Bishop of Rome, in order to favor evening communions, has lately relaxed it so far that only a fast of two hours is required in the case of solid food, and one hour after liquid food; so that one may dine at six and communicate at half-past eight. This is equivalent to breakfasting at nine o'clock Sunday mornings, and going to Mass at eleven. Seriously, there are other things besides food we might require the people to fast from—especially the Sunday paper. For it is more important that the mind be free to receive Christ than that the stomach be empty.

The breaking of the loaf was obviously the necessary preliminary to every meal. We might suppose therefore that it was a gesture often remarked upon. Some of us, indeed, though we have no loaf on the table, speak, innocently though profanely, of "breaking bread" when we would indicate the hearty hospitality of any secular meal. But, in fact, this expression was never used, so far as we know, in Jewish literature; and among Christians it was always understood to refer to the impressive gesture of Christ. We may suppose that Jesus broke the loaf at every meal he partook with his disciples, as he certainly did when he fed the multitude in the wilderness. Therefore it was a phrase fit to use as a distinctive name for the Eucharist, with which at the Last Supper it was solemnly associated. The supper in the wilderness was Christ's farewell to the multitude, the supper in the upper room was his farewell to the Apostles.

A name which was used to describe the whole action of the Eucharist must surely be significant, and must at least denote specifically an essential part of it. What then is its significance?

It has been thought that it signifies pathetically the broken body of Jesus. But in fact The Lord's words at the Last Supper were very laconic: "This is my body, for you," is all that St. Paul reports (1 Cor. 11:24), and, according to the best texts, the Evangelists give substantially the same report—except that in St. Luke (22:19, 20), where the text is uncertain, we read, even in the Revised Version, "my body which is given for you," corresponding with the pathetic phrase, "my blood which is poured out for you"; and in St. Paul's account a phrase which is more certainly interpolated, "my body which is broken for you." But this notion of the significance of the breaking of the bread ignores the fact that Jesus used this gesture significantly on other occasions, probably at every meal; it is not in accord with the earliest tradition, and is in striking discord with the fact upon which St. John, 19:30, 33, laid so great a stress (in conformity with the proscription of the Law, Ex. 12:26, that no bone of the Paschal lamb should be broken) that the body of Jesus was *not* broken.

The phrase, "my body which is *broken* for you," is evidently designed for liturgical use. It appears as early as the end of the second century in the *Testimony of Hippolytus* and would naturally crop out in the texts of the Gospels. It was ardently adopted by Calvin, who of course regarded it as Scriptural, and it constitutes now the principal pathos of all Reformed Liturgies. It does not, however, appear in the Roman rite, nor in the text of our Liturgy, although unfortunately it is implied in our rubric which directs that "here" (i.e. where the words of institution are recited) the priest is to break the bread.

To the English Reformers the breaking of bread was only a ritual gesture. In fact, it was so regarded by the Roman Church at that time—without reflecting that a ritual gesture was not exactly what one might expect of Jesus. Our Reformers thought that, at all events, this gesture had to be performed, because the Lord had done it. The only question was, Where? They did not feel bound to follow the Roman practice, in which they were inclined to discover so many errors; and so they were easily seduced into following the custom of the Presbyterians. And on the face of it nothing could seem more natural than to break the bread at the place where in the recital of the words of institution it is said that Jesus broke it. But, in fact, this is not doing what the Lord did; for all the reports agree in saying that He broke the bread *after* He had given thanks. Therefore we should do it after the conclusion of the Eucharistic prayer, where the *fractio panis* is found, not only in the Roman Mass, but in all Catholic Liturgies. So, after all, the Roman practice was not erroneous in this respect, whereas ours is. It might be said that in the Reformed Liturgy of the Church of England this act comes *nearly* at the end of the Canon—because the Canon was cut short at this point. But this excuse cannot be made for our American Liturgy, which has completed the truncated Canon. With us, the priests who in breaking the host try their best to produce a frangorous sound which rends the heart by its pathos may plume themselves upon being Catholics, but in this instance they emphasize the Calvinistic interpretation of the Breaking of Bread.

Our error, though it was due only to a little misunderstanding, is not a trifling error, since it obscures the fact that the Breaking of Bread, though it does not express the whole thought of Communion, is an important part of it. At an earlier time this was well understood in the Church of Rome; for the *Liber Pontificalis* records that Pope Sergius I ordered the *Agnus Dei* to be sung by priest and people during the *fractio panis*. This means during the distribution of the elements.

"Distribution," as I remarked in a previous chapter, may be criticized as a cold word. But here it indicates, not a mechanical act, but a feeling act of fellowship, of sharing, of communion. The Breaking of Bread could therefore very well be used for the whole action of the Liturgy, since, in a sense, it was the Communion.

In this case we have not only to distinguish the two senses (fellowship *and* communion) of the word *koinonia*, but we must in a measure separate them, hold them apart.* In this instance it

* In saying this I do not at all assent to the notion so laboriously worked out by Hans Lietzmann (*Messe und Herrenmahl*, pp. 174 ff., 186 ff.), that

means more particularly sharing or fellowship. If at every meal Jesus was accustomed to break the loaf with great solemnity, it could only be understood as an expression of fellowship among the disciples who did in fact share with one another what they had. At the Last Supper Jesus attached to it for the first time a deeper meaning, but not a meaning altogether different. The deepest ground of Christian fellowship is communion *in* Christ. What "in Christ" means we shall consider in the next chapter. But the Breaking of Bread lays stress upon human fellowship. This, though it is not the culminating act of the Liturgy, is a matter of no little importance. It is a common observation that in the act of Communion each individual communicant, intent upon his relation to God, which exalts his sense of individuality, is inclined, more than in any other act of worship, to ignore the presence of the others, and therefore needs to be reminded that only as he is incorporate in the mystical Body of Christ, the blessed company of all faithful people, has he this individual relation to God. Moreover, the Breaking of Bread is not only a striking expression of fellowship, but it implies such practical expressions of solidarity as the Liturgy illustrates in the Offertory and expects the disciples of Christ to exemplify in daily life, outside the *domus ecclesiae*—not to say outside the Church.

---

the liturgies of Hippolytus and Serapion represent distinct and incompatible conceptions of the Holy Communion: the one, characterized by the names "The Lord's Supper" and "The Breaking of Bread," being a fellowship meal only, in remembrance of many meals the disciples had partaken with Jesus, without any reference to the Last Supper; while the other (following Paul and Mark) was essentially a remembrance of Jesus' sacrificial death. But certainly The Breaking of Bread and The Lord's Supper (a name which St. Paul used) should remind us that from the very first the Holy Communion was a fellowship-meal. But it was (even according to Lietzmann) the thought of the actual presence of the risen Lord which made this meal sacred. We now clearly express the thought of fellowship by the "parish breakfast," but it is more aptly and more profoundly expressed in the Liturgy. We may reflect that, if the bread were now distributed as abundantly as it was in early times, there would be no need of a breakfast following the Holy Communion. It seems not unlikely that, as the use of the name suggests, the Breaking of Bread was so predominant a part of the Holy Communion that on occasions it might have been performed without the use of "the cup," as it certainly was by St. Paul on a sinking ship (Acts 27:35), or without wine in the cup (cf. Lietzmann, *op. cit.*, pp. 239 ff.), as some encratic sects preferred.

Therefore the Breaking of Bread is to be regarded as a part, the human side, of the Holy Communion, which in the next chapter will be regarded on its divine side. Also it points forward to "Catholic Action," which is the theme of the last chapter.

In the solemn act of breaking the bread, the priest, acting as the representative of Christ, doing what the Lord did, acts alone. Here the people do not act with him; they are in the position of recipients. But if they are truly responsive to such instruction in brotherhood, they cannot be said to be passive. Their response to the Breaking of Bread may be action in the deepest sense.

The formal response of the people to the Breaking of Bread was the Kiss of Peace. This is the most express recognition of the fact that the Lord's Supper is a fellowship-meal, an expression of Christian brotherhood. The people were accustomed, as the early liturgies attest, to "greet one another with a holy kiss," at the beginning of the mass of the faithful. In the Roman Liturgy this expression of fellowship was aptly enough deferred until after the Breaking of Bread; but it is deplorable that the people were no longer expected to participate in this expression of brotherhood. Indeed only a vestige of this custom remains when at a solemn Mass the celebrant kisses the deacon, and he in turn the other clergy at the Altar—if this is not commuted into kissing a plaque which is called the *pax*. This is perhaps symptomatic of the loss of the sense of fellowship in the Roman rite. In our day and among our people we cannot hope to restore this early practice, partly because men and women are no longer segregated in the church, and partly because with us the kiss is now regarded exclusively as an expression of *eros,* not of *agape.* But at least we can keep this early practice in mind as an explicit witness to the social character of the Sacrament of the Lord's Supper. Having it in mind, the people, as they rise to go to the Altar, might feel instinctively impelled to clasp the hand of a neighbor, this being the modern equivalent of the kiss of peace.

CHAPTER FOURTEEN

HOLY COMMUNION

DIVINE OPERATION

About the Holy Communion St. Paul says, in 1 Cor. 10:16, "The cup of blessing which we bless, is it not a communion [participation] in the blood of Christ? The bread which we break, is it not a communion in the body of Christ?" This rhetorical question expects confidently an affirmative answer. If the Apostle had made a dogmatic affirmation to this same effect, we could not be so sure that he was expressing the common conviction of the Church. Men hold various views about the Holy Communion, but this is the only Scriptural view. If we had not this saying of St. Paul's and the discourse reported in the sixth chapter of St. John's Gospel, we should have no way of knowing what conceptions the Apostolic Age attached to a sacrament which was the most distinctive feature of Christian worship—except as we act on the very plausible assumption that the conception of it which was current in the second century, the early Catholic age, was not radically different.

It is comforting to note that these words of St. Paul confirm substantially the Catholic view. Consequently, we dare not understand the words body and blood "in a pickwickian sense." The bread and wine are symbols, certainly; but we may not say "*only* symbols"; for we are to understand that when God makes them symbols, he makes them *real* symbols, makes them to be what they signify. Yet we are not taught to shut our eyes and affirm that the bread and wine are so transformed that they have ceased to be what to our senses they still appear to be. On the other hand, if at the instant of Communion we treat these symbols as sacred, and believe that they have been made sacred by God, it would require a prodigious agility of mind to treat them the next moment as though they were profane, as though they were common bread and wine. This, at all events our Liturgy plainly forbids us to do; and by this we are distinguished from all Calvinistic Protestants—from Arminian Protestants, too, for that matter; that is, from Methodists as well as from Presbyterians, Congregationalists and Baptists. It is dolorous that we are thus distinguished, for by this distinction we are also divided. The rubric of our Prayer Book which prescribes that, "if any of the consecrated Bread and Wine remain after the Communion, it shall not be carried out of the Church; but the Minister and other communicants shall reverently eat and drink the same," was added tardily to protect the Church of England from the encroachment of Calvinistic practices which treated the consecrated bread and wine only *as if* they were the Body and Blood of Christ, and were to be so regarded *only* in the act of Communion.

I cannot easily suppose that the early Christians when they broke the large loaf were as meticulous as Catholics now are about the crumbs. But certainly St. Paul did not take lightly the words Body and Blood. Neither did he endeavor to rationalize them; yet he does imply a certain intellectual operation which is necessary for "discerning the Body" (1 Cor. 11:29). For him, the bread and wine are indeed the Body and Blood of the Lord. For him, this was an objective fact—not dependent upon the exercise of pious imagination, which for a moment can make these symbols sacred, and just as easily reduce them again to the level of the profane. Hence the man who eateth and drinketh unworthily does not consume mere bread and wine, but he "eateth and drinketh damnation unto himself," and his condemnation is that he does not discern the Lord's Body. He is therefore "guilty of the Body and Blood of the Lord" (1 Cor. 11:27-29). "For this cause," says St. Paul, "many among you are weak and sickly, and not a few sleep." Alas, what was said so long ago of Christians in Corinth might be said today.

Yet with all this St. Paul says nothing to satisfy our curiosity. He is speaking here of what in another place (Ephes. 5:32) he calls "a great mystery," the relation between Christ and His

Church. We should remember that what we call sacraments were first called mysteries, and are still so called in the Eastern Churches. The Latin name *sacramentum* is significant too; for it meant in the first place the soldier's oath of obedience to his general, and later the oath of allegiance which the holder of every office in the Empire was required to make to the Emperor. But it would be well if we still spoke of every sacrament as a mystery; for this would remind us that sacraments can be understood only in so far as they have been revealed. This is the characteristic of what in the New Testament are called mysteries, and the use of this word is no longer exposed to the danger of confounding the Sacrament with pagan cults.

I am not bold enough to go further than Revelation goes in explaining the Sacrament of the Lord's Supper. In following consecutively the action of the Liturgy we have only now come to the point where we must consider the sacramental action. What sort of action is that? I have remarked already that every sacrament puts us in the humble position of recipients. We simply receive, and can do nothing even to deserve the gift. The action therefore in this sacrament is God's action. It is a sacrament *ex operatione Dei.* To us the *modus operandi* is not revealed, and we ought not to pretend to know it. I have already made due apology for using in time past the term *ex opere operato;* but really the words quoted from St. Paul almost seem to imply it, and perhaps the Roman Church may understand it in a tolerable sense. Indeed, Roman Catholics like to call the Sacrament *Opus Dei.*

At all events, the Sacrament is not man's action. At the most it might be said that man does something when he apprehends it by faith, that being the hand by which we grasp "the things not seen." But then in turn faith is not our own, but is the gift of God (Ephes. 2:8). Our Liturgy rightly instructs us that only by faith can we "draw near" enough to receive this Holy Sacrament. Faith is exhibited especially in the reception of the Sacrament, as something which is essentially invisible, and therefore not to be "gazed upon nor carried about," but duly used. But faith pervades the whole Liturgy, being the postulate of every prayer. Who would even come to the Eucharist without faith? I have perhaps emphasized sufficiently the part of hope in the Liturgy. About faith it is hardly possible to say enough. But as this is an aspect which no one is likely to ignore, I shall say no more about it here.

By faith we know that we have received the heavenly gift. It is not a sense of taste, nor any other kind of feeling, which gives us this assurance, although this sort of Methodism is common even among us. But why say "Methodism" when so much sentimentalism is exhibited in modern Catholicism, especially in relation to the Holy Communion! At least this degree of passive action we should like to experience, and perhaps think it a duty to experience, or perhaps think it a special privilege. "O taste and see that the Lord is good," might be said innocently by the Psalmist in old times; but it is perilous when we apply it to the Holy Communion and declare in ecstasy that it is "so sweet!" I am attracted by a more austere Catholicism. If the Eucharist were a bitter drug, I should be content with the assurance that it is the drug of immortality, the antidote of death.

The Holy Communion, though it is indeed a viaticum which God provides for this present life, while we are running the way of his commandments, is fully appreciated only when (as in the sixth chapter of St. John's Gospel) we regard it eschatologically, as a viaticum for our last mysterious journey. In our present pilgrimage we need it often, and in the hour of death we have not ceased to need it. If this were made, as once it was, the most prominent thought in the Eucharist, the hope of immortality would surely be a more lively hope. For in the Eucharist we have not only a pledge of life eternal, which perhaps once in a lifetime might suffice; but we have a frequent reminder of it. And that we need to have—lest we forget. We can forget not only the past, but the future; not only the gift we have received, but the promise. Because this Sacrament is a promise of joy to come, we cannot fully "taste" it now.

Because the Roman Mass, as it is now commonly understood and celebrated, lays a greater emphasis upon the Sacrifice than upon the Communion, it may have prompted the Calvinistic tradition, unconsciously and against its will, to regard even the Communion as a means of forgiveness for sin. This being a popular error rather than an ecclesiastical dogma (for it has no place in the Calvinistic Liturgies) is the more likely to infect us. We can defend ourselves against it by the observation that it has no Scriptural warrant. It is only as forgiven sinners we come to the Holy Communion. Of course, the Body and Blood, separated as they are in the Sacrament, mean death. They refer therefore to the Sacrifice; but they refer back to it as something already accomplished. The Sacrifice promises the forgiveness of sin, but the Communion promises more—it promises life. It must be admitted that in some early forms of the Epiclesis, and in the words addressed to the communicants in some of the ancient liturgies, the forgiveness of sin is mentioned prominently; but surely this, which is the effect of the Sacrifice, is not a thought which should be predominant in the Communion.

In the Communion the predominant thought is communion with God, which is the result of forgiveness. This implies God's presence, or more specifically the presence of Christ. The Lord's saying (Mt. 18:20), "Where two or three are gathered together in my name, there am I in the midst of them," was doubtless not applied exclusively to the Eucharistic assembly, but there Christ's presence is, in a way, visibly represented and most sensibly felt. The presence of Christ is the mystical element in the Sacrament. But the Biblical expression for the experience of Christ's mystical presence is St. Paul's phrase, "in Christ" (2 Cor. 5:17 and elsewhere) and the "ye in me and I in you" of the high-priestly prayer reported in St. John's Gospel (14:20). A sense of the presence of Christ which does not go so far as that, is not really mystical. In the Eastern Liturgies, the Elevation of the Host, coming after the Eucharistic prayer, is an invitation to communion, and is accompanied by express words of invitation: "Holy things to holy persons." If the Elevation, as in the Roman rite, stands in no obvious relation to the Communion, and is regarded as being in itself the culmination of the Liturgy, it does not express the characteristic Christian experience denoted by the phrase "in Christ." It is so far from expressing this mystical experience that, like the adoration of the reserved Sacrament, it may even denote a reluctance to *do* what the Lord commands us to do in remembrance of him. That is to say, it may indicate a disposition to shirk the searching question posed by Kierkegaard: "Can a man be a Christian without being a disciple, and a disciple without being a follower?" It is significant that after the "triumph of the Church" under Constantine, when Christians ceased to communicate frequently, they also ceased to call themselves disciples, reserving that name for the early followers of Jesus. If the Roman Mass, as it is usually performed, has shifted the accent from the last to the penultimate syllable, from the appropriation of Christ's sacrifice in the act of communion to the miracle of consecration and the presence of Christ upon the Altar, as a sacrifice offered for all, even if it is not appropriated, this change is not anywhere prescribed by the text of the Liturgy, but is indicated by the tinkling of a bell. The Church of England found itself in precisely the same situation after the Reformation, though it adopted a more radical solution, which placed the emphasis not upon the Sacrifice but upon the Offertory. For although the Book of Common Prayer expected a celebration of the Holy Communion on every Lord's Day, the Church found itself obliged by the lack of communicants to make the best of a bad situation and conclude the Liturgy with the collection, resting ignobly content with a *missa secca,* the Ante-Communion. Neither of these defections from the ideal can be ascribed to priestly machinations, for they were evidently due to popular delinquency. You can lead the horse to water, but will he drink? And on their part the people have reason to be reluctant to communicate frequently—not in so far as, being sinners, they necessarily "fall short of the glory of God," but in so far as they personally feel convicted of the severe charge made by William Law in the *Serious Call,* that they "have not so much as formed the bare intention of pleasing God in all their actions." For the Holy Communion, though it is a sheer gift, is a gift which implies a definite disposition, the intention to be a disciple of Jesus Christ. Given this intention, God may be relied upon to do the rest; and indeed the Holy Communion is the means graciously provided for the amelioration of our imperfections and the healing of our spiritual sickness.

In early times the Holy Communion was regarded as a foretaste of the celestial banquet which the disciples of Jesus were to enjoy with him in the kingdom of God. This image was a familiar one to the Jews (Lk. 14:15); in a way the feeding of the multitude in the wilderness was a pledge that they who had followed Jesus here should eat with him in the kingdom of God; and at the Last Supper the Lord encouraged his disciples to look forward to this bliss when he said (Mk. 14:25, and cf. not only the Synoptic parallels but Lk. 22:30), "Verily I say unto you, I will no more drink of the fruit of the vine, until that day when I drink it new in the kingdom of God." The celestial banquet furnishes the imagery in terms of which the eschatological hope is brought into the closest relation with the Eucharist. It is significant that in the Roman catacombs during the second and third centuries the picture of the celestial banquet was very frequently used as a symbol, almost a hieroglyph, of the Lord's Supper. This symbolism fell into disuse as the eschatological hope paled, or was transmuted into the more rational thought of immortality. For us it is perhaps no longer an available symbol; but at least we should associate with the Holy Communion the hope of heavenly bliss of which it is a pledge. I would expand upon this theme here, if I had not already dwelt upon it sufficiently in another chapter of this book, as well as in *The Short Story of Jesus*, pp. 107-115, and in my recent book on *Early Christian Art.*

CHAPTER FIFTEEN

CATHOLIC ACTION

OUTWARD ACTION

The term Catholic Action is now commonly used to denote the activity which Christian men, and laymen in particular, exercise in the social and political world in favor of the interests of the Church and of the Christian way of life. This is a broad theme, too big for any book, and one which can be dealt with more appropriately in a periodical which is free to take account of new situations as they emerge. But my theme is even broader; for I have in view all practical activities, whether of individuals or of groups, both within the fellowship of the Church and as far beyond it as the eye can reach. And yet with this broad theme I can deal briefly; for I have no notion of indicating specifically *what* is to be done, but would only stress the fact that action of a very practical sort, outward action in the world as well as in the fellowship of Christ's religion, is implied in the Liturgy and prompted by it.

Our thanksgiving after the Communion very properly reminds us when we leave the church of "all such good works as God has prepared for us to walk in." These words were inscribed in bold letters upon the front of a parish-house belonging to the Church where I first served as curate. Some pious people complained that it was a desecration to inscribe the words of the Liturgy upon a house dedicated to what was then known as "institutional Christianity." Certainly, not all works are "good works," and in this generation there is some doubt about the "institutional" works which a while ago were enthusiastically sponsored by the Churches. But the ways which God hath prepared for us to walk in are manifold; and works which are prompted by good intentions are positively good, even if they come to naught. Hence they are properly referred to a Christian motive. Works which are prompted by love for God and man stem naturally from the Liturgy.

Without love, what would the Liturgy be? Hitherto I have not spoken of love as a part of the action of the Liturgy—simply because I would not use the word in a context where it might be thought to indicate only internal action. Here, however, where we are speaking of external action there is no danger of incurring St. John's scornful reproach that we "love with the tongue" (1 Jn. 3:18). But how are we to show "in deed and in truth" our love of God?

One will hardly come to the Holy Communion without some love for God, nor leave without finding love kindled to a warmer flame. For there Christ is openly depicted as crucified before our eyes (Gal. 3:1). We have there an experience to which St. John gave classical expression (1 Jn. 4:10,19): "Not that we loved God, but that he loved us, and sent his Son to be the propitiation for our sins. We love him because he first loved us." I am inclined to think that the Epistle of St. John, no less than the sixth, the fourteenth, and the fifteenth chapters of his Gospel, was a commentary upon the Lord's Supper—which, strangely enough, he did not report. At all events, it describes exactly the inward action of the Liturgy, up to the point where it must issue in outward action—or else strangle and be suffocated. St. John was one who could talk much about loving God without thinking of it vaguely. In immediate connection with the words quoted above he says, "Beloved, if God so loved us, we ought also to love one another." This sequence, illogical as it may seem, is absolutely central in St. John's thinking. It answers a question which must arise whenever we profess to love God—the question, What are we to *do* about it? But this same sequence, which is more compelling than formal logic, is the central thought of the Liturgy, in which communion with God is the ground of true fellowship among men. It is not in vain we recite Christ's commandment to love God *and* our neighbor, although this is expressed clearly enough in the action of the Liturgy.

It is important for us to recognize that the transition from love of God to love of men is not justified merely as a psychological sequence but is the *commandment* of the Lord. This is a word which St. John reiterates again and again, at least fifteen times (Jn. 13:34, 14:21; 15:10, 12, 14; 1 Jn. 2:3, 4; 3:22, 23, 24; 5:2, 3; 2 Jn. 4, 5, 6). Commonly the commandment is that we shall love one another as God loved us, or that he who loves God must love his brother also; but in the last instance cited here it is expressed in the most general terms: "And this is love, that ye should walk in his commandments. This is the commandment, even as ye heard from the beginning, that ye should walk in it." St. Paul (2 Cor. 5:14) has in mind the compulsive authority of the commandment when he says, "The love of Christ constraineth us."

It is the more important for us to dwell upon the word "commandment," because the wholesome Catholic emphasis upon "the Law of Christ" (which belongs to the earliest Catholic tradition) was not only relaxed but scornfully repudiated by the Protestant Reformation—with the result that for us, so far as we remain under that influence, there is nothing absolutely binding but the Moral Law, conceived pretty much as the Stoics conceived of the Law of Nature, the distinctive Christian obligations having no longer any effective sanction, so that even the Dominical precept is not a "bounden duty and service." This is the consequence of the rigid and radical opposition between law and faith, and between faith and works, which both Luther and Calvin decreed. It is hardly necessary to say that no contrast of this sort can be found in the words of Jesus as they are recorded in the Gospels. Kierkegaard remarks upon the impudence of Luther in pitting an Apostle against the Lord. In fact St. Paul was not so radical, for he spoke (Gal. 6:2) of "The Law of Christ."

If we do not enter the church with at least so much love for our neighbor that we are ready to forgive him, and do not leave it with a sense that love is a commandment which prescribes something we must do, we have come in vain to the Holy Communion, and have gone away without experiencing its action.

After the Communion we may rightly be in haste to go forth in order to do what love enjoins. Some may think that the prompt dismissal after the Communion which I have proposed is far too unceremonious. But what could be more unceremonious than the dismissal with which the Roman Mass originally concluded: the *Ite, missa est* (Go, you are dismissed), which hardly left the people time for a hasty *Deo gratias* as their thanksgiving after the meal? The ritual of the Passover expressed a feeling of haste which in a measure transformed it from a mere memorial of an accomplished salvation into a forward-looking sacrament like our own. For in Ex. 12:11 the Israelites were required to eat it thus: "Your loins girded, your shoes on your feet, your staff in your hand"—as though, like us, they expected to receive in this sacrament their marching orders.

I now imagine that we are already out of the church, facing the tasks of the world, which, though we may expect it to be hostile to our enterprise, is nevertheless the world which "God so loved that he gave his only-begotten Son." Although our first interest is "the household of the faith," there is nothing in the great wide world we may not be called upon to do "as for God's laws."

But here, on the threshold of the church, we must pause for a moment to reflect upon the saying recorded in Jn. 6:28, 29: "What must we do that we may work the works of God? Jesus answered and said unto them, This is the work of God, that ye believe on him whom he hath sent." Outward action which does not stem from faith may be either good or bad—for St. Paul's saying (Rom. 14:23), "whatsoever is not of faith is sin," was not meant to apply generally. The inward action which we have been contemplating is relatively pure; but outward action is inevitably mixed. It is as though the Body and Blood of Christ were transmuted again into the common elements of bread and wine, the spiritual transmuted into the material and temporal—as it was in the Incarnation. Outward action is always perilous; with the best of intentions it may result in doing good or harm. But we are not free, like Lao-tze, or like the Quietists, to desist from action and rest content with non-action. We, with our "loins girded," have our marching orders, the commandment which requires us to act, come what may.

With this warning in mind we may venture to hallow all our actions, even our most obviously secular occupations, by regarding them as our "vocation and ministry." This phrase is sanctioned by our Prayer Book, where it occurs among the forms of prayer to be used in families. Nevertheless we must use it cautiously, remembering that it is not Scriptural. The word ministry as it is used in the New Testament means service in and for the Church; and the word calling (vocation) always points to "the upward calling of God in Christ Jesus" (Phil. 3:14), or to "the heavenly calling" (Heb. 3:11). We owe this phrase, in the sense we now attach to it, to Luther. It was doubtless well meant—meant to elevate to a religious level our humblest and most secular occupations. This thought has permeated Protestantism so thoroughly that we hardly recognize it as a modern invention. In itself it is a noble thought, and it has been welcomed by Roman Catholics. But we are prompted to be cautious when we observe that the effect, instead of levelling up, has been to level down, to obscure more and more the difference between the secular and the religious, to treat the earthly "calling" as though it were a substitute for the heavenly calling. The common use of the words calling and vocation (instead of avocation) attest the truth of this allegation. It may be said that this, more than anything else, accounts for the fact that, the "counsels of perfection being ignored, the bourgeois Protestantism of today has become sheer worldliness."

I am not inclined to say more about action; for to sit and coin felicitous phrases about action is so remote from real action that it may become a detestable occupation.

But I must say one thing about the social action which confronted and challenged us after the termination of the second world war. Many are aghast at the proposals of Malvern and subsequent Christian conferences, and still more at the pronouncements of the Archbishop of Canterbury, thinking that they indicate a movement too far to the left, as it is called. It has been said wittily that everybody fears communism . . . except the Russians. I said recently to a group of clergymen that as Christians we do not need to fear it, seeing that it accomplishes, though rather roughly, a Christian ideal. Evidently I was misunderstood, for one of the brethren objected that we have no right to force our ideals upon others. Indeed I was thinking that "the others" might force this ideal upon us, and I was hoping that we might have the grace to bear it. Communism is not agreeable to me. But certainly Christians are now called upon to *do* something by way of a thoroughgoing social reform—not merely to put up with it patiently. In this we face all the perils inherent in outward action —and we must face them bravely. Hitherto (especially here in America) we have been merely playing with the word democracy. Now we must do something about it. The crisis of this time demands something more than the good works and almsdeeds which Dorcas did. I remember (perhaps because it is sonorous) a sentence of Arnold Toynbee's which I read for the first and last time nearly sixty years ago when I was a youth in college: "For democracy is sudden like the sea, and like the sea it grows rough with storms and sweeps away many precious things; but, like the sea, it reflects the light of the wide heavens and cleanses the shores of human life."

And finally, inasmuch as this book will probably be read by the clergy chiefly, I should like to say something about our vocation as ministers of the Gospel, pointing out that this ministry is exercised not only in the celebration of the Liturgy, but that from the Liturgy, from the whole action of it and from every part, we derive an incentive to "make full proof of our ministry" (2 Tim. 4:5), the fullest proof being, not in the Church and in the performance of the Christian cult, but in the world, in every sort of Christian endeavor, whether we are dealing with Greek or barbarians, with the wise or the foolish, where nevertheless we can say, "I am not ashamed of the Gospel, for it is the power of God unto salvation" (Rom. 1:16).

Part II

Important Non-Essentials

HOW TO PERFORM THE LITURGY

1. POSITION OF THE ALTAR

(Plates I, IV and V-IX)

Central to the program of Liturgical Reform, though by no means the project most easily carried out, is the location of the Holy Table between the clergy and the people. I cannot affirm too emphatically that this is not a revolution but a reform, a return to early Catholic practice. To us it may appear revolutionary if we have never seen an altar which is not built like a shelf against the wall. It seemed revolutionary when by royal authority the Reformed Church of England was required to remove the altars from the deep monastic choirs and to place the Holy Table near the people. Because this was done under Calvinistic influence and without a profound understanding of the early Catholic practice, the altar was not long maintained in this position, except as the distinction of an Evangelical party which did not know what to do with a table in that position and therefore expected the priests, instead of ministering behind it, to kneel upon high cushions at either end, looking very much like the cherubim hovering over the Mercy Seat. I myself have sometimes had to take that embarrassing position, especially at Holy Trinity in Philadelphia. It is very ironical that now the table in that church, which in Phillips Brooks' day was placed upon the chord of the apse, has been shoved against the wall, just at the instant when a Catholic effort is being made to restore the Holy Table to its proper place, and just about the time when in the same city Dr. Stuckert, Rector of the House of Prayer, was cleverly contriving to build beneath his church a chapel resembling a crypt in the catacombs, with the cathedra behind the altar. Dr. Stuckert was likely justified in thinking that among us he was the first to celebrate in this position. But I learn that several parish churches in the United States which have recently been built by Benedictines can boast of having the altar in the right place. I am told that about eleven years ago the Roman Catholic Primate of Holland required that all new churches must be built with this possibility in view, that is, with the altar at such a distance from the wall that the priest could celebrate behind it, if he chose to do so.

Dom Albert Hemmenstede, one time Prior at Maria Laach and later superior of a little priory in New Jersey, told me with becoming modesty that he was the first to institute this change. The Abbot of Maria Laach permitted him to erect an altar of the antique sort in the unused crypt dating from the twelfth century beneath the monastic church. He tells me that the monks liked the arrangement, but that the nuns who came to worship there, and not a few laywomen, were greatly embarrassed by the thought that the celebrant could see them and might be watching them. There was no danger of that, he said, for a monk was taught to cast down his eyes; but he admitted that a secular pastor might be tempted to look around to see what members of his parish were present and how they comported themselves. He concluded reluctantly that perhaps there was some reason for the later development which required the priest to turn his back to the people.

Doubtless there was a reason—but was it a good reason? The Presbyterians have never showed any embarrassment at finding themselves face to face with their pastor at the Holy Communion. Father Hemmenstede, however, was reflecting upon difficulties peculiar to the Church of Rome when he remarked that during the Mass the people were absorbed in their private devotions. Such individualism finds no encouragement in our Communion, where all can hear and understand every word of the Liturgy and are expected to follow it. And yet with us too, though for a different reason, the congregation in the act of worship is almost completely resolved into its primary units, each man praying by himself, even though all are praying the same prayers. This is also true, though perhaps to a less degree, of Protestant worship. The worshiper is alone in the crowd, and the more intent he is upon communion with God, the less he is aware of sharing this communion with God's people. This situation is so natural to us that many will be incredulous at hearing it criticized. We are likely to regard it as an ideal situation when all are so completely absorbed in prayer that the priest forgets that he is ministering to the people, and the people are unaware of one another. But observe that it is precisely for this reason the Protestants universally speak of "communing" in the sacrament of the Lord's Supper. That is what they do. We, however, continue to use the traditional word "communicate," and that means, or ought to mean, that we share the Sacrament in common and are aware of it.

But the people have not only a fellowship in the communion but in the prayers and in the sacrifice. The invitation *Orate, fratres* in the Roman Mass declares this expressly: "Pray, brethren, that my sacrifice and yours may be acceptable to God the Father almighty"; and the gist of the movement called "Liturgical Reform" in the Church of Rome is the zeal to make this fellowship real, and consciously real. In part, it seeks to accomplish this end by prompting the people to make audibly the responses, the Confession, the *Kyrie,* the *Gloria,* the Creed, the *Tersanctus,* which for centuries they have supinely relinquished to the server and the choir; and in part by encouraging them to recognize that the whole action of the Mass is their action conjointly with the celebrant, even where he alone utters the words. It is commonly conceived that the usurpation of sacerdotal power is due exclusively to the selfishness of the priests. Alas, it is more often due to the indolence of the people, their supine cowardness, their unwillingness to do their part. They prefer that the priest should do in their stead what a Christian is required to do. The first part of this program, which the reformers seek to realize by the use of what is called "the dialogue Mass," the Anglican Communion attained by reciting the Liturgy in the vernacular.

When the chief emphasis is placed, not on the communion, but on the sacrifice, and that not a sacrifice made in common, it is natural enough that the priest should lead the people to the altar and therefore have them behind him. In the Church of Rome, where, in spite of the protests of the reformers, many people come to witness the miracle of transubstantiation and conceive that the climax has been reached at the elevation, it is indifferent where the priest stands. But in the Church of Rome there is now a prodigious effort to restore the practice of communion, and among us great emphasis is placed upon the importance of what we call "corporate communion." The corporate character of the Holy Communion is most vividly represented when the clergy and the people surround the Holy Table. If the fellowship (that is the other word we use to translate the New Testament word *koinonia*) is not vividly realized then, in sharing the one loaf and the one cup, the parish breakfast is not an adequate substitute.

It was a misunderstanding on the part of the Calvinists to complain of the altar built against the wall on the ground that it represented a pagan conception. No pagan altar was ever placed against a wall, and, except in the case of Buddhist altars, the people surrounded their altar. Constantine had a predilection for building churches on a centralized plan, either round or else cruciform with arms of equal length. He had good reason for building at Jerusalem a round church, the Anastasis, to mark the place of our Lord's Ascension, and the Church of the Apostles at Constantinople was round in order that his own memorial column might stand in the midst of the columns of the Twelve Apostles; but in other cases too he seems to have desired to place the altar in the center. That was clearly a reminiscence of paganism. It was an idiosyncrasy which had no enduring effect, for it was opposed to the tradition which was embodied in the basilica. The early Church did not cherish the ideal of placing the altar in the middle where it would be surrounded by the people indiscriminately. On the contrary, it required that the clergy should be distinguished by their position at the Holy Table. In the first stage, when all sat at the table, the clergy occupied the "chief seats"; at a later stage they had the only seats. The arrangement of the basilica precisely defined the office of every grade of the clergy.

Although the Roman Catholics encounter some special difficulties in restoring the altar to its proper place, yet on the whole it is easier for them than it is for us. For we must remember that what we ill-advisedly call the Roman Church is the Church of Rome, or rather, to use the New Testament expression, the Church in Rome. Being in Rome, that Church cannot regard it as an innovation to insist that the altar be in the midst, for so it is in every basilica where the Bishop of Rome or his vicar celebrates, and so it is also in every church big or little which was built before a late period in the Middle Ages (Plates I, IV and V). It is so natural there to imitate this ancient custom that when our American church of St. Paul-within-the-walls was built by my predecessor, Dr. Nevin, with the aid of that admirable architect George Edmund Street, the episcopal chair was built against the wall of the apse with the altar in front of it. But of course neither the American priest nor the English architect could divest their minds of the prejudice that an altar must be adorned by a retable and that surmounted by two candles (at least), two vases of flowers, and a big cross between them. The consequence was that the bishop was completely snuffed out when he sat in that chair, and since 1895 no bishop, so far as I know, has been modest enough to occupy the seat appointed for him, though in itself it is a magnificent throne. After my departure it was moved by impious hands to the conventional position on the Gospel side, and (partly to hide the disfigurement of the wall) the conventional Anglican dossal was hung behind the Altar. Lately it has been restored to its proper place. But even the Church of Rome and in Rome will have to overcome some traditional prejudices before it can return to the earlier tradition advocated by the reformers. For even in the Basilica of St. Peter, and even in the ancient Basilica of St. John Lateran, and indeed on every papal altar in Rome the candlesticks and the altar-cross obscure the celebrant from the people in the nave more thoroughly than if he had his back to them and were facing the wall.

So the reform now advocated is a drastic one, even though it is plainly a reversion to the older custom. To us who are uninformed, or only vaguely informed, about the customs of the Catholic Church before the Middle Ages it will seem undesirable in the highest degree—"but, thank God, unfeasible," someone will exclaim. "What! an altar without candlesticks or cross, without even the vases of flowers which are so dear to the neo-catholicism (or neo-paganism) of our day that they have been adopted even by our ultra-Protestant brethren as the entering wedge of ritualistic embellishments! How uncatholic!" And yet in this country, wherever the Benedictine reformers have their way, this thing has been done. For my part I am willing enough to leave it to the Methodists to "say it with flowers"—there are other and more sober ways of expressing devotion to God. Of course candles are very nice, but I cannot forget that until the period of barbarism which succeeded the downfall of the Roman Empire they were considered a very inferior means of illumination. The only candle used ritually in the Church at an early date was the Paschal candle, and that with its lofty candlestick stood upon the floor. Olive oil was justly preferred, and lamps were commonly *hung* over the Altar. The Cross also could be hung, or it could be erected upon the rood-screen.

Certainly it would be easier to carry through a reform which involved only a change in the position of the altar, leaving its ornaments unchanged, and it would be still easier if the celebrant were not expected to face the people. Yet even the easier part of this reform would be difficult for us, accustomed as we are to see the backs of priests and to expect the altar to be at the furthest possible remove from the congregation and planted against the east wall of a deep monastic choir. The deep monastic choir which strikes us as so "churchly" is characteristic of the churches of Northern Europe, which was Christianized by monks, more especially by friars, and therefore at so late a date that there are few monuments to remind us of early ecclesiastical practice. The long monastic choir has a certain sublimity, but what the celebrant says when he stands at the further end of it and with his back to the people might as well be uttered in an unknown tongue—unless he shouts so loud that those near the altar are deafened.

But this is a difficulty only to Anglicans. In Southern Europe the high altar even in monastic churches was commonly in front of the choir, that is, between the choir and the people. At an early date, perhaps as early as the fifth century, there had been a tendency to enhance the mystery of the cult by hiding the altar by a curtain from the eyes of the people. From this was developed the iconostasis of the Eastern Church, but in the Western Church this tendency left no other trace but the rood-screen, and the use of side altars brought the people into the closest relation to the sacred mysteries.

On the other hand, the shape of the altar itself underwent a change in the West. Originally it had been a small table not much more than a yard square. In the West during the Middle Ages it became oblong, having approximately the length of a man, owing doubtless to the custom of burying beneath it the body of a martyr. But it is significant that the size of it did not vary with the size of the church. The most prodigious basilica had an altar no larger than had a tiny chapel. Some years ago at the meeting of our General Convention the altar in the Convention Hall was enlarged to a prodigious size to correspond with the bigness of the building. That is not in accord with the Christian tradition. In a great basilica like St. Peter's at Rome the importance of the altar is emphasized not by enlarging it but by erecting over it a greater ciborium or *baldacchino.*

The ancient position of the altar between the clergy and the people was of the utmost importance for doctrine and discipline —especially for the doctrine of the ministry. Accordingly it is of the utmost importance today that the altar should be restored to its original position.

But for us there is the rub. I imagine a tremendous outcry. "What! Do away with the reredos, the dossal, the retable, and sweep away all the altar furniture!" For my part I cannot take this objection very seriously. The chalice and the paten, perhaps the pyx, would still be on the altar during a celebration, and the missal or the book of the Gospels might remain there permanently, the cross or the crucifix might be hung above it, lamps could be hung from the ciborium, as was the ancient custom, or, if we persist in using candles, then the candlesticks, like that of the paschal candle, might be planted on the floor, and all that need be swept away is a lot of *brass.*

To me it is appalling to think of the thousands of tons of brass used upon Anglican altars. Brass, though it is a base metal (an alloy of iron and copper), has its uses in industry, and disagreeable as it is to the touch and quick to tarnish, it is used alas, in the home only too frequently for door-knobs, andirons and lamp fixtures. There is no sanction in ecclesiastical tradition for its use in the church, and yet our altars are loaded with brass and surrounded by brass. This bad custom threatens to corrupt the world, for our Protestant brethren when they essay to enrich their worship learn from us to enrich it with brass. It is a mercy that no one has yet thought of making chalices of brass. But the richest altars no less than the poorest must have a brass cross, two or else eight brass candlesticks, perhaps as many as six brass vases, a brass book-rest, perhaps brass doors for the tabernacle, beside it we plant a brass processional cross, before it perhaps we swing a brass censer, we fence the altar from the people with a brass rail (instead of inviting the communicants to approach a narrow table properly spread with a linen cloth), before it we place a brass lectern, likely a brass pulpit also, and the walls of the chancel and the nave are disfigured by brass memorials of the dead. The most arduous duty of the sacred confraternity called the altar guild is the polishing of all this brass. It would be a great blessing if the Government were to requisition in behalf of the defense effort all the brass that is to be found in the churches. Think how many brass buttons it would make!

I cannot conceive how this base metal attained with us the reputation of being the holy metal *par excellence,* unless perhaps because we were led astray by the use of the word "brass" in the Bible, where properly bronze is meant—as when the Book of Exodus describes the appurtenances of the altar of the Tabernacle (27:3): "And thou shalt make its pans to receive its ashes, and its shovels and its basons and its flesh-hooks and its fire-pans: all the vessels thereof thou shalt make of brass." Bronze (an alloy of tin and copper) is indeed a noble metal, and it has always been used along with silver and gold upon pagan as well as upon Christian altars. For my part I should prefer gilded bronze (or even gilded wood) to silver and gold, partly because, in accordance with the earliest tradition of the Church, the poor are the "altar" upon which gold and silver are properly lavished, and partly because in our good land, alas, where precious metals cannot be carried through the streets except in armored cars protected by armed men, and where the people are far too enlightened to fear the commission of sacrilege, it is not safe to display objects of intrinsic value in our churches. The few churches I know where there is much silver and gold in evidence create grave anxiety for those who are responsible. But this is hardly a sufficient reason for using brass and for using so much of it; it may rather reconcile us to the necessity of sweeping away the ornaments from our altar, so that again the altar may by its position symbolize the communion of priests and people (that is, of the whole Church) in the one Bread. Even the Papal altars, though they are in the right place, do not aptly symbolize this communion, inasmuch as even there medieval custom has erected between the priest and the people a barrier consisting of the altar-cross and the candlesticks. Sublime as these things are, they must be regarded as a parasitical sublimity of the altar. The tons of silver and gold which according to the *Liber Pontificalis* were in the fourth and fifth centuries bestowed upon the churches of Rome for their adornment did not for the most part load the altar, and if we might dare to use such precious gifts we could find some other place for them than the top of the Holy Table.

But from this digression I return to the main point. The main point is that the altar should be in the right place. If the altar of the Church were simply a place of sacrifice, like every pagan altar, and like the altar of burnt-offering outside the Tabernacle and the Temple of the Hebrews, it would be appropriate enough for the priest to go before the people and therefore turn his back upon them as he leads them to that dread place to which he alone may venture to draw near, and though it would perhaps be rather queer it would not be altogether unseemly to build it like a shelf against the wall. But such was not the Christian tradition for well over a thousand years—and this for the good and sufficient reason that what we call the altar is first and foremost the Holy Table. If calling it an altar obscures the fact that it is a table, we ought to give up calling it an altar. It is the Holy Table which symbolizes the sacramental unity of the Church. Accordingly it is appropriate that the Church should gather around this table. Without doubt in the early days when the disciples broke bread from house to house they all sat at the table. When the company of believers became too numerous for this it was a matter of course that the men who were most highly revered in the congregation, who had been accustomed to sit in the chief seats when every one sat at table, should continue to sit there when the greater number had to stand at a distance during the prayer of thanksgiving and approached the table only to receive the Sacrament. Such persons were of course the apostles, prophets and evangelists. But if no such eminent persons were present, there were in every assembly at least elders, that is, older men, who would sit at the table, and one of them must preside, pronouncing the blessing as Christ did, breaking the bread, doing everything as Christ did at the Last Supper, being in fact the representative of Christ, Christ's vicar if you will. That was the most eminent position in the Church, whether it was occupied by an apostle or by an elder. Ultimately the dignity and authority of the bishop was defined by that position, and so also was the character and authority of the presbyters in the earliest stadium. For at the beginning of the second century (that is, in the days of St. Ignatius of Antioch) it was the presbyters who were likened to the Apostles, while the bishop was likened to Christ himself. Hence it was natural for Ignatius to say, "When ye are obedient to the bishop as to Jesus Christ . . . . be ye obedient also to the presbyters as to the Apostles of Jesus Christ our hope" (*Ad Trall.* c. 2); "Plainly therefore we ought to regard the bishop as the Lord himself" (*Ad Ephes.* c. 9). Or the bishop was exalted by a still higher analogy when he was regarded as "the type of the Father." "In like manner let all men respect the deacons as Jesus Christ, even as they should respect the bishop as being the type of the Father and the presbyters as the Sanhedrin of God and the band of the Apostles" (*Ad Trall.* c. 3). The deacons are here regarded as serving the bishop as the Son serves the Father: "The bishop presiding after the likeness of God and the presbyters after the likeness of the council of the Apostles, with the deacons who are also most dear to me, who were entrusted with the serviceable ministry of Jesus Christ" (*Ad Magn.* c. 6, *Ad Smyr.* c. 8). At all events the presbytery is always compared with the council of the Apostles, and all three orders—the bishop, the presbyters and the deacons—are commonly associated together in a way which plainly reflects their concrete relation towards one another as defined by the places they occupied at the Lord's Table, where the bishop and the presbyters as his assessors sat behind the table facing the people, and the deacons stood, as their serviceable ministry required. When Ignatius says, "With your reverend bishop and with the fitly wreathed spiritual chaplet of your presbytery and with the deacons who walk after God" (*Ad Magn.* c. 13), he seems to have in mind the half circle of elders seated on either side of the bishop's cathedra in an apse such as we find in the earliest basilicas. The half-circular arrangement of the presbyters' seats seems to explain the figure of speech he employs in *Ad Ephes.* c. 4, where he says that the presbytery is "attuned to the bishop like the strings to a lyre."

The Christian basilica (i. e. royal house—we say "the Lord's house") was also properly regarded as *domus ecclesiae* (the house of the Church) and was therefore planned expressly to accommodate the Church as it assembled on every Lord's Day for the celebration of the Holy Communion, its most distinctive sacrament, which also characterized most clearly the nature of its organization. The altar by its position between the clergy and the people dominated the plan. Although during the course of the Middle Ages the altar was generally removed from its proper position and thrust back against the east wall, yet the ground-plan of the basilica was not substantially changed by later styles of architecture (the Romanesque, the Gothic etc.), except by the introduction of the monastic choir, and therefore it is generally possible without too much difficulty to restore the altar to its appropriate place.

In 1901, when I published a textbook on *Christian Art and Archaeology,** though I furnished many illustrations of the position of the altar in early times, I did not venture to propose that we should revise our present practice; for it had not yet entered into my heart to believe that a return to the ancient practice of the Church might be possible. Now, however, when in the Church of Rome such a reform is advocated and in many places

* Sold in the United States under the name of *Monuments of the Early Church* and frequently reprinted by the MacMillan Company—until, to my contentment, it was suppressed by the government of the United States during World War II, on the plea that the metal plates were good for making bullets.

is put into effect we cannot dismiss it as unpractical antiquarianism. Antiquarian it certainly is not, for the primitive position of the Holy Table is as important today as ever it was for the understanding of the meaning of the Eucharist and the character of the ministry. Moreover a return to the primitive custom is important today in the interest of reunion. For though our Protestant brethren occasionally imitate the brazen decoration of our altars and occasionally thrust the Holy Table against the wall, yet the tradition of the Reformed Churches requires that the Lord's Table be near the people and that the pastor and the elders shall sit behind it.

When in 1904 I published a discussion of *The Church and its Organization* (with perhaps too much evidence of erudition), and when twenty years later in the *Problems of Church Unity* (which vainly sought to attain popularity by suppressing every semblance of learning) I rehearsed briefly the principal argument of the first with the intent of proving that the original position of the Church about the altar graphically defined the character and authority of the Christian ministry—even then I was too faint-hearted to believe that the primitive custom might ever be restored. These two books can no longer be bought—not, alas, because the editions were sold out, but because Longmans did not find it profitable to deal in them, and finally they were "destroyed by enemy action." And yet now when this has become practical politics, now when in view of the theme of this chapter I read again these books objectively after the lapse of many years, it would not be candid of me if I were to suppress the conviction that they are good books; indeed, being now an old man, I am bold enough to say that they are the best books written on this subject in my generation, and that it was not creditable to my generation that it ignored them. But at all events they are "books in being," they can be found in public libraries, and I am told that lately in Great Britain there has been a revival of interest in them, I therefore assume that any one who really desires to follow the theme of this chapter further will consult them.

I refer here also to my recent work on *Art in the Early Church*, written with much labor to replace the antiquated book of half a century ago, and published by Pantheon Books. It is my swan song, for it broke my back with the task of reproducing nearly five hundred pictures. It is appropriate to mention it here, for it contains many pictures which illustrate themes which are here prominent, especially the subject of ecclesiastical dress. This is a case which exemplifies the importance of a book "in being"; for since this new book of mine is potentially in the possession of every reader, it may be assumed that one who is interested in the ancient monuments here referred to can find adequate reproductions of them there. If I had not produced that bigger book, I should have felt obliged to provide more pictures in this little one.

2. PREPARATION

INTROIBO

(Lines from the forty-third Psalm with its antiphon and the *Gloria,* to be said alternately by the priest and server.)

In the name of the Father, and of the Son, and of the Holy Ghost.
Amen.
I will go to the altar of God,
Even unto God my exceeding joy.
Give sentence with me, O God, and defend my cause
Against an ungodly people!
O deliver me from the deceitful and unjust man!
For Thou art the God of my strength.
Why hast Thou cast me off?
And why go I mourning
Because of the oppression of the enemy?
O send out Thy light and Thy truth,
That they may lead me,
And bring me to Thy holy hill,
And to Thy tabernacles!
Then will I go to the altar of God,
Even unto God my exceeding joy;
And upon the harp will I praise Thee,
O God, my God!

Glory be to the Father, and to the Son, and to the Holy Ghost. Amen.
I will go to the altar of God,
Even unto God my exceeding joy.
Our help is in the name of the Lord,
Who hath made heaven and earth.

I know very well that this preparation is not found in our Prayer Book; when it is used by us it is treated as if it were not properly a part of the Liturgy, and in the Church of Rome for a long time past it has been treated as if it were not properly a part of the Mass, although it is printed in the Missal and is an appropriate beginning. Even before the Reformation it was regarded as the private preparation of the priest, which might just as well be said in the sacristy; and for that reason it was omitted in the reformed Liturgy of the Church of England.

But surely there must be something dreadfully Romish and Papistical in these prayers that are recited at the foot of the altar, for otherwise the Reformed Church of England would hardly have discarded them, leaving no prayers of preparation to be said humbly at this place, although some such preparation is obviously seemly. So one might think very plausibly. But as a matter of fact there is no grave fault to be found in these prayers; even from the point of view of Anglican Evangelicalism they are (except, it might be, for references to saints in the *Confiteor*) not only innocent but edifying. What happened was that, in the Church of England at the time of the Reformation, these prayers at the foot of the altar were, as I have said, falsely regarded as the private preparation of the priest and no more than that. In our Liturgy, where we use a language known to the people and pronounce every word in a tone audible to them, it is questionable if the people will not be more vexed than edified by any authorized insertion which has to be said *secrete,* i. e. in a tone audible to those about the altar, and which is regarded as a private prayer of the priest. The prayers at the foot of the altar will surely be irritating to people who have not the slightest notion of what is being said and can find no light upon it in the Prayer Book. The case is different in the Church of Rome where everything is found in the Missal and can be read in the vernacular by the people, and where what I venture to call the godly celerity of the Roman priest saves even the private prayers from being tiresome. He who uses these prayers in our Church might at the very least instruct the people by placing in every Prayer Book a leaflet on which they are printed. Moreover it is clearly desirable that in places where there is a choir the *Introit* should be sung at this point, if the people will not join in the *Introibo*. It is a prime principle of godly celerity to cover with a hymn the intervals during which something is being said which cannot be heard by all the people, or something is being done and not said, as for example when the corporal is spread on the altar and when the chalice is cleansed.

The Server

Inasmuch as the prayers at the foot of the altar are commonly in use among us and are almost invariably used when the priest has a server, they cannot be simply ignored as an inepitude when we are considering how the Eucharist is to be celebrated. One may decide for or against the use of them, but one cannot decide wisely without knowing what they are. Clearly these prayers have intrinsic qualities which powerfully recommend them, yet they perhaps will not be used, certainly they will not be used rightly, if they are regarded as the *private* preparation of the priest. Nothing is really private which is done with so much solemnity before the eyes of all, but obviously this is not the private preparation of the priest, seeing that the server or other ministers have an equal part in it. Neither can it be regarded as an adventitious and superfluous addition to the Liturgy, although it is true that in the Roman practice of today the confession, the very same confession which was made by the priest and the server, is made by the people immediately before the Communion, and the same prayer of absolution is said. But this repetition betrays the assumption that the prayers at the foot of the altar represent the private or personal preparation of the priest and the server. Nothing could be further from the truth, for properly this should be regarded as the confession of priest and people, and surely for the people as well as for the priest no place is more appropriate for such a preparation by confession and absolution than the very beginning of the Liturgy, or, if you prefer, before the beginning. If the people join in the confession here, it would not need to be repeated before the Communion. Instead of saying that no place is more appropriate, I would say that no other place is equally appropriate. We need preparation for communion in the prayers of the Church no less than for communion in the sacrament. We have lost all sense of this need, just in proportion as we have lost a sense of the difficulty and of the reality of prayer. But St. Chrysostom, protesting against the growing habit of non-communicating attendance at the Eucharist, exclaimed, "If you are worthy of the Sacrifice, why not receive the Sacrament? If you are unworthy of this, neither are you worthy to join in the prayers. . . . You say, 'I am unworthy'—are you then not unworthy of that communion which is experienced in the prayers?" (*Hom. iii in Ephes.*)

Churches which use a server have a compelling reason (though it does not always effectively compel) to use also the prayers of preparation at the foot of the altar, for this is the only place where the server appears clearly in his true character, it is the only situation where we can readily perceive the appropriateness of Oscar Wilde's remark that the server at the Mass is the last vestige of the Greek chorus.

But to appreciate this remark fully (perhaps more fully than did Wilde himself) one must be acquainted not only with the purpose of the chorus in Greek tragedy, but also with the early Christian way of regarding "those about the altar." The Greek chorus was the audience, not as being auditors of the poet's lines but as witnesses of the actual tragedy. In a similar way those about the altar represented the Church. They were not representatives of the people in the sense of our political theory of representative government, which was completely foreign to the notions of the early Church, but they represented the people ideally, or rather they were ideally the Church. When it was no longer possible for the whole multitude of the faithful to sit at the table, those who actually sat there, being of course the most highly esteemed disciples, the nucleus of the Church, could be regarded ideally as the Church, so that what was done by them was done by the Church. For example, when the clergy elected their bishop this counted as an election by the Church, and the people had only to acclaim their decision. Nothing could be more remote from this whole range of thought than our notion that the interests of the people and the clergy are in a measure opposed, so that the people, like the *tiers état,* need to elect delegates to represent them and defend their separate interests. No, the clergy (i. e. "those about the altar," as they were significantly called in the second century) were ideally the representatives of the people, they acted in their interest not only, but in their behalf and in their stead—not, however, as delegates, not as though they derived any authority from the people, for in the Church there is no authority but God's will. Difficult as it must be even for Catholics—perhaps especially for Catholics, and perhaps for all Christians but Quakers—to get through their heads this primitive and early Catholic notion, it must be evident that the prevailing view which sharply contrasts clergy and people is a profoundly pessimistic view, a dismal view, which gives neither clergy nor people their due. The estimation which during the early centuries was accorded to those about the altar, i. e. to the bishop, the presbytery and the deacons, applies now in a small way to the priest and his server. Thus the server is not merely the last vestige of the Greek chorus, but he is the last vestige of the early conception of the clergy as ideally the representatives of the people. Hence Roman Catholic liturgists, if they are well informed, recognize that the prayers at the foot of the altar, even when they are said by the celebrant and the server alone, are so far from being private prayers that the priest after the *Confiteor* asks the *people* to pray for him, and that the *Confiteor* of the server is to be regarded as the confession of the people. Whatever the practice of the Church of Rome may be, the rubrics of the Mass prescribe that the priest shall begin by saying *In nomine Patris,* etc., in an "intelligible voice" and shall recite the *Introibo* in a "distinct voice" (*clara voce*), and also that in the *Confiteor* all who are about the altar (*circumstantes*) even if the Pope be amongst them (*etiamsi ibi fuerit Summus Pontifex*), shall join. So it is plainly the Catholic ideal that all who are about the altar should take part in this preparation, though in our Church I have never seen it done.

To this vestige I am fain to cling, although it is so small a vestige of a great conception which prevailed in the days when at every Eucharist the bishop, the presbytery and the deacons were present at the altar. At Rome during the third century, when the bishop could no longer be present in every Church, it was the rule that "there shall be two presbyters to every Church." How comfortless it is, both for the celebrant and for the people, when one priest stands alone at the altar. I have often wished that the vestry would join me there, and I have envied the Presbyterian pastor who has the support of the elders. But at least we may have the server—and with that we have ideally the people at the altar.

A Macedonian cry from St. Vincent's Guild asks for help in defending the servers against the encroachments of visiting clergymen. It is assumed that the priests of the parish can be relied upon not to behave in a manner unbecoming a clergyman and a gentleman. But the priests who occasionally are present to lend aid to the celebrant—how ought they to comport themselves? Of course if they are acting as deacons and subdeacons and are dressed for the part, they supplant the acolytes in most of their functions. The last word on the ritual comportment of ministers at a solemn mass was said by Dr. Frere in a little pamphlet which he sent me just before he died. I need say no more about that. But suppose the visiting presbyters are there only to preach, to read the Epistle or the Gospel, and to help to communicate the people. Then let them do what they have been invited to do. There are surely places appointed for them where they can sit and stand and kneel. Let them not crowd the servers from their place on the steps of the altar. The situation is so simple that a word to the wise should be sufficient. But likely there will be no server present, and in that case it is appropriate for the priest to perform the functions of the subordinate minister—indeed it would be very improper for him not to do so.

The Confiteor

I assume as a matter of course that if we make the *Confiteor* in this place we will not use exactly the Roman form but will expurgate, as we now do, the mention of Mary ever Virgin, Michael the archangel, John the Baptist, the holy apostles Peter and Paul, and "all the saints," in whose presence the Romans make their confession to almighty God and whose prayers they solicit. I too am accustomed to omit them, but reluctantly, only for fear of offending the weaker brethren. "Reluctantly," I say, for though undoubtedly it is a stimulus to our high endeavor as we climb the steep ascent to reflect that we are compassed about by so great a cloud of witnesses, yet to my mind it is no less salutary to think of these witnesses when we can hardly stand upright or when we stumble and fall, and it is a comfort to think that such witnesses as they will surely not be indifferent to our plight.

At this point I must write out the *Confiteor,* for the same reason that I wrote out in full the *Introibo.*

The priest makes his confession as follows:

I confess to almighty God, to blessed Mary ever Virgin, to blessed Michael the archangel, to blessed John the Baptist, to the holy apostles Peter and Paul, to all the saints, and to you brethren, that I have sinned exceedingly in thought, word, and deed, *through my fault, through my fault, through my most grievous fault.* Therefore I beseech blessed Mary ever Virgin, blessed Michael the archangel, blessed John the Baptist, the holy apostles Peter and Paul, all the saints, and you brethren, to pray to the Lord our God for me.

I prefer not to say much about the manual acts of the celebrant, except when they are visible to the congregation. Here I need only remark that the repetition, *mea culpa, mea culpa, mea maxima culpa,* is not only a pungent expression of penitence but is intended also as an occasion for beating the breast thrice. This custom is so natural and so significant that, even in case a man were making his confession perfunctorily, such a gesture might perhaps prompt a profounder sense of contrition. In our Liturgy there are other places where this gesture is appropriate: in the General Confession the phrase, "by thought, word, and deed," suggests the triple gesture of penitence, and I suppose was coined for it; and another occasion for it is presented less obviously by a phrase near the end of the Canon: "unworthy, through our mainfold sins, to offer thee any sacrifice."

In response to the priest's request that the brethren pray for him, the server as the representative of the people prays as follows:

May almighty God have mercy upon three, forgive thee thy sins, and bring thee to life everlasting.

It is appropriately the priest who says the Amen. Thereupon the server, representing the people, makes the same confession, except that instead of "you brethren" he says "thee father"; and the priest offers the same prayer of absolution, to which the server responds with Amen. Then the priest concludes with a prayer for himself as well as the people:

May the almighty and merciful God grant us pardon, absolution and full remission of our sins.

To this the server responds with Amen, and the priest and the server say alternately the following:

Thou wilt turn us, O God, and bring us to life,
And Thy people will rejoice in Thee.
Show us Thy mercy, O Lord,
And grant us Thy salvation.
O Lord, hear my prayer,
And let my cry come unto Thee.
The Lord be with you.
And with thy spirit.

Here the priest, going up the steps, says before he kisses the altar:

Take from us our sins, O Lord, that we may enter with pure minds into the holy of holies; Through Christ our Lord. Amen.

With this we have reached the end of the prayers at the foot of the altar in the Roman rite, for the next thing is the *Kyrie*. It is surely evident that there is nothing Papistical about these prayers. On the contrary, they are more strikingly evangelical than anything that is to be found in our Book of Common Prayer, or than any Protestant formula of worship, for the fact that priest and people are reciprocally active in precisely the same measure, making to one another the same confession and offering in behalf of one another the same prayer of absolution. Only it would doubtless be more in accordance with the earliest practice, and also with our own, if in all this the people took an audible part, were directly active, not active only through their representative the server. So it is with us when at a later place in the Liturgy we make our confession. But, alas, with us there is no one who prays for the absolution of the priest. It is not even perfectly obvious that the priest makes the confession on his own account and not rather on behalf of the people. There is the same ambiguity in the prayer of humble access, where it might be supposed that the godly priest is speaking only in behalf of the people when he says, "We are not worthy," whereas *Domine, non sum dignus,* is unequivocal.

Perhaps it is not to be expected that the people, who hitherto have been ignorant of the content of these prayers, might now be ready to take part in them audibly; but at least where they are said the people ought to be made familiar with them, and to this end, as I have already remarked, these prayers ought to be inserted in all the Prayer Books in the pews. Moreover, if I am right in maintaining that these are not private prayers, they ought not to be mumbled but should be pronounced clearly and in a tone audible to those about the altar, if there are any other ministers there, and in that case, it seems to me, it would be appropriate for all those about the altar to take audible part in them.

The Server Again

I have used the word server here rather than the grandiloquent title acolyte, not merely because the latter word is highfalutin but because it is misleading. It is my belief that the acolyte was in the earliest stage equivalent to subdeacon, both offices being at that time peculiar to Rome. But at all events the acolyte belonged then, as he does now, to the clerical order, and the assumption was that he was seeking a higher degree, namely, the diaconate, eventually the priesthood. Perhaps it is this notion, or rather a slight trace of it, which prompts us to select young boys as servers. Sometimes we see young men performing this function, but in our Church one rarely sees an old man acting as server. And yet it is obvious that an adult Christian serving in this capacity would be more clearly representative of the people of God. Moreover, it seems to me that the server, be he man or boy, would be more clearly representative of the people if he were not vested in cassock and cotta but dressed in his ordinary clothes. It is inevitable that after living for twenty-five years in Rome I have a tendency to Romanize. I am attracted especially to the simplicity of the Roman ways—when they *are* simple, as in this instance they are. I know that to many of us such simplicity as this may seem almost sacrilegious. Yet that is a prejudice which can be overcome. During the first world war the chaplain of a Canadian regiment, conducting to Rome a number of his men who were on leave, asked permission to celebrate in our church at an early hour and inquired if I could lend him a cotta for his server. Of course I could, but I urged that it would create among his soldiers a greater sense of solidarity if one of their number were to serve at the altar in his military uniform. That chaplain assented dubiously but was convinced by the experiment. This practice is universal in the Roman Church, and in no situation is it more clearly appropriate than in the army and navy. Yet perhaps in the school or university it is equally appropriate. Certain it is that a different sort of boy or man, and by no means a baser sort, would be more readily inclined to act as server if he were understood to be a representative of the people rather than a humble servitor of the priest.

Posture of Celebrant

I have no intention of instructing the server how he is to perform his functions. I can leave that to St. Vincent's Guild. I am concerned here only about the conduct of the priest. I remark at this point that he *stands,* even when he makes his confession. This observation is more important than at first sight it may appear, for it means that the celebrant is always to stand at the altar, *never* to kneel. We cannot follow consistently this ancient practice, for at the time of the Reformation the Church of England had lost sight of the reason for it, and consequently our rubrics prescribe that at two places the celebrant shall kneel, namely, at the General Confession and at the Prayer of Humble Access. This therefore the celebrant must do. But he need not suffer these two exceptions to obscure utterly for him and for the people a very ancient tradition. He should be scrupulous not to kneel where he is not commanded to kneel, neither before the Liturgy begins, nor when it is finished, neither when he takes the communion, nor after he has received it, nor at any other place whatsoever. Evangelical Anglicans, even when they are desirous of complying with Catholic practice, are all the time flopping upon their knees—to the secret vexation of the congregation, which is not always ready to accept at its face value this superfluous exhibition of fervent piety. At times when a genuflection or a profound reverence would be appropriate the "Evangelical" (so I shall call him for convenience, though I know that no such thing exists any longer, but only ex-Evangelicals, ex-Liberals, or vague Christians) are likely to sink down upon both knees and remain there for an appreciable time . . . as though they were engaged in prayer. It seems to be impossible for them to realize that a reverence before the altar, the cross, or the Gospel, or the host, even if it be a genuflection, is simply an act of homage and does not in the least imply a prayer, any more than does a lady's curtsy to a queen. The most distinctive institution of Islam, the prostrations, though we commonly think of them as prayer, and though it may seem to us a peculiarly earnest sort of prayer because the worshiper repeatedly touches his forehead to the ground, is in fact nothing of the sort, it is not even a silent prayer, although it is certainly worship.

If with unmannerly zeal I insist upon the upright position of the celebrant it is because this too is a vestige of a very old custom, and it would be deplorable if we were to forget altogether that kneeling is not the only posture appropriate to prayer. Although in the earliest age the disciples doubtless sat at the Lord's table, and although in a subsequent age, when the people stood, the bishop and presbyters continued to sit, yet after the third century at latest it was customary for the clergy as well as the people to stand throughout the Liturgy. Kneeling at all events was prohibited on the Lord's Day, and until the ninth century at least the people received the communion standing and bending reverently. Is it a light danger we incur when we suffer the celebrant to kneel as often as he likes, and thus to obscure the one important vestige which remains of an early Christian practice?

Unfortunately the other clergy who are about the altar must kneel, unless they are vested as deacon and subdeacon and follow strictly the Catholic ritual. So it must be, for they have sunk to the position of servers, and it is appropriate that the server should kneel as the representative of the people, who for a thousand years have knelt during the Liturgy, except when they hear the Gospel and say the Creed.

The Lord's Prayer

The Lord's Prayer, with which our Liturgy begins might be regarded as the last remaining vestige of the prayers at the foot of the altar, except that it was in fact no part of them but rather was substituted for them. It is now left to the discretion of the priest whether he will omit the Lord's Prayer; but if he says it, either aloud or *secrete,* it must of course be said at the foot of the altar, and the collect which follows, though it is still a part of the preparation, he must say from the top step, and before the middle of the altar, where he is about to rehearse the Ten Commandments, "turning to the people."

Kissing the Altar

At this point in the Roman rite the priest for the first time kisses the altar. Because to my mind it is more than questionable whether we who have no such tradition should revive this custom, I shall not call attention to the other occasions when the celebrant might kiss the altar. Personally I am inclined also in this instance to Romanize, yet I do not do it, because I know that this action would seem to the people an effeminate affectation. Sometimes I have felt prompted to kiss the book of the Gospels, and sometimes I have yielded to this prompting, because this may be done in a way which is not obvious to the people. When first I went to Italy it was far more usual than now for male acquaintances to kiss one another when they met on the street, now it is chiefly my clerical friends who expect me to kiss them. How different the situation is in America! For us the kiss is predominantly an erotic expression. Among us, alas, it could not occur to the most pious layman to kiss the priest's hand, nor to the priest to kiss the bishop's ring; no vestige is left of the kiss of peace with which the people once greeted one another at the Eucharist, not even do those about the altar kiss, and to kiss *things* as a token of veneration is so totally strange to us that we regard it as an abominable superstition. Such being our situation, a general revival of this ancient practice is clearly impossible, and a partial revival of it, that is, the adoption of it by a few, would only be regarded as a strange idiosyncrasy and would constitute an unnecessary divergency in custom, when, alas, we already have more than enough. I am ready to suffer reproach with the people of God—but not for such a cause as this.

The Decalogue

The Ten Commandments are still a part of the preparation. Presumably they were inserted in the Book of Common Prayer to take the place of the prayers at the foot of the altar which were discarded, but of course they are not to be rehearsed at the foot of the altar, for in pronouncing them the priest is not in the position of a penitent (it is not he who says, "Lord, have mercy"), but he is in the position of authority. The priest is to "rehearse distinctly" the Commandments, it is not said that he must read them, but in my judgment he would do well to do so, however perfectly he may have memorized them, for they were written and engraven on tables of stone and do not depend for their authority upon the pathos with which the priest might pronounce them, whereas the Summary may well be supposed to be written upon our hearts and had best be repeated "by heart." The rubric requires that either the Ten Commandments or the Summary or both shall be rehearsed, and that the Ten Commandments (with permission to omit what the Westminster Shorter Catechism calls "the reasons annexed") shall be said "at least one Sunday in each month." I could wish that the clergy did not need to be reminded that *the* Sunday when it would be most improper to omit them is Pentecost, which is the celebration of the giving of the Law. And it must not be forgotten that though the Spirit is a gift, the Law too is a gift, one of God's greatest gifts of grace. Catholics at least should not too abruptly oppose the Law to the Gospel, since it was characteristic of early Catholicism to regard the Gospel as the New Law. It is certain that the rubric must be obeyed, and it is a very dubious assertion that the rehearsal of the Ten Commandments in the Liturgy is strange to the Catholic tradition, inasmuch as the *Didache*, which is the earliest direction for the prayers at the Eucharist, seems to imply something of the sort. The use of the *Kyrie* in the Roman Mass implies, if not the rehearsal of the Commandments, at least a vivid sense of their obligation.

THE *KYRIE*

The fact that in our prayer book the *Kyrie* is printed in three lines may justify us in repeating it in this brief form, but it surely does not exclude the traditional custom of repeating each line thrice in alternation with the minister—but, alas, we may not say it in Greek, in the language of the Apostles, which only in this instance is used in the Roman Liturgy, and was used in the First Prayer Book of Edward VI.

The Collect which follows is obviously more appropriate after the Decalogue than after the *Kyrie,* and probably for this reason the use of it is left to the discretion of the priest.

As for the *Kyrie,* it is perhaps a little difficult for us to conceive that for a long time the predominant language in the Church of Rome was Greek and that its earliest liturgy must have been in that language—although everybody knows that St. Paul did not write his Epistle to the Romans in Latin. The *Kyrie* is the only vestige of the earliest liturgy. It is not without significance that in this instance the Greek language was preserved, as a fossil is sometimes preserved in a rock and gives a clue to its origin; and neither is it fortuitous that precisely this feature was preserved. It is as natural as was the preservation in the New Testament, and presumably in the Apostolic liturgy, of the words *Abba* and *maranatha,* for these Aramaic words express the distinctive Christian faith in God as Father, and the distinctive Christian hope: The Lord cometh. So too does the *Kyrie* express the distinctive Christian note in worship. Feuerbach, intending to heap scorn upon Christianity, points with infallible accuracy to a distinctive trait when he says, "Whereas the pagans mingled the exultation of sensuous pleasure with the cult of the Gods, the tears and sighs of a broken and contrite heart were for the early Christians an essential part of divine worship." Yes, the *Kyrie* expresses an essential part of Christian worship, and a distinctive part. I do not say, however, that this is the predominant character. It needs to be remembered that here, immediately after the *Kyrie,* the Roman Mass has the *Gloria in excelsis.* It does not argue well for the taste of our Reformers that they transferred this to the end of the Liturgy. Our Reformers did well, perhaps, to translate the *Kyrie* into English—but why did we abbreviate it? That in fact was not the fault of the Reformers, for they provided that the *Kyrie* should be said ten times, i. e., after each commandment of the Decalogue. It is we in America who have abbreviated it, for when we have discarded the use of the Commandments, all we have left is a threefold *Kyrie:*

Lord, have mercy upon us.
Christ, have mercy upon us.
Lord, have mercy upon us.

Whether this is said or sung, it makes no deep impression. It is evidently only a vestigial survival. Maybe it was because of timidity our revisers printed only these three lines; at all events, it can hardly be supposed that now we are prohibited from saying nine times "Lord have mercy upon us," seeing that till a short time ago we were required to say it ten times. I print the ninefold *Kyrie* in the form traditionally used, putting the response of the people in italics:

Lord, have mercy upon us. *Lord, have mercy upon us.*
Lord, have mercy upon us.
Christ, have mercy upon us. Christ, have mercy upon us.
Christ, have mercy upon us.
Lord, have mercy upon us. *Lord, have mercy upon us.*
Lord, have mercy upon us.

Certainly this is a much more serious expression of our dependence upon God's mercy; and the Church, both in the East and in the West, has abundantly furnished for it the most impressive music. I may say that, if the music is not impressive, the thing becomes tedious.

3. ABOUT VESTMENTS

(Plates III, IV and V-XI)

The priest when he approaches the altar of God is of course already vested—the only question is *how.* I am dealing with this question rather tardily, but obviously something must be said. Though I do not say it perhaps as briefly as I might, yet I am reluctant to give the subject undue importance by treating it as a separate chapter, so I append here what I have to say on the subject.

The chapter on "Ecclesiastical Dress" which I included in

my book on *Christian Art and Archaeology* made due acknowledgment (as I do again in this little disquisition) of my indebtedness to the studies of Mgr. Joseph Wilpert, particularly to his pamphlet on the *Gewandung der Christen in den ersten Jahrhunderten,* which was published in Cologne in 1898 and for the first time throws a clear light upon the subject of ecclesiastical vestments, a light derived from a thorough knowledge of ancient monuments both Christian and pagan. Although I was expounding the views of a Roman Catholic scholar, that chapter perhaps gave scant comfort to "Catholics" who are zealous for the restoration of the traditional vestments. Here, in view of the different character of this book, I endeavor to give them all the comfort I can without ignoring the historical facts. Perhaps, in spite of a purpose to be brief, I have included many observations which are more interesting than edifying, or which at all events are not strictly pertinent to the question what vestments we ought to use. But since these incidental remarks are not elsewhere available in English, I may be forgiven for jotting them down; and if sometimes they are perhaps a bit upsetting to preconceived views, "Catholics" may find some consolation in the fact that, logically or illogically, I reach conservative conclusions.

It is easy to deride the use of a distinctive dress for the clergy, and perhaps as easy to defend it. I propose to do neither. The fact that all religions, including the religion of Israel, have required their priests to dress in a distinctive way in order to make it evident that they were priests goes to show how human the thing is. But this might be regarded as an argument against the use of a distinctive dress for the Christian ministry, seeing that Christ and His Apostles were not distinguished from their fellow-citizens by any article of dress. In early Christian art Christ and the Apostles were almost invariably represented in the Greek tunic and pallium which had become the cosmopolitan dress of the Roman Empire, in contrast to the toga, which was the distinctive dress of Roman citizens and by no means worn by all of them. This is a plausible tradition, and it prevailed until modern times when we have become accustomed to think of them as clad in outlandish oriental garments.

But whether the Christian ministry ought to have a distinctive dress is hardly an open question, seeing that until lately Protestant ministers, if they did not wear the dog collar, were commonly distinguished by the white tie (the scanty vestige of the medieval amice, which, as it was worn by "clerks" in the broader sense, was once common also to lawyers and still persists in the dress tie) and commonly wear a preaching gown in the pulpit. The only question which agitates us now is what the priest ought to wear when celebrating the Holy Communion. At the present time we have no uniform custom. The greater part of our clergy wear the surplice and stole. There is nothing much to be said for the use of the surplice on any occasion, except that it is white and that actually it is in general use, in spite of the fact that we have absolutely no legislation on this subject. Both these considerations are arguments of the greatest importance and clearly outweigh the fact that of all the vestments which actually have been used in the Church the surplice is the most unreasonable and topsy-turvy—a fluttering linen garment worn over heavy garments of wool, if not over a fur coat. St. Augustine (*Sermo* 37, 5) ordained that for undergarments linen should be worn and for outer-garments wool. That is reasonable, especially in a warm climate like North Africa, and even in Rome a linen garment was commonly worn beneath the woolen tunic. The surplice is also the *latest* invention in the way of ecclesiastical vestments, indeed it is the only *invention,* for all the other vestments in use in the Church are traceable to garments worn in common life. It is only very remotely that the linen surplice can be traced to the woolen tunic. But all this we must forget. I am glad to forget it; for actually we use the surplice and clothe our choristers in the small surplice or cotta, as many of our Protestant brethren are fain to do. But sometimes we clothe our servers or acolytes in the long tunic with close sleeves (the *tunica alba* or alb), and with that they are better clad than most priests, and also girded in a seemly manner. For the alb is a real garment, dating from the most ancient times, and we can readily forget that under it is hidden a complete modern dress, even to the barbarian trousers. Although the surplice (including its variant the cotta) was not introduced until late in the Middle Ages and is therefore the latest vestment, the time as well as the reason of its origin is obscure. What prompted the use of such a vestment was presumably the consideration that the Mosaic Law required the Levitical priesthood to be clad in pure linen garments when they were exercising their functions in the Tabernacle. The mystical interpretation of Church vestments, which in the Middle Ages was a common theme for pious lucubrations, sought erroneously to refer the origin of them all to the Old Testament—and by this, as Mgr. Wilpert says, wrapped the whole subject in the profoundest obscurity. To this was due the invention of the surplice, and perhaps also the custom of making the long tunic or alb out of linen. The alb was worn by all orders of the clergy, for it is an indispensable garment, whatever else may be worn over it; and when as in modern times the ordinary street dress is worn beneath it and it is no longer needed for warmth, it might just as well be of linen. Now that the Old Testament precedent has been shown to be irrelevant to the origin of ecclesiastical vestments, the question may be raised whether, instead of using linen for alb and surplice and cotta, we might not use one of the newer silk-like fabrics, which equally are of vegetable fibre and are not so easily soiled, nor so easily rumpled. But perhaps this is a vain suggestion, for I know that any argument for economy in the Church is likely to be despised and resented.

It was a matter of course that the surplice was white when it was made of linen, for linen is not (or rather was not) easily dyed. But for the white color of ecclesiastical vestments there was also New Testament precedent which had a decisive influence from the earliest time. At the Transfiguration of our Lord even "His garments became glistening, exceeding white, so as no fuller on earth can whiten them" (Mk. 9:3). The mention of the "fuller" shows that our Lord's garments were of wool. But white was the color of light, the appropriate color for Him who was "the Light," and also for "the children of light" and "the saints in light." Hence in the book of Revelation the four and twenty elders around the throne were "arrayed in white garments" (Rev. 4:4), and the "great multitude which no man could number, standing before the throne and before the Lamb" were likewise arrayed in white robes. "These are they," it is said, "which came out of great tribulation, and they washed their robes and made them white in the blood of the Lamb" (Rev. 7:9, 14). It must be remembered that these were favorite themes for the decoration of the apsidal wall of the church or its façade in the fifth and sixth centuries, and that these figures were always in white. The frescoes of the catacombs testify to an earlier predilection for this color; for almost invariably Christ and the Apostles and the saints (except female figures) are represented in white, whereas all but sacred personages are dressed in colored garments. Thus a preference for white as the color of church vestments was very early and very emphatically established, and this is a consideration which reconciles me to the surplice. Surely many who know no such reasons for the choice will feel instinctively that white is appropriate in Christian worship. We can imagine that a need for the white surplice was keenly felt in the Middle Ages when not only dalmatics, chasubles and copes were dark in color but the dress of the monks was black and lugubrious.

Although my studies have focused my own interest upon the early Christian centuries, I am not an archaeologist of so quaint and curious a sort that I could wish to abolish the surplice because it was not in use before the Middle Ages. After all, it has been worn for nine hundred years, the bishop's rochet derives from it, and it is the only ecclesiastical vestment most of our clergy use. The name *superpellicium* indicates that in the first instance it was worn over the fur coat (*pellicia*) which the clergy were obliged to wear in the cold churches of Northern Europe. This accounts for the necessity of very wide sleeves. Ceremonial law required that the fur coat should reach to the ankles, and in the earliest picture we have of the surplice it was so long that only the edge of the coat appears. It was rather topsy-turvy to wear linen over fur, or even over wool, yet we cannot but think it more seemly for the clergy to dress in white. The earliest mention of such a garment belongs to the middle of the eleventh century. There was a tendency later to shorten it for convenience; but Rome was so conservative that until the fifteenth century (as may be seen on Plate VI) it reached nearly to the hem of the cassock. A short surplice (the cotta) is long enough for an altar-boy or a chorister, but I wish the clergy would reflect that a greater length enhances their dignity. Alas, I see priests celebrating at the altar who do not know how humorous it seems when even the alb comes hardly below the knees. Percy Dearmer made a valiant effort to restore in the Church of England the long, full surplice worn by the Protestant reformers. This is really important if the surplice has to do duty as a substitute for the alb, the chasuble, the dalmatic, and the cope. I suppose that "Percy Dearmer surplices" can still be bought from the St. Dunstan Society in London. I wore them for many years. Yet I must confess that a picture Percy Dearmer furnished in one of his essays is not so convincing as are some of the advertisements by clerical tailors. Theirs is an art which has for me a peculiar fascination of antipathetic sympathy, inasmuch as it is able to transform a minister of Christ into a clerical figure to which everything human is alien—except a smug conceit. I have made a collection of such pictures and find it chastening to review them. But in spite of them all, I have here ventured to provoke a choice in favor of the long surplice by placing it on Plate VI alongside an example of the Rococo surplice so dear to the Counter Reformation.

I searched for an abhorrent example which might perhaps deter my brethren from wearing such frippery. I had in mind a thousand and one graven images of St. John Nepomuk which adorn the wayside shrines of Bavaria and Tyrol. But, alas, in one of the most complete art libraries, and with the help of learned professors of the faculty, I sought for such a thing in vain. What I wanted was a mediocre work of art, and that, naturally enough, no one takes the pains to publish. What I found was a statue made to adorn an eighteenth century palace, by an admirable Bavarian wood-carver, Joachim Dietrich, which was thought worthy of a place in the Kaiser Friederich Museum at Berlin. I had never before seen St. John Nepomuk presented in so favorable a light. This picture, instead of being deterrent, is seductive. It evidently would be a shame to wear a surplice so long that it would hide the beautiful cassock, made of the richest material, and so tastefully designed. And if over it all I could throw a costly sable cape (such as this saint seems to have worn in all weather), I might be converted to the short surplice—lace and all. Yes, I understand now why the Counter Reformation has such a compelling attraction for finely fibered souls. Yet I have plainly posited here an either/or, and I trust timorously to the persuasive appeal of a pre-Reformation example, a picture of the ordination of St. Lawrence (Plate VI) painted in the Vatican by dear Fra Angelico of Fiesole, depicting the dignified dress worn at the end of the fifteenth century by two priests in the court of Pope Nicholas V.

But now we encounter the scruple whether the surplice can properly be worn by the celebrant at the Eucharist. Some are fearful perhaps lest the sacrament might not be quite valid unless the priest wears a chasuble. In the second century, ironically enough, Tertullian, who himself preferred the pallium as the dress for Christians, whether in church or out of it, and wrote a book to extol this garment, found himself obliged to denounce a superstition which was concerned with the scruple whether a man could rightly say his prayers without putting *off* the chasuble (or *paenula*, as it was then called) in accordance with pagan custom. Tertullian suggests sarcastically that St. Paul may be supposed to have left his *paenula* behind in the house of Carpus (2 Tim. 4:13) because he had taken it off there to say his prayers (*De orat.* c. 12). The issue was a practical one because soldiers commonly wore the *paenula* (including the soldier who made the bold confession which prompted the work *De corona militis*) and could not be expected to take off their uniform when they came to the church to worship.

This reference to St. Paul's chasuble may suggest the reflection that perhaps he wore it in celebrating the Eucharist. Yes, that is likely enough—especially when aboard the boat threatened with shipwreck he "broke bread in the presence of them all" (Acts 27:35). But perhaps only on that extraordinary occasion; for in St. Paul's day the *paenula* or *phenoles* was hardly an indoor garment but rather an overcoat, more especially a rain-coat, having a hood (*cucullus*) to pull over the head in case of a storm. As such it was a very appropriate garment for such a traveler as St. Paul. As it was made of heavy wool, or more rarely of leather, it may well have been of use to him in his cold lodging or perhaps a colder prison in Rome. It came into common use as an outer garment in the course of the second century and into general use during the third, eventually replacing not only the Roman toga but the Greek pallium, garments which, though they were more elegant were less convenient because they might readily fall off. The *paenula* could not fall off, for essentially it was a poncho such as is now used in Mexico and in our own South West. *Casula,* which was one of the Latin names for it, describes it well: it was a snug little house or cabin. Commonly it was a rectangular piece of cloth taken just as it came from the loom and about twice as long as it was broad. A hole was left in the middle through which the head could be passed. In its more elegant form it was elliptical. In Greek, besides the names I have mentioned, it was called *phainoles* or *phainolion,* in Latin *amphibalus* or *planeta.* Judging by the early frescoes and mosaics the color was commonly a dark chestnut, tending to red or yellow, and without any adornment. By its darker color it contrasted with the woolen tunic or dalmatic over which it was worn, for it was commonly made of a light brown wool, the natural color of a favorite breed of sheep.

In spite of sumptuary laws which sought to suppress this outlandish garment, the chasuble steadily made its way into popular favor, so that Juvenal could say (*Sat.* 3, 171) "throughout a great part of Italy no one wears the toga except the corpse," and Tacitus (or whoever wrote *De oratoribus,* cf. c. 39) remarks that it was quite common for advocates, though they were proud to be called *togati,* to argue a case before the judge when dressed in the *paenula,* notwithstanding that it restricted them on every side and cramped their style as orators. Not more, however, than the toga; for Tertullian in arguing in favor of the pallium (*De pallio,* c. 4) asks his opponent to tell him "on his conscience" whether it was not rather a burden than a dress, and whether he was not rather bundled than clothed in it. Roman sculptures reveal that the *paenula* worn by laborers and the common people generally was often very scanty, too scanty to embarrass them in their work. But evidently persons of high standing like the advocates wore a more voluminous garment, and it goes without saying that ecclesiastical personages would be careful for the dignity of their dress, especially in the performance of their office, and this presumption is substantiated by early Christian art. They are often represented in the long-sleeved tunic reaching to the feet (our alb), although this had been reprobated by the Romans as an effeminate dress, and over that a dalmatic, not quite so long but longer than usual. But if priestly personages were careful to dress with dignity, it was not so with philosophers and prophets. Early Christian art took pains to depict the prophets in scanty attire—not only John the Baptist, but the Prophet Isaiah. Greek philosophers too affected a simple dress, the *tunica exomis,* which was a scanty tunic fastened only over the left shoulder and leaving the right arm and part of the breast bare. In the Second century Justin Martyr wore the *tunica exomis* and insisted that it was the only proper dress for the Christian preacher. He did not carry his point, however, and in the following century St. Cyprian of Carthage (*De bono patientiae,* 2, 3) protested vigorously against the use of the philosopher's dress. Up to the fourth century the pictures in the catacombs depicted ecclesiastical personages in the long tunic and pallium. Only in one case does it happen that a bishop is clad in the *paenula.* That is to say, the clergy in the performance of their office dressed as others did in every-day life. When St. Jerome says (*In Ezech.* 13:44) that "the divine religion has one dress for divine service and another for common use," he makes it clear in the same passage that he was not thinking of garments of a different form, but of clean garments, perhaps of a finer texture, the difference between every-day clothes and Sunday-go-to-meeting clothes. Till late in the Middle Ages ecclesiastical ordinances prescribed on the one hand that priests were not to celebrate in their every-day tunic, and on the other hand that they were not to wear the liturgical tunic except at holy functions. After the fourth century the chasuble (*paenula*) was so generally used that the lower grades of the clergy to whom it did not properly belong as an ecclesiastical dress were required to take it off when they entered the church. Most of the clergy, however, were expected to wear it. Mgr. Wilpert refers to the *Ordines romani,* some of which are posterior to the year one thousand. The first *ordo* prescribes that the subdeacon is to hold with his chasuble the sacred pallium and the *mappula* of the Pope; the fifth reckons the chasuble among the garments to be worn by the priests, the acolytes, "and the other lower grades in the Church"; and in the eighth it appears among the vestments of the acolyte, the subdeacon and the presbyter, whereas the deacon at the moment of his ordination was to exchange it for the dalmatic. At a time when all the clergy except the deacon wore the chasuble the different grades were presumably distinguished by the cut of their garments or by the fineness of the material.

Since the Reformation the Lutheran ministers in Scandinavia have worn no other ecclesiastical vestment except the chasuble. That was natural because they retained no other office of public worship except the Holy Communion. In Sweden they have been progressive enough to introduce matins and evensong. This innovation is still opposed in Denmark because it is thought to savor of Romanism.

So soon as Constantine granted peace to the Church it was natural that there should be an effort to distinguish by their dress more definitely than before the different grades of the clergy; for under the Empire nearly everybody was in uniform: the soldiers were distinguished not only from their officers but also from soldiers of other regiments; civil functionaries were in part distinguished by their dress, in part by some special ornament, and even artisans of different sorts dressed differently. There is nothing improbable therefore in the statement of the *Liber Pontificalis* that Pope Sylvester required that deacons should wear the dalmatic in church. Until about the beginning of the sixth century the dalmatic was the distinction of the Roman deacon exclusively, and in view of the proud eminence the Roman deacons enjoyed (above the presbyters, as St. Jerome complained) it is not amazing that Gregory the Great gave to several foreign bishops the privilege of wearing the dalmatic, and that later the use of it by bishops became so common that St. Isidore of Seville describes it as the "sacerdotal tunic." He further describes it as *tunica candida cum clavus expurpura,* showing that in his time both the dalmatic and the tunic were white (Plate III). The *clavus* was a narrow strip of color running over each shoulder from one end of the garment to the other. Originally it was the adornment of the tunic, but when that was covered by the dalmatic (which was simply a looser tunic with broader sleeves) this ornament was naturally transferred to the latter garment. Either could be made of wool or of linen according to the climate.

But I return to the chasuble, which is the garment of most interest to us in the present unity of discourse. So far as we can judge from early pictures it was the distinctive dress of bishops and presbyters. The dress of the other orders was definitely defined by the sixth century, as we see in a mosaic of the seventh century in the Chapel of St. Venantius in the Lateran Baptistry (Plate III). The vestments remained subtantially unchanged till late in the Middle Ages, although the eleventh century fresco in the lower church of St. Clement in Rome (fig. 9) shows that there were temporary fluctuations in fashion, for here St. Clement wears a chasuble which is long behind but cuneiform in front, like the *paenula* Wilpert discovered in classical monuments and called "the baroque *paenula*." The fiddle-back chasuble now commonly worn by Roman priests did not appear till very late in the Middle Ages and is to be explained by the necessity of restoring to the priest the free use of his arms when the chasuble had become stiff with gold embroidery and covered (to use Robert Browning's phrase) "with all the needlework of noodledom." In spite of the fact that in the picture mentioned above St. Clement wears a purple chasuble, this garment was commonly unadorned, and until the thirteenth century, when the custom arose of varying the color *pro qualitate temporis,* it generally retained the traditional chestnut color. It remained essentially the practical woolen garment which had been so long in common use, except that the hood was naturally omitted when it was no longer worn out of doors unless it was covered by the cope, which to this day has retained its hood, though only as a vestigial adornment. Thus it was only because of the characteristic conservatism of religious usages that in the course of the Middle Ages the vestments worn by the clergy in the church became substantially different from the common dress in civil life. The dress which once was common in the Roman Empire was retained by the clergy when it had ceased to be worn outside the church and when the barbaric breeches had given the classical style of dress the *coup de grâce.*

I will speak briefly about the stole and the maniple. The origin of the scarves which are worn by the clergy as insignia of rank (including the sacred pallium of the pope) was for the first time explained by Mgr. Wilpert in *Un Capitolo di Storia del Vestiario,* 1899. Stole is a very late word which has served to obscure the essential difference between the insignium of the deacon and the scarf which was worn by presbyters and bishops. The former was not properly a scarf but a linen towel or napkin thrown over the left shoulder (Plate IV, 7) or the left forearm. It was called *orarium,* and this word by a false analogy was transferred to the stole of the presbyter. But the word had nothing to do with prayer (*orare*) but indicated that this towel was to be used for wiping the mouth (*os, oris*) as well as the hands and the sacred vessels. It was appropriate to the practical service the deacon had to render at the altar, and often it was woven in the form of what we call Turkish toweling. On the other hand, the stole worn by presbyters and bishops is derived from the woolen scarf which commonly was thrown about the neck, not only as a protection against cold but for comeliness and dignity. For it must be remembered that neither the tunic, nor the dalmatic, nor the chasuble provided any covering for the neck. When by the process of *contabulatio* the neck-scarf had become the mere strip which we know as a stole, it still served as a distinction of grade, but inasmuch as it no longer protected the neck, it is natural enough that at a very late date the amice was introduced to serve as a collar. The linen maniple (*mappula*) served the same purpose as the deacon's napkin but may be regarded rather as a handkerchief. It could serve as a distinction because in those days the handkerchief was a rare luxury. But in Rome, where bishops, presbyters, and deacons were sufficiently distinguished by other marks, the maniple was obviously not needed, and Wilpert remarks that it "was never held in much esteem in the Eternal City," although it often appears in early pictures. This observation may dispose Anglo-Catholics to dispense with this vestment, which, now that it is made of silk and has thus lost all pertinence to its original use, has become not only redundant but absurd. As a matter of fact, I seldom see it used.

In view of these facts, what are we to do?

I am not sorry to think that the facts do not furnish us with any excuse for affirming that the sacraments of the Church cannot be rightly administered except by a clergyman who is clad in the traditional vestments. But it is hardly logical to conclude that because the traditional vestments have no connection with the Levitical priesthood, cannot be traced to the Apostolic age, have their origin in the common dress of the early Christians, and therefore can hardly endure the mystical interpretations which have been foisted upon them, *ergo* they should be despised and eschewed. It would be still more illogical to affirm that the surplice, because it was the last vestment to be introduced, and the only one which was sheerly invented, but by a sort of historical accident was the only one commonly in use in England after the Reformation (though the Lutheran Churches in Scandinavia have always used the chasuble), is not only to be preferred above all others, but to be used to the exclusion of all other vestments. No, I should think rather that everyone might be impressed by the fact that for fifteen hundred years the chasuble has been the distinctive dress of the Christian priesthood. I should think that this must count for something. To me of course as an archaeologist it counts for much—and yet as a Christian minister I have not commonly worn it.

At this time in our Church there are good reasons for wearing the chasuble—and also good reasons for not wearing it. I can best illustrate them by my own case. When I began my ministry nearly half a century ago I found myself in a diocese where the use of the chasuble was rare and was almost invariably associated with the High Churchmanship which was then in vogue but now is disparaged by "Catholics," that is to say, it was associated with a petty emphasis upon trifles. During nearly a quarter of a century, when I was chaplain of "the American

Protestant Episcopal Church of St. Paul in Rome," which except for a short while was the only American Church in which Protestants of all denominations could worship, it would not only have been inexpedient but in the deepest sense unwise to repel anybody by adopting a use which, however reasonable, was then a subject of contention, and essentially was "indifferent"—although especially with regard matters which are indifferent to the faith I was loath to distinguish myself from the Church of Rome.

Now the situation is materially changed, at least in many parts of our country. Now, both within our Church and without it (at least among people who are at all inclined to approach us), there is not much left of the spirit which brought the Bishop of Lincoln to trial for having candles on the altar and was inclined to descry in the use of the *Agnus Dei* a tendency to Papistical superstition. Some may attribute this change to a decline in religious fervor. I do not. It might even mean an increase in charity. Today the layman may wisely see in the use of the chasuble a precarious assurance that the priest, to the best of his knowledge, is resolved to preach the faith once delivered and to maintain in the face of a vague and recreant Protestantism loyalty to the Christian tradition and solidarity with the Church as a whole. Although this expectation may often be deluded by the ignorance, stupidity, or narrowness of the priest, yet it is nearly the only external sign we have to go by. On the other hand, a priest who would make himself known as a Catholic will wish to do so by this token, if it can be done without a breach of charity. And a priest who wishes to make himself known, not as a Catholic pure and simple, but as a Romanizing Catholic, can do so effectively by demonstrating a special predilection for the fiddle-back chasuble, for the biretta, or for any of the modern Roman practices which the liturgical reformers in the Church of Rome are eager to abolish.

Perhaps not many of us wish to advertise ourselves as Catholics. Unfortunately this is still a party name. Hence for many years I have scrupulously refrained from calling myself a Catholic. But not long ago, in reading a book by an eminent Protestant professor of theology who would commonly be regarded as a Liberal and who belongs to the most liberal denomination, I was so profoundly impressed by its arraignment of American Protestantism for its recreancy to the decisive positions of the Christian faith that I decided then and there to call myself henceforth a Catholic, as a demonstration of my antagonism to all this vague faith and vague unbelief, above all to the prevailing tendency to resolve Christianity psychologically into a mere religion and to explain away the tremendous paradoxes which are plainly stated without being explained in the dogmas of the Church. In thanking the author for his book I let him know of this resolution, and to my surprise he replied as follows: "I feel reasonably sure that were I a secularist and now were converted to Christianity I would need to enter the Roman Catholic Church, or if I had been bred in that Church so that I could fight from within against its aberrations I would be in no temptation to leave it for Protestantism. As it is I have no choice but to do my duty as I see it in the particular stream of Christian life and organization and in that order of the universal Church to which I have been 'called.'" These are weighty words, a significant sign of the times. Genuine Christian believers are all of them faced today by the same problem. I would not of course confound with these weighty words the comparatively trivial matter of wearing the appropriate Eucharistic vestments. But these words suggest that those who are resolved to do their duty in that particular stream of Christian life in which they are "called" might now call themselves Catholics without implying a narrow party spirit, and might, if circumstances permit, give notice of this by wearing the Eucharistic vestments.

It goes without saying that I am not advocating the use of the chasuble *alone*—as if one were to wear an overcoat without anything else. I assume that under it is worn the Classical *tunica alba,* girdled as it ought to be, long enough to be visible below the chasuble; that there is also a stole—and the medieval amice to serve as a collar. Yes, and (incongruous as it is) the medieval cassock which recalls a period of history when monasticism had a potent influence even upon the secular clergy. And underneath all this (still more incongruously) there is the complete dress (barbarian trousers and all) which is characteristic of this modern day. Yes, it is a strange conglomeration, but it is not fortuitous, it is a historical concretion. For my part I can attach to it a significance which reconciles me to its incongruity. *Homo sum*—I dress substantially like every other man in my time and place. But over and above that I am a historical man, I am a Church-man. This means that "nothing that is human is alien to me." I say this humbly, but I can say it proudly. I am thankful that I am not cut off (may I say without a taint of Phariseeism, "as other men are"?) from the medieval heritage which was so definitely Christian even if it were crudely so. I am thankful that through this medium I am in touch, more feelingly and more vitally than most modern Humanists are, with the Classical culture of Greece and Rome, which in turn was the medium through which the Gospel was most adequately expressed to the world. I do not attach undue importance to the fact that St. Paul wore the tunic and chasuble, but I like to remember it, it brings me closer to him as essentially my "contemporary"—Kierkegaard would say. And so this whole dress which is traditional for the celebrant at the Eucharist, this whole historical concretion, symbolizes what I am, or what I fain would be: a modern man, in deep and essential sympathy with, and not without some knowledge of, the Medieval mind, and through that of the Classical mind, and through that of the Christian mind—a man with a past which he consciously possesses. This is what I understand by a Humanist.

I could wish, however, that instead of using costly chasubles of silk, heavily embroidered, which fall in awkward folds about the body, we might use, at least in the less opulent parishes, the antique chasuble of light wool, without adornment, chestnut in color, without reference to the variety of the seasons. This wish is not prompted chiefly by an archaeological or by an aesthetic interest; it is prompted rather by an interest in simplicity, perhaps by the same considerations which explain in part the prevalent use among us (and among us alone in Christendom) of a white linen chasuble, because it is less fussy, less pretentious, and more economical. It would be a great blessing if in poorer churches only one chasuble were needed, the stole being sufficient to indicate the season.

But for my part I should be glad to see the linen chasuble displaced by a silk one, if only it were perfectly plain, sufficiently light to fit snugly, and of a color (it might even be white) which did not vary with the season. Silk is after all an animal tissue like wool and appropriate enough for an outer garment; whereas a chasuble made of linen shrieks not only against reason but against all ecclesiastical tradition, both early and late. Chasubles of shantung silk are available now, and they look good to me. Besides the reputable reasons cited above for using a linen chasuble there are other reasons so far from reputable that they cannot be publicly confessed. Chief among them is the consideration that as an "entering wedge" a white chasuble made of the same material as the surplice would hardly be noticed by the people—so that the priest would be able to get away with it. The people would say, "Well, after all, since the material is the same, what difference does the form make?" The priest will think, "If only the form is the same as a real chasuble, what difference does the material make?" This is not honest.* The priest would not say of a linen sheet that because it has the same form it is therefore a blanket. I am hotly opposed to the linen chasuble for the reason that it is initially dishonest, as an entering wedge. In a later stage is it not so plainly disingenuous, for I notice that gradually it is becoming embroidered with orphreys—first in white, and then more

* Alas, after I had committed myself *in print* to this position, "circumstances beyond my control" compelled me to go out and buy a linen chasuble. At least it was near-linen—some sort of mercerized material, which did not look unseemly, and by the ignorant might be taken for a sort of surplice. At a very difficult time I was serving as Student Pastor in my university, and I had reason to fear that the colored chasuble I was wearing might be distasteful because it was strange to some youths coming from parts of our country where such things are hardly known. And then what happened? Nothing could be more ironical! One Sunday I absentmindedly entered the Chapel without any chasuble at all. I sent the server to fetch one from the distant sacristy—and, naturally enough, what he brought was an embroidered silk chasuble in the color appropriate to the season. This I took to be an intimation that I need not wear again the near-linen vestment.

boldly in color. When once it has become embroidered all over with silk what can I say against it? Nothing. For I cannot well refuse to admit that the chasuble of Thomas à Becket which I have often admired at Anagni is a real chasuble, although the ground of its rich embroidery is heavy linen. Presumably it was left by the great Archbishop of Canterbury as a gift to Pope Boniface VIII when he made his visit *ad limina,* not at St. Peter's but in the Castle of the Gaetani at Anagni—a very precious gift, for at the end of the thirteenth century no such embroidery could be made in Italy.

As for the rochet and chimere, the distinctive dress of Anglican bishops, what can be said to recommend it as a Eucharistic vestment? Well, I can say nothing, for it goes without saying that I have never had it on, and it would not be seemly to talk about something of which I have no experience. As a street-dress (which it was meant to be) it seems a bit cumbersome. It may feel comfortable to one who is inside it, but to the outsider it appears chimerical. The word chimera is defined by the Oxford Dictionary as "a wild impossible scheme or unreal conception."

I cannot bear to republish this imperfect account of clerical dress without adding something to make it seem less unworthy. I conceive that many readers will be glad to see in my *Art in the Early Church* reproductions of the two most important monuments bearing on this subject which have come down to us from the Middle Ages. They are also the earliest, for they both belong to the Carolingian Revival, which was not only a revival of classical learning but of classical art. They illustrate therefore the period of transition between early Christian modes of dress and the Medieval. It is worth while publishing them because, though they have often been published before,* they are not all of them available in any English book, indeed nowhere are they adequately reproduced except in costly folios.

* One of them, the Frankfort Missal, by O. M. Dalton: *Catalogue of Medieval Ivories,* London, 1912; both of them by Rohault de Fleury: *La Messe,* Paris, 1883; F. X. Krauss: *Geschichte der christlichen Kunst,* Freiberg in B., 1897; and by many others, but nowhere so adequately as by Adolph Goldschmidt: *Die Elfenbeinskulturen,* 4 vols. folio, Berlin, 1914-26, and by Louis Weber: *Einbanddecken,* folio, Metz and Frankfort am M., 1913, which comments fully upon the Drogo Sacramentary.

The earliest monument illustrated in my book (Pl. 128) consists of two ivory tablets which were carved evidently for the front and back covers of a sacramentary written in France not later than the middle of the ninth century, although now they are far separated, one of them being at Cambridge in the Fitzwilliam Museum, the other in the Stadtbibliotek at Frankfort on the Main. The second is composed of eighteen ivory panels, all by the same artist, which still adorn the covers of the Drogo Sacramentary (made for the bishop of that name in Metz), now in the National Library in Paris (Pl. 126, 127).

I need not describe completely pictures which are visible to the eye, and yet for an understanding of the details some comment may be necessary.

I shall speak first of that which comes second among the illustrations (Pl. 128). As it certainly was made for a sacramentary, which of course was a Gregorian sacramentary, I conjecture that the archbishop depicted on the front and back covers was meant to represent Pope Gregory himself. It is not uncommon to find St. Gregory depicted on the cover of a sacramentary; but ordinarily he is represented writing at his desk. In this case I am tempted to make this conjecture because of the little books the deacons hold firmly and ostentatiously in their hands. I cannot conceive what they might be, unless they are the famous *Regola pastoralis* of St. Gregory, which was so highly esteemed in Gaul at this very time that Hinkmar, Bishop of Rheims from 845 to 882, required the deacons to hold it in their hands and take their oath upon it when they were ordained to the priesthood. With this clue in mind it seems not unreasonable to suppose that the other acts for which Gregory was famous are represented here: on the one side where he leads the choir; and on the other where he begins to read the Canon which he composed. The sacramentary lies open on the altar, and on it is clearly inscribed the *Te igitur* as far as *benedicas hec* [*sic*] *dona.* On the other cover the psalter is open on the desk at the 24th (25th) Psalm, the first two verses being plainly legible: *Ad te levavo animam meam, deus meus, in te confido, non erubescam neque irredeant me inimici mei, etinam universi qui expectant* [instead of the Vulgate reading: *sustinent te*] *non confundentur.* This Psalm was the introit for the First Sunday in Advent, the first day of the year. It is evident that the choir is singing lustily, and the bishop, whose mouth is closed, seems to be waiting for the song to end before he begins the *Kyrie eleison.* On the other cover the bishop is likewise silent, waiting, as it seems, for the choir to finish the *Tersanctus* before he begins the *Te igitur.* The singular notion of Dean Ladd that the five men before the altar are presbyters who repeat aloud with the bishop the prayer of consecration founders upon the obvious fact that these men are *singing* while the bishop is silent. Moreover, it is not perfectly sure that these men are presbyters. They are tonsured, but because their backs are towards us we cannot see whether they have stoles. It was generally believed that Gregory was responsible for the introduction of the Roman chant as well as for a revision of the Canon, both of which still bear his name, and it may well be that this was in the mind of the artist.

The five singers dressed in the cappa with a hood might have been meant to recall St. Gregory's activity as the first founder of well established monastic houses in Italy. But from Amalar, author of *De ecclesiasticis officiis,* written in the year 820, we learn that the cappa (which here and in the Drago Sacramentary is for the first time represented in art) was worn especially by the *cantores.* We see, however, from the cover of the Drogo Sacramentary that it was worn also on certain occasions by the bishop. It is the antecedent of the pluviale or cope, though at this stage it was shorter, hardly as long as the chasuble, and was evidently not open in front. Neither garment was ornamented, as they are depicted here, but the chasuble is distinguished by having a square yoke, whereas the cappa has an opening triangular in front, with an obvious pleat which descends to the border of the garment, suggesting that originally it was a cape.

In the ninth century the chasuble (*casula, planeta, Phainoles*) had not ceased entirely to be used as the common dress of the people, and in ecclesiastical use it was thought appropriate for every grade of the clergy. We see here that all of them wore an alb reaching to the ankles and girded in such a way that no part of the girdle appears. We can be certain that no cassock was yet worn under it. But above it was worn, not by the singers, but by the bishop as well as the deacons, a dalmatic which almost completely covered the alb. In Roman times it was accounted effeminate for men to wear a long tunic (alb), and yet because it lends much dignity to the wearer St. Hippolytus was represented in the *tunica talaris* in the famous statue which was made of him at the end of the second century. The dalmatic too was short in classical times, and we may suppose that to make it more dignified it was lengthened in the Middle Ages, only to be cut short again when the style changed. The dalmatic here worn by the bishop is a very elegant garment, but it is exactly like that of the deacons. All are decorated alike by a narrow stripe (*clavus*) which passing over each shoulder descends to the border of the garment before and behind. This was the customary decoration of the tunic, then of the dalmatic, in Roman times; but here it was accompanied on each side by an embroidered design which looks like a series of interrogation marks. A curious feature is a fringe around the cuff of the *left* sleeve, and there only. We might refuse to believe our eyes if Amalar did not apprise us of the ritual rule in Gaul which prescribed a fringe for the left sleeve only. Although in Rome the deacons wore the dalmatic, the Pope bestowed it as a special privilege upon archbishops in Gaul and in Spain, just as he did the pallium, which in this case the bishop wears as the only mark of his episcopal rank. He wears also the stole, which is ornamented at the bottom and ends with a fringe. We may note that neither the amice nor the maniple appears here, though both can be seen on the covers of the other sacramentary.

The altar is square, with a frontal which appears to me of hammered metal, and is covered only for a few inches by the embroidered end of an altar-cloth. Besides the open sacramentary and the closed book of the Gospels, there is nothing on the altar but a chalice with two handles and a paten on which lie three pieces of bread shaped somewhat like a pretzel—apparently not so large as the hooplike breads which in the eleventh century fresco in St. Clemente (Plate V in this book) we see carried to the altar by a man and a woman. Two candlesticks planted on the floor behind the altar bear candles which are hardly as high as the bishop's shoulders. The bishop stands of course behind the altar. His hands are spread open before his breast but not extended. We are supposed to understand that the ciborium supported by four Corinthian columns is really over the altar. The artist followed a common convention when he put it in the background so that it would not hide what was being done. The Drogo Sacramentary exhibits curtains which hang between the columns and are pulled aside.

When I speak of the Drogo Sacramentary (Pl. 126 and 127) I need not say much about the dress of the many figures it depicts. It is not so instructive on that score, because the scale is much smaller, and because the artist does not delineate the details with such remarkable precision. On the other hand, these eighteen ivory reliefs afford a great deal of information about ceremonial. They tell their own story so well that I need not do much more than indicate the themes. It is likely that some of the panels have been displaced in the course of so many centuries; but here I follow the present order, from left to right and from above down, as we read a book. Both covers are succinctly interpreted in the captions printed below each. The date of the sacramentary is thought to be earlier than the year 835. For it was in that year King Louis the Pious ordained the celebration of All Saints, and the prayers for that day were added to the manuscript some time after it was written.

Beginning with Plate 126, we have the baptism of Christ, his commission to his disciples, and the Ascension; and then a series of sacramental acts (continued on the other cover) which the bishop performs in compliance with this commission. The first panel represents the ordination of two subdeacons to the diaconate. Of the two priests standing behind the ordinand one holds the stole which is to be presented to the newly made deacon, and the other lays his hand upon the shoulder of the subdeacon while the bishop lays his hand upon his head. It is notorious that Amalar, in opposition to St. Gregory, contended for such participation of presbyters in ordination.

No. 2 represents the baptism of Jesus. There is a harmless reminiscence of an ancient artistic convention in the introduction of a little river god, who pours from a jar the water which makes the Jordan and at the same time (in conformity with a singular trait in early Christian iconography) raises the water to cover the naked body of Jesus.

In No. 3 the trees indicate that the scene is out of doors and that we are to understand this as Jesus' last appearance before the Ascension, when, according to Mt. 28:18-20, he charged his disciples to preach and baptize among all nations.

In No. 4 the bishop on Maundy Thursday blesses the oil. Three clerics have about their shoulders a sort of shawl which is likely a silken scarf, and one of them presents to the bishop an ampula of oil.

In No. 5 the scene is a closed room, indicating the appearance when Jesus gave his Apostles authority to bind and to loose (Jn. 20:19-23).

No. 6 represents the consecration of a church and its altar. Note that several persons carry on a bier the sacred relics which are to be buried under it.

No. 7 represents the confirmation of the newly baptized. Here the bishop wears the cappa—and this is, so far as we know, the first instance of a bishop's use of it.

In No. 8 the bishop, now wearing the chasuble, blesses the water of baptism. A cleric on the left carries a pail of holy water for asperging the tank, and one on the right has an ampulla of oil.

In No. 9 the bishop stands ready to baptize an infant who is held in the font till the bishop immerses him. In the background are mothers carrying their children. This is the ceremony of the Great Sabbath, the eve of Easter. Evidently No. 7 ought to follow this. The proper order for the ceremonies in Holy Week would be: 4, 8, 9, 7—i.e. blessing the oil, blessing the water, baptism and confirmation. Note that the font is not the same water receptacle shown in No. 8 and that the room is a different one.

On the back cover (Pl. 127) all of the nine panels describe the ceremony of the Mass. As a sequence to the ceremonies of Holy Week this may be regarded as the Easter Celebration. I conjecture that the original order was: 6, 5, 1, 3, 4, 7, 8, 2, 9. But I follow here the order in which the panels are actually placed.

No. 1 represents the position of the clergy and the people during the reading of the Epistle. The bishop is seated on his throne, the presbyters seated beside him on a low bench covered with a cloth. The deacons stand, as do the people in the background. Three acolytes carrying candles stand before the altar, and behind them stands the *schola cantorum.*

No. 2 represents all the clergy at the moment when they make a profound reverence before the altar. The attitude shown here is more solemnly reverential, it seems to me, than the later attitude of genuflection. What this moment was we cannot be sure, since the present order of the scene is not a reliable guide. Commonly it is thought that this was the moment after consecration. Weber, who has commented on this monument more fully than others, believes that the clergy as soon as they came in from the sacristy made their reverence before the reserved Sacrament. But we can see that there was no place for the reserved Sacrament *on* the altar, and we know that for this reason it was commonly reserved in another place, which by analogy was called a ciborium.

No. 3. The bishop gives to his clergy the kiss of peace. The book of the Gospels is already on the altar.

No. 4. The bishop kisses the Gospel. At one corner of the altar stands a deacon holding a maniple. This is the only instance where the maniple occurs in this sacramentary. It was more appropriate to a deacon than to a priest. In fact it was from this the deacon's stole was derived. It was originally a towel.

No. 5. Posture of the clergy at the *Kyrie* or at the Creed. The bishop steps up to the dais on which was his throne and faces it, i.e. he faces the east. All the clergy have turned in the same direction and consequently stand behind the bishop. Here for the first time the deacons and subdeacons are in full number—the symbolical number of seven which was established very early in Rome. The subdeacons are not distinguished by their dress from the acolytes: they wear a girded alb.

No. 6. Procession of the clergy from the sacristy to the altar—the scene which obviously ought to be first. The bishop does not yet wear the pallium, which presumably will be given him at the altar.

No. 7. Presentation of the oblations. In the first instance the bishop is represented at the parapet which encloses the sanctuary. There a woman kisses his hand while she presents a loaf, and a flask of wine is received by the archdeacon, on whose garment (dalmatic) one can plainly distinguish the clavus. In the second instance the bishop has already deposited the loaf on the altar and is ready to receive other oblations from the hands of the clergy. In raising his right arm the bishop makes visible the sleeve of his dalmatic.

No. 8. The consecration. With his right hand the bishop makes a gesture of benediction above the chalice (without touching it), and it appears as if perhaps several presbyters before the altar are making a similar gesture as co-consecrators. The bishop reads from the sacramentary which is held up before him by a clergyman.

No. 9. The communion. The bishop first puts the bread into the hands of one of the presbyters—who kisses his hand. The other clergy stand ready to communicate in their turn. They do not kneel as they come forward.

The description of these monuments has led me far beyond the point to which we now have to return. For the next topic is the Mass of the Catechumens. The fact is that while I was adding a little to this book I was totally rewriting my work on Early Christian Art (*Monuments of the Early Church*), and between the two I grew confused, putting in this book what perhaps ought to go into the other.

4. MASS OF THE CATECHUMENS

Here, before the Collect of the Day, we have for the first time in our Liturgy the reciprocal greeting of the priest and the people:

The Lord be with you.
And with thy spirit.
Let us pray.

It goes without saying that at this point the priest turns to the people, for he is addressing them. He "spreads and joins his hands"—but about this gesture I prefer to say all that I have to say once for all in connection with the Prayer for the Whole State of Christ's Church.

Fortunately the last revision of our Liturgy introduced the traditional greeting at this place, for here begins the part which roughly corresponds to the Mass of the Catechumens in the early Liturgies, the part devoted to instruction, to which therefore persons preparing for baptism were admitted, which was called a mass (*missa*) because before the prayers began all who were not in full communion with the Church were invited to leave, with a formula not unlike the *Ite, missa est* with which in the present Roman rite the faithful are dismissed after the Communion, from which that part of the Liturgy now takes the name of *missa* or mass. I use the word "mass" freely and without embarrassment because in view of the derivation here indicated (and in spite of the opprobrious connotations foisted upon it by religious controversy) it is and remains the most noncommittal term, and therefore the handiest term we have for the Eucharistic ceremony, especially in this book which contrasts the Mass of the Faithful with the Mass of the Catechumens. For that reason it was freely used by Luther and by the Lutherans long after the Reformation. It was only the Reformed (that is, the Calvinistic) Churches, including the Church of England, which from the first rejected it. When in the Eastern Liturgies the deacon cries at the conclusion of the Mass of the Catechumens, "The doors! The doors! Recognize one another," the situation implied by this is one which as a matter of fact did not persist beyond the fourth century, for the prevalence of infant baptism and the assumption that all men in Christendom are Christians made it impossible to carry out the fiction that the Church like the Greek mysteries was a secret society which might be expected to repel outsiders with the Virgilian warning:

Procul! O procul este profani!

"Avaunt! Keep your distance, ye uninitiated!" It is fortunate that the early Catholic *disciplina arcana* did not last longer, for it was not a primitive custom. We learn from the fourteenth chapter of St. Paul's First Epistle to the Corinthians that an "unbeliever" might be admitted to a meeting where the Christians were not only "prophesying" but speaking in tongues, and doubtless praying. Yet very properly there remains in all the Liturgies, including our own, a distinction between the Mass of the Catechumens and the Mass of the Faithful. It is true that this distinction is no longer clearly drawn, inasmuch as prayers precede the Mass of the Catechumens, at least one prayer, the Collect of the Day, is included in it, and it concludes with the Nicene Creed as a confession of faith. Nevertheless this part is still plainly enough distinguished from the Mass of the Faithful by the fact that it is devoted predominantly to instruction, to the reading of the Scriptures and to the sermon. The Creed need not always be recited, and in this place it may be regarded as a compendium of the doctrines which have just been read and preached. This part therefore can still be aptly used for missionary propaganda—far more aptly, I may say, than Morning Prayer, to which, very absurdly, we were accustomed not long ago to attach it as a superfluous appendix. It is more apt for this purpose because logically the sermon ought to come immediately after the Scriptural lessons it is supposed to expound, and also because this part is not encumbered with prayers in which the outsider cannot reasonably be expected to join. But of course in Christian lands we are in hopeless confusion about the aim of a missionary service, not knowing who are the outsiders, or whether there are any such, and having the ironical task of converting to Christianity people who are already Christians, since they have already been baptized, a task, as Kierkegaard observes, which is doubly difficult because these persons must first be disabused of the illusion that they are Christians.

This important part of our Liturgy occupies less than two pages of our Prayer Book. Indeed, apart from the rubrics and the Creed (which is printed in full), there are only five lines, namely, the reciprocal greeting and the acclaim of the Gospel before and after it is read. But this is natural, for the Collect is found in another place, the Epistle and Gospel perhaps in another book, and the Sermon, it is to be hoped, in the head and in the heart of the priest. So, after all, this may be the longest part in the Liturgy, and even when there is no sermon it occupies a considerable space of time.

THE COLLECT FOR THE DAY

The priest is to say the Collect of the Day immediately after the reciprocal greeting and presumably at the same place—and of course spreading and joining his hands. As usual the rubric does not indicate where he is to stand, but no one has ever had any doubt that he must stand on the top step, facing the altar at the "South" end where he is about to read the Epistle.

There may be more than one collect he is obliged to say, for in Advent and Lent there is the Collect for the season, there may be one for the octave and one for a commemoration, etc. It is the rule that when there is more than one collect there should be three, and for this emergency our Prayer Book has obligingly made provision. It ought to be understood too that the solemn termination ("Who liveth and reigneth etc.," or whatever the phrase may be) is to be said only after the last collect. It is not so solemn when it is several times repeated, and if it does not happen to be attached to the last collect said, the ending is awkward.

THE EPISTLE AND GOSPEL

That the minister should turn to the people when he reads the Epistle and the Gospel is so evidently appropriate that when an Anglo-Catholic reads them with his back to the congregation it is an intolerable solecism. It apes the Roman practice, but it finds therein no justification. It was natural enough for Roman priests to slump into their present practice of reading the Scriptures with their backs to the people, and also of mumbling the prayers, for all was uttered in an unknown tongue, and often there was no congregation. But now the liturgical reformers in the Church of Rome strongly decry this practice, and in fact such a practice has never been in vogue at a solemn high mass, that is, when there is supposed to be a considerable congregation, for then the acolyte who holds the Gospel has his back to the people and the minister who reads it faces them. It was in order that the Gospel might easily be heard by all the people that the marble ambone, which is still a prominent feature in many of the churches in southern Europe, was erected in front of the chancel. And even today, after the priest has read the Gospel in Latin facing the altar, he turns about to face the people when he reads it again in the vernacular.

I wish it were superfluous to say that after the priest has turned to the people to announce the Gospel he ought not to swing around towards the altar with the book of the Gospels in his hands at the moment when the people acclaim it with the *Gloria tibi,* for that is to show scant respect for the Gospel, which at that moment is the most holy thing in the church and should be solemnly exhibited to the people. Unfortunately it is not only the "Evangelicals" who have a liking for this military evolution. We have far too many maneuvers of this sort. Ordinarily there is not a separate book for the Epistles and Gospels, and since the invention of printing there perhaps has never been one for the Gospels alone; but there is the altar-book which contains them along with the prayers, and for the minister to leave that book on the altar at this moment and take in his hands a small edition of the Prayer Book is another way of showing scant respect for the Gospel.

At this point, that is, before announcing the Gospel, the scrupulous Catholic will make the sign of the Cross: on his forehead, before his lips, and upon his breast. But why do I say "Catholic," and why "scrupulous"? One might think that Evangelical fervor would prompt one to consider and give expression to the fact that the Gospel one is about to read makes demands upon a man's mind, upon his lips, and upon his heart. But far be it from me to prescribe either to priests or laymen when they should make upon their own person the sign of the cross. In common worship this must be determined in part by what other people do. At the conclusion of the Creed one may well feel that there is a peculiar solemnity in the act of signing one's body with the salutary sign of the cross at the moment when one makes confession of one's faith in the resurrection of the dead. It may be used as a sign that one accepts and appropriates an absolution or a benediction. It may be made upon entering and upon leaving the church, and at the conclusion of the prayers. This sign can of course be made very unostentatiously—but it may also be ostentatious, and it may be made too often. I am inclined to plead for temperance even in religious practices—and to fear "lest one good custom should corrupt the world." At a later point I have occasion to characterize genuflection as a baroque custom, dating from the Counter Reformation. Of course no such thing can be said even of the excessive use of the sign of the cross, since we learn from Tertullian that before the end of the second century it was practiced in common life with a frequency which seems to our sober sense extravagant. But the too frequent use of it in the Liturgy we may characterize by a term which to my mind is far more disparaging, we may call it Byzantine. For the Byzantine Liturgy observed no *ne quid nimis* in the use of the cross either as a gesture or as a decoration, a decoration which degenerated into filigree. In the Western Church perhaps it was the use of the austere crucifix which restrained men from a frivolous use of the cross.

Our rubric says that the Epistle and the Gospel shall be read by "The Minister appointed." That is hardly precise enough. "The Minister" at Morning or Evening Prayer may be a layman. No one is less disposed than I to belittle the part of the layman in common worship, but in this case the vague expression of the rubric does not in fact leave anybody in doubt, for it has always been the custom for an ordained minister to read the Epistle and the Gospel at the Eucharist. This is a sign of respect for the Holy Scriptures. In our Ordinal the bishop expressly gives *authority* to the deacon "to read the Gospel in the Church of God." Our rubric is so indefinite only because it would leave the celebrant free to ask another presbyter or a deacon to read the Epistle or the Gospel—and of course it does not prohibit him from appointing himself, as ordinarily he must do simply because there is no other clergyman present. If there is another clergyman among "those about the altar," the celebrant would do well to appoint him to read the Gospel. It would be rather queer, however, for the celebrant, if he is only a presbyter, to appoint a bishop to read the Gospel, inasmuch as ideally that is the deacon's part. It is a traditional fiction that the two ordained ministers who assist the celebrant at the Eucharist are respectively deacon and subdeacon.

Our rubric prescribes the formula we are to use in announcing the Epistle and the Gospel. In practice we pretty nearly agree in the way we announce the Epistle, and we generally agree in going beyond the form prescribed and saying, for example, "The Epistle [for the Tenth Sunday after Trinity] is written." Very wisely, I think, for we cannot be sure that in the congregation there may not be some persons so benighted that they are not quite sure what Sunday it is. I remember instances when I as a traveler have been so ignorant. But perhaps on Saint's Days this little addition is not so necessary. The rubric does not prescribe for the rare cases when the "Epistle" is taken from the Acts of the Apostles or from one of the Prophets, but the phrase "For the Epistle" which introduces such passages clearly enough suggests that we should say, for example, "The portion of Scripture appointed for the Epistle is written in the sixty-third chapter of Isaiah, beginning at the first verse." It cannot perhaps be affirmed that the rubric forbids us to say, e.g., "The Epistle is written in the third chapter of [the Epistle of St. Paul to the] Philippians," but I have no doubt that we are expected to say simply "the third chapter of Philippians," for it is awkward to repeat the word "Epistle," and it is a mark of respect to the Holy Scripture to assume that the people know that "Philippians" is an epistle and that it was written by the Apostle Paul. If uniformity is desirable in this little matter, it can be attained only by agreeing upon the use of the simpler phrase.

In our way of announcing the Gospel we are not in such close agreement. It is rare for any one to say with an affectation of elegance, "The Epistle is written in *that* of St. Paul to the Philippians," but I have only too often heard, "The Holy Gospel is written in *that* according to St. Matthew." I can hardly call this a crime, but it is certainly bad taste. There can be no doubt that the rubric expects us to say simply, "in St. Matthew." Our formula is complicated enough anyway when we have to announce the chapter and verse, as clearly as we ought to do. Because the Roman formula dates from a time when the Bible was not divided into chapters and verses it is much simpler: "Continuation of the Holy Gospel according to St. Matthew."

Our rubric prescribes that all the people shall stand at the reading of the Gospel. This is traditional, but it is also very evidently appropriate as a mark of respect for the Gospel and as an indication that the people are prepared to go forth and do it. For the Gospel must not only be heard but done.

The people stand therefore and look towards the Gospel. It is only accidentally that they are facing East, the altar being (perhaps) at the east end of the church. The celebrant and his ministers also look towards the Gospel, although they may be facing West and looking away from the altar. On the other hand, in saying the Creed both priests and people face the East, or in the direction which is ritually assumed to be the East because of the position of the altar.

Our rubric does not prescribe in what attitude the people are to hear the Epistle, and for this reason our customs are discordant. It might be argued that for the Epistle too we ought to stand because that was the custom in the early Catholic Church. But this merely means that it was once the custom for the people to stand throughout the entire service, even during the sermon, and rightly enough no one now feels like standing at the Epistle because we wish by a difference of posture to demonstrate a peculiar reverence for the very words of our Lord, although the Epistles too are full of the Gospel and in some respects proclaim it more expressly than do the Gospels themselves. Hence at the Epistle some continue to kneel and some sit, often those about the altar kneel while the people sit. It is difficult to make the people do what they are not accustomed to do. But clearly it would be more respectful to remain kneeling at the Epistle, and if the reasons for and against kneeling were evenly balanced, the consideration that kneeling is the position in which we *remain* is enough to turn the scale. Because this is the simpler way I prefer it, not because it is the Roman way. The frequent changes of posture characteristic of our practice are very disturbing to worship, and fortunately they are not prescribed by our ritual. By Morning and Evening Prayer we have had training in acrobatic agility, which is trying to the aged and imposes a hardship upon strangers who are not acquainted with our ways; for naturally they are not so much afraid of the devil as of not knowing when to do what other people do. Perhaps nothing has so much narrowed the influence of our Communion. Let American Protestants sit throughout their worship (European Protestants do not), but let us kneel at the Eucharist. Of course I mean, kneel upon our knees, not upon our foreheads. If there be no sermon, we have no need of chairs at the Eucharist except to support the feeble when they kneel, and only one change of posture is required—that is, when we stand at the Gospel and the Creed.*

THE GRADUAL

The chant which is appropriately sung before the Gospel gets its name from the fact that it accompanied the minister as he solemnly ascended the steps (*gradus*) of the ambone. Since our Prayer Book now graciously concedes that "here may be sung a hymn or anthem," we ought unfailingly to take advantage of this permission. If the congregation is capable of singing a hymn, there is no more appropriate place for it. Our congregations, alas, are not capable of singing anthems. They could of course be taught, but I see no prospect of that in America. When I was living in Peking and attending regularly the Anglican Cathedral I was profoundly impressed by the fact that Bishop Norris had taught his immense congregation of Chinese to sing heartily all the parts which belong to the people in the Liturgy. Before going out as a missionary he had had as a parish priest in England experiences which convinced him that the greatest impediment to the propagation of the Gospel is the choir, the choirmaster and the organ. Consequently he would have none of them, and he was his own precentor. If the Chinese can do it, why not we?

* Fortunately at the Eucharist the people are not obliged to make frequent changes of posture, as we do at Morning and Evening Prayer, to a degree which is unknown in any other Church in Christendom. Even there we could at least avoid the military evolution the choir is expected to make whenever the *Gloria Patri* is said. This is not a Catholic custom. I remember that it was first introduced into America at Trinity Church in New York on the visit of H.R.H. Albert Edward Prince of Wales. It spread like a pestilence. Indeed it is not an innocent foible which people should be allowed to practice because they think it pretty. The congregation cannot be expected to attach any particular significance to the Catholic custom of turning to the East at the Creed when they see the clergy and the choir wheeling about with military precision whenever the *Gloria Patri* is said or sung.

Doubtless we would if we had to. It is said that if you throw a child into the water, the extremity of his need will teach him to swim. But generally we have choirs to sing the anthem. If to gratify the exhibitionism of the choir an elaborate and difficult anthem has to be practiced and sung, it might be best to sing it here, although of course not every anthem is appropriate as a gradual and no long anthem is appropriate at this time when the congregation of God's people must be upon their feet to salute the Gospel. I cannot say that an anthem is inappropriate also at the Offertory "when the alms and oblations are being received and presented," as another rubric permits; but there too it is expected to be appropriate to the place, to be "an offertory anthem," and this consideration, if it were reflected upon at all, would somewhat cramp the style of the choir. I confess with shame that in the cathedral where I am Honorary Canon they once sang "The Star-Spangled Banner" at this place. If, however, there is a sermon, it is by no means so evident that an anthem is appropriate at this place. I would far rather, especially if I were the preacher, have a hymn following the sermon, a rousing hymn in which all the people could join. I would far rather have the hymn here than before the sermon, for I am content to mount the steps of the pulpit without musical accompaniment and would prefer to begin the sermon in a very sober tone. If the people were really stirred by the sermon, they would want to express themselves at once, and they would feel the more need of self-expression after they had for so long a while been listening to the parson in a relatively passive attitude. To compel them then to listen to the choir would be (or, alas, it is) the most effective way of quenching the Spirit.

There is nothing in which we are more united than in the custom of standing at the Creed and facing the East, and yet strangely enough our rubric has nothing to say about this, absolutely nothing. There is no statutory law to prohibit us from kneeling at the Creed or sitting. How many of our rubrics simply assume a knowledge of ecclesiastical tradition! And here we have a tradition which is not only universal but very ancient—far more ancient in fact than the custom of saying the Creed at the Eucharist. For the position at the Creed was determined by the fact that in baptism the neophyte stood in the font and faced the East, the direction of the rising sun, when he made his profession of faith (which in the Western Church was the so-called Apostles' Creed), after having faced the West in making his *abrenuntio,* the renunciation of the devil and all his works.

The Nicene Creed is very properly in place after the Gospel because it summarizes the teaching of the Scripture; but because it was not originally a constituent of the Liturgy it is not always recited in the Roman Mass, and our rubric permits us to omit it under certain conditions. The conditions specified in the rubric practically nullify this liberty, for it may be omitted only "if it hath been said immediately before in Morning Prayer," and doubtless this has in view the antiquated custom of saying Morning Prayer as an introduction to the Holy Communion and was prompted by the desire to avoid "vain repetitions." Nevertheless by a strict interpretation of this law it may be made to cover the case when Morning Prayer has been said *immediately* before but not by the same congregation. Perhaps some may have no scruple about omitting the Creed even though Morning Prayer has not been said "immediately before." I am not scrupulous, but on the other hand I am not eager to find an excuse for omitting the Creed, even at a nuptial or a funeral Mass. For in our day, when we have barely lived through a period of vague Christianity, the Creed seems as important in the Liturgy as the back bone is to the human body. It seems almost ironical of our rubric to permit us at any time to substitute for the Nicene Creed the baptismal confession which we call the Apostles' Creed. For not only has this never before been used in any Catholic Liturgy, but I have never heard it used in our Church. As an attempt to evade Catholic doctrine this substitution would be found disappointing. Of course the Creed *ought* to come after the sermon and immediately before the Offertory, for it is not properly a part of the Mass of the Catechumens but of the Mass of the Faithful.

GENUFLECTION

I must speak here of the custom of making a genuflection at the *incarnatus est,* and in this connection I would speak of the

practice of genuflection in general, neither recommending it nor condemning it. If ever it is appropriate, it is at this place in the Creed and at the consecration of the bread and wine as the Body and Blood of our Lord, that is, at the recital of God's humiliation and at the sacramental repetition of it. For though we reverence every name by which God is known, yet we show a more marked reverence by bowing at the name of Jesus, the human name for God, which denotes the voluntary humiliation of God in becoming man. Such a show of reverence is in our age peculiarly important, and it is important that it should be emphatically demonstrated; for it is not merely an expression of our faith, but, since Christianity cannot help being in a certain measure polemical, it is a public demonstration, indeed a public rebuke, and a rebuke not only of the infidelity which denies the Incarnation, but more especially of the self-complacent humanism which entertains not the remotest suspicion that to God it might be a humiliation to become man.

It is this consideration which prompted me to practice genuflection, and that all the more because I ministered for many years in Rome and was jealous of allowing the Church of Rome to show a more marked reverence than I. But I have always used this gesture temperately. I have never lost sight of the fact that in the Church of Rome genuflection is a comparatively modern innovation, characteristic of the Counter Reformation, though in Southern Europe it seems to have come into use in the fifteenth century, that therefore it was no part of the Catholic heritage of the Church of England, and that consequently Anglo-Catholics who discard genuflection in favor of a profound inclination of the body (*à la Sarum* etc.) can claim to be more consistent with their principles than are the more numerous imitators of Rome. It might also be urged that a profound inclination of the body is really more reverential than genuflection. On the other hand it is not nearly so conspicuous. That may be an advantage—but it also may be a disadvantage in the case of a gesture which is meant to be a demonstration of our faith and at the same time a rebuke to unbelief. When weighing the pros and cons we may also reflect that genuflection is more expeditious. This is in the interest of "godly celerity"—especially when one is passing in front of an

altar—but godly celerity may be overdone. On the other hand no precise definition of a reverential bow can be given, hence no general agreement can be expected about the proper angle of inclination; it may be exaggerated with pretension to superior piety, or it may degenerate into a little nod such as one might bestow upon an acquaintance in passing. It is an advantage that the act of genuflection can be precisely defined as touching (or almost touching) the right knee to the floor, but the tempo unfortunately is left undefined, and how often it is to be performed cannot be exactly determined if it is understood as a sign of reverence for Christ present in the Sacrament, for then one might think that we ought to genuflect all the time, or rather that we ought to get down on our knees and stay there.

Genuflection as it is commonly practiced offends against the maxim *ne quid nimis* because essentially it is Baroque. This does not condemn it absolutely in my eyes, for I have learned tardily to appreciate the Baroque, especially in architecture and sculpture. The Baroque was the characteristic expression of the Counter Reformation, and I have learned also to appreciate the value of the Counter Reformation, appraising it no less highly and no less critically than I do the Protestant Reformation, but I protest against the smug notion that either reformation was a permanent "settlement," and I recognize that today the Baroque does not reflect aptly the spirit of the Church of Rome, least of all the spirit of that group which is zealous for liturgical reform. The fault of Baroque art is its too-muchness, it does not know where to stop; even in architecture it has no limits rationally prescribed, for it is not functional, as the embellishments of Greek and Roman and Gothic architecture were originally. The practice of making innumerable genuflections is Baroque in the highest degree; it deserves to be called Rococo, and its too-muchness has the unfortunate effect of obscuring the significance of the genuflections which are made at a place where they are obviously appropriate, i.e. before the mystery of the Incarnation, as a sign of veneration for the humility of God.

Even if not all can be expected to agree where the line is to be drawn, it certainly must be drawn somewhere, and in our Communion it must be drawn soberly and severely, for there is

nothing in the Roman Catholic ritual more offensive to the majority of our people than the practice of genuflection. And yet genuflection is a more marked token of reverence than a lowly inclination of the body. Maybe that is the chief objection to it. It cannot be ignored or overlooked, especially when it is made at the Creed when every one is standing. When made at the Words of Institution it will not be so much remarked, for then the congregation is kneeling, and when the celebrant genuflects after making his communion even the "Evangelicals" might condone it, in part because the "Evangelical" celebrant is prone to make his communion kneeling, like the rest of the people, in part because they will regard it as an indication that the priest is making a little prayer, and this they think a nice thing for the priest to do at any time. Perhaps it might not be too extravagant a use of "economy" to let them think so, though, as I have said, a genuflection no more implies a prayer than does the sign of the cross or the Mohammedan prostrations or the gesture of touching one's hat.

During the few years I have to live I probably shall continue to practice genuflection at the Mass whenever I find myself amongst those who do it. Yet I wonder whether it is wise or charitable to adhere to a custom which, even if few were to resent it, the majority will certainly not follow. For I do not believe we can reasonably expect to attain uniformity in the practice of this custom even within our own Communion, and the prospect is still less promising if we have in view the possibility of union with Protestant brethren of other denominations. Protestants who in other respects might be willing to unite with us can hardly be expected to conform readily to this practice.

And what can we say to persuade them that this custom is fit at all times to be law universal in the Church of Christ? It cannot be said that it has been practiced *ubique semper et ab omnibus.* It is significant that it was adopted at that particular moment in history when the theory of absolute monarchy was so absolutely in the ascendant in Europe that both Protestants and Catholics accepted it as a matter of course, as almost the only thing they could heartily agree upon. Calvinism was then so popular because it interpreted God in terms of the absolute monarch, as a

God who has decreed for his own glory whatsoever comes to pass; and it cannot be accounted strange that at the same time the Church of Rome introduced the custom of genuflection, which was the etiquette required in the court of the absolute monarch, where every courtier bent the knee to his soverign. It is pretty certain that the practice of genuflection in the Church could not have arisen spontaneously at any other period of history, least of all in our day, when there is no absolute monarch left, indeed very few monarchs of any sort, and when the respect shown to the Leader, the Führer, the Duce, though perhaps it is more heartfelt, is less ceremonious. So far as I know, it is only in England a subject is expected to fall upon one knee before his sovereign, and that is required only when one does formal obeisance for some special favor bestowed by the monarch.

I am very far from meaning to imply that it might be possible to feel too much reverence for God, but perhaps one might demonstrate one's reverence too conspicuously, and certainly it would be unseemly to express it in unusual ways, for example, by standing on one's head. The manner of showing reverence for God will always be influenced by the ceremonial customs of civil life. In the early Catholic Church under the Roman Empire the practice of genuflection in the Mass would have seemed extravagant, for until an oriental etiquette was introduced in the Byzantine court neither Romans nor Greeks were accustomed to gestures of subservience. I am very far from drawing the absurd inference that we have no need to show any reverence for God because in our day, especially in America, where every man is as good as another and a great deal better, we show no marked reverence for anybody. But the fact that this inference has been drawn very generally, confirms my thesis. American Protestants will neither stand nor kneel in prayer, they think this a too obsequious sign of reverence—like the Quakers, who will not even take off their hats in the meeting house—and therefore, in accordance with a well known psychological law, they inhibit the feeling of reverence by suppressing its appropriate expression. Genuflection, though it does not imply a prayer, may by the fact that it expresses reverence actually evoke it, and in any case it is better than a prayer without reverence.

In general I am not an advocate of the golden mean, and hence I am not enthusiastic over the claim of the Church of England to be the *via media,* and yet I must admit that there is some truth in the thought that at the present juncture our Church is fitted, perhaps called, to serve as a bridge, and that therefore it is our manifest duty to act upon a maxim calculated to conciliate uniformity not only within our communion, but, so far as may be possible, in the Church at large. Bridge-making has from ancient times been regarded as a priestly function, a pontifical function, and the most exclusive title of the Bishop of Rome is that of Pontifex Maximus. I remember that Julius Caesar built his bridge with *tigna bina sequepedalia,* but whether with genuflections an ecclesiastical bridge can be built we have reason to doubt, in view of the fact that it is not used in the Eastern Church and is abhorred by most Protestants. In fact it is used by only a small minority in our own Communion, and even when the clergy genuflect in the Creed, only a few in the congregation follow them. So the use of genuflection introduces a discordancy which is more observable than a discordancy in faith, whereas it seems likely that the congregation would concordantly follow their priest if he were to content himself with making at the *incarnatus est* a lowly inclination of the body.

And yet, after all, genuflection is now the Roman custom, and that is an argument of prodigious weight. Perhaps the impossibility of getting the congregation to follow the celebrant on the one occasion when the people are not upon their knees might be simply accepted, with the understanding that "those about the altar" act for the people when they perform this gesture of reverence.

I have been accustomed to write on more serious themes. Here I have employed so many words about a mere ritual gesture, viewing it aesthetically, historically, dogmatically, psychologically, and philosophically . . . without reaching any conclusion! Yet in view of the antics I see performed in many places, what sympathy I have felt for the Baroque is turning into a sour antipathy.

THE SERMON

We come now to a more substantial subject and one upon which I could dwell with more pleasure did not the character of this part of my book exclude all considerations which are not merely formal, as formal, for example, as the question how the preacher should be dressed. How the sermon should be composed, or even how it should be delivered, is another story and a long one. Here we must assume that every preacher is well acquainted with the Holy Scriptures and thoroughly instructed in the doctrines the Church has deduced from them, that from a rich Christian experience he knows how to bring forth things new and old, and that he has an advantageous exterior and a sonorous vocal organ—although, alas, if he possesses these latter advantages he will likely be taken away from our parish and made a bishop. We might almost assume that every preacher is a prophet and expect that the Holy Ghost will dictate to him what he is to say. But even in that case we may have something to tell him which he needs to know. And yet we would not hamper him; for the place of the sermon is the one place in the Liturgy where the priest may properly claim to be himself, free from the restraint of ritual prescriptions. And this being the only place where he may exercise such freedom, everything which plainly reflects the personality of the priest or his individual idiosyncrasies, whether it be parochial announcements or special prayers, must be pronounced in this place. I do not mean necessarily in the pulpit but in the interval between the Creed and the Prayer for the Whole State of Christ's Church, and not at the place where he stands to recite the Divine Liturgy. The celebrant cannot invoke his liberty as a preacher to justify the license of introducing into the Liturgy prayers which because of their sentimentality or because of their form or because of their content are in strident discord with our liturgical tradition; and such prayers are actually mixed up with the Liturgy when they are uttered immediately before the Prayer for the Whole Church and at the very place where that prayer is said. This practice has become all too common, but it is plainly unlawful. It is so far from being permitted by our rubric that it is implicitly excluded by the permission which is granted: "Here the Priest may ask the *secret* intercessions of the Congregation for any who have asked the prayers of the Church." By italicizing the word "secret" I do no more than call attention to the obvious meaning of the rubric, which permits the priest to name the persons who desire the prayers of the Church and presumably to indicate the nature of their affliction, in order that the congregation may with this "intention" offer the prayers prescribed in the Liturgy. For the priest to insert other prayers at his "discretion" not only *is* unlawful, it ought to be unlawful, for it is a grave infringement of the rights of the people. At this place the priest is not at liberty to insert even such prayers as he may find in other parts of our Prayer Book, and still less, of course, the prayers which he gathers from every conceivable source, even from his own head. And yet with this I do not mean to condemn entirely the use of such prayers or to disparage the use of free prayers. On the contrary, I value them in their proper place, that is, in connection with the sermon, the place which allows for liberty of prophesying. The people are willing to put up with almost anything from the pulpit, but the prayers pronounced before the altar are prescribed, and the people are legally (not virtually, alas) protected from the whims of the priest.

So, if he will, let the preacher begin his sermon with a prayer. Only let not the people kneel for the brief prayer which is then uttered. Commonly they are standing when the priest enters the pulpit (either immediately after the Creed or after the singing of a hymn), so let them remain standing. Frequent changes of posture are disturbing to all and are difficult for the aged. And let him, if he will, conclude the sermon with a prayer. Whether a prayer of petition or an ascription of praise is more appropriate depends upon the sermon or rather upon the note with which the sermon ends. If it is a penitential sermon (but how rare such sermons are, it is feared that they will "throw a coldness over the meeting"), then of course a penitential prayer is in place, and of course the people will be invited to kneel. But for my part I prefer to end even a penitential sermon on a note of thanksgiving or of hope, which would well accord with St. Paul's noble ascription: "And now unto him who is able to do for us very much more exceeding abundantly than we can ask or think, according to the power which worketh in us, to him be the glory in the Church and through Christ Jesus, unto the age of the ages." In another place I shall speak of the propriety of using a bidding prayer *after* the sermon. The common custom of prefacing the sermon with a compendious profession of faith, "In the name of the Father, and of the Son, and of the Holy Ghost. Amen" may justly be regarded as a formal assurance to the people that they will hear the truth and nothing but the truth. Such an assurance was never more needed than today. It is regarded as a "Catholic" custom, but it might be commended to "Evangelicals" by the plausible inference that every one who rose to speak in the Apostolic Church gave some such assurance of fidelity to the truth as it is in Jesus; for in 1 Cor. 12:3 it seems to be implied that the compendious creed, "Jesus Christ the Lord," prefaced every address, every prophecy.

It is very instructive to observe that the Book of Common Prayer assumes that "the sermon" is to be delivered here and here only, that is, at the beginning of the Liturgy and immediately after the reading of the Scriptures. For us this piece of instruction is very necessary, seeing that for several hundred years we have, without knowing it, been living in ignominious subjection to the Calvinistic notion that the sermon ought to come after the prayers. In Calvin's prayer book, the "Directory for Worship" (the only prayer book which contains nothing but rubrics), it is prescribed that after many prayers have been said, including the so-called "long prayer," which the Puritans stretched to an hour and a half, the sermon should be preached —after which there remained nothing to be done but to take up the collection and dismiss the people with a blessing. It is making too much of the sermon to make it the climax of divine worship. There is no justification for putting the sermon in this position— unless it might be supposed that the congregation was so much moved by the sermon that every one felt impelled to go out at once and do what the preacher said . . . without waiting to ask God's help. On the other hand, this makes too little of the sermon, for it ignores the consideration that the sermon might prompt the people to pray and make it possible for them to pray heartily together. It ignores the fact that public worship in the sense of common prayer is a difficult art and a goal rarely attained. Perhaps our "Catholic" brethren would not be so much inclined to belittle the importance of the sermon if they used it in the right place and conceived of it as an aid to devotion. At all events this attitude of theirs is evidently very far from being Catholic when we consider the high esteem in which the sermon is held in the Church of Rome and how able are her preachers. The sermon is not to be disdained unless it is contemptible, unless it is a sermon which does no good. It is significant that the "Catholic" priests who disparage the sermon are commonly men who are unable to preach. What they say about the sermon is to be understood as "compensation" for their inferiority. That may be condoned only if they don't "overcompensate" and make out that without being Ministers of the Word they are able ministers of the new covenant. Seeing that most sermons are ineffectual I have been inclined to welcome the suggestion that there might be decreed a moratorium on sermons—but that only with a view to making confession of the irregularities commonly practiced in the stewardship of the heavenly treasure and giving time to make good our deficiency. That the banks should remain permanently closed would not be so great a calamity as to have the pulpits always empty.

Of course the sermon ought to come after the Scripture lessons which it may be expected to explain, but equally of course it ought to come before the prayers. Although our Prayer Book gives no countenance to the Calvinistic notion, we are so completely in subjection to it that when Morning or Evening Prayer is said it is taken for granted that the sermon will *follow*. The English Reformers had in fact no thought of associating a sermon either with Morning or with Evening Prayer, but being acquainted with the Catholic tradition, they would doubtless have preferred to put it before rather than after, or they would have put it after the Lessons. Since we commonly put the sermon in a preposterous place, the cart before the horse, it is not to be wondered that persons who come more particularly to hear the sermon are a little impatient at the prayers, perhaps express their discontent by saying that it "takes too long to read the minutes of the last meeting." This judgment is perhaps not merely a condemnation of the perfunctory way the prayers are read. If the Archangel Gabriel were to read them, his angelic trumpet voice might fall upon deaf ears. It is not merely difficult, it is impossible for outsiders to take part heartily in our Morning and Evening Prayer, which, being a condensation of monastic offices, expect and require the utmost familiarity, the familiarity which comes from saying them daily. It is with this expectation the Prayer Book proposes them for use without the help of a sermon. They are the furthest possible remove from an evangelistic or a missionary service designed to bring in outsiders. The Mass is more apt for that purpose, more particularly the Mass of the Catechumens with which we are now dealing.

When apart from the Eucharist a sermon is to be preached it may justly be regarded as the principal event on the program, and it would be well, not only for a missionary purpose but for the better instruction of the faithful, to give opportunity to hear sermons unaccompanied by prayers, or with a few prayers and hymns following it. This is today the practice of the Church of Rome. It gives due importance to the sermon and allows due time for it. In Italy it is expected that such a sermon will last an hour and a half, with a little intermission to allow the preacher to rest without leaving the pulpit. We have something like this in the so-called Three Hours Service on Good Friday—which is three hours for the preacher and, alas, perhaps half an hour for the people who come and go. In the Church of Rome it is also expected that on such occasions the preacher will be a real preacher who has something to say and knows how to say it. It is not assumed that such preachers are always available. To this end there are preaching orders. Of course it cannot be expected that there will be enough real preachers to preach at every Eucharist every Sunday. So we might begin with the requirement that every priest be prepared to "explain the Gospel." Until the Protestant Reformation the Church was never under the illusion that every priest as such might be capable of preaching. In the earliest age apostles, prophets, evangelists, and teachers, were the only preachers, and not till the charismatic ministry was disappearing did the bishops diffidently assume this function—not for a long time the presbyters, for before they assumed to preach there were monks like Athanasius. But surely the parochial pastor should be competent "rightly to divide the word of truth," to preach in a humble but edifying way, at least to explain the Gospel of the day. Starting with that humble task (which is really the highest task and one upon which a lifetime might profitably be spent), rather than with the ambitious task of composing a conventional sermon with three heads and as many subdivisions under each, with an exordium and peroration as well, a conventional sermon which sets out with a striking text and gets away from it as fast and as far as possible, divagating into every field of knowledge with which the preacher is not competent to deal—starting with this humble task, beginning with a simple explanation of the Gospel, the simple parish priest is sure to become an edifying preacher.

Our rubric prescribes the place for the sermon, but it does not tell us who is to preach. Ordinarily, on account of the paucity of ministers (and they must always be too few if they have to be paid), it may be taken for granted that the celebrant will preach; but as he is permitted to appoint other persons to read the Gospel and the Epistle, he doubtless may appoint another to preach. "Here followeth the Sermon," is a rubric so laconic that we are left without any instruction as to who may be accounted legally competent to preach. Well, since we have no law covering this situation the decision is left to our reason, and it surely is reasonable to affirm that any one who is virtually competent to preach may be appointed to deliver the sermon. Even women are not excluded by any express law of our Church—but on that point I agree heartily with St. Paul. From St. Paul, however, we derive no encouragement whatever for excluding laymen from the pulpit. It is very "convenient"—no one is more ready than I to admit it—that ordinarily the pastor of the parish should preach. If he is a man who has the respect and confidence of his people, his sermon will be more edifying to them than that of a more eloquent orator. It is of course in the highest degree inconvenient that any one should preach at the Eucharist who is not able to communicate in the Sacrament; but I can see no inconvenience in inviting a layman to preach if he is not only formally a member of the

Church but is an exemplary Christian—provided he can do it well, perhaps better than any ordained minister who is available, and perhaps more acceptably, more tellingly, for the very fact that he is not a clergyman, that it is not his profession to preach, not his "living." We have Catholic precedent for this, as well as evangelical precedent from the earliest age, for during the greatest period of the Middle Ages the friars were well nigh the only preachers, and at that time the friars were not ordained. It is true that in our Ordinal the priest when he is ordained is given "authority to preach the Word of God." This sounds like a real and universal authority; it might also seem to imply that no others have authority to preach. But strangely enough the Bishop attaches a string to this authority granted to the priest when he adds the clumsy phrase: "in the congregation where thou shalt be lawfully appointed thereunto." So in the last resort it is the vestry electing him which confers this sublime authority upon the priest! I wish this provision had not been added, for then the priest might have felt authorized to preach in the street, in a theater, or wherever the people might be found ready to listen to the Word of God. I remember in this connection that Dr. Martin Luther once expressed the opinion that "a church is no place to preach the Gospel in." In the critical time ahead of us, if it is not already upon us, the most important preaching will perhaps be done outside the churches, where the layman has pretty much the same authority as has the priest, and if there are now any laymen who are able to preach the Word of God, they might well be given practice by preaching in the churches before they go out to preach to the world.

Even with regard to the sermon, a ritual question emerges which we cannot avoid: How is the preacher to be dressed? I do not ask how he is to be vested, for that would in part be begging the question by implying that at least he must wear something different from his ordinary clothes. But if this is a "must," it is not one which has any sanction in our law. We have absolutely no prescription how the preacher is to be dressed. Generally we feel no embarrassment about this lack, indeed we are commonly unaware of it, for it is so much a matter of course for the preacher to wear a cassock, a surplice and a stole or tippet, with perhaps an academic hood thrown in, that any other dress seems queer to us. But of course if a celebrant properly vested is also the preacher, he cannot well put on a surplice; he divests himself of the chasuble and goes to the pulpit dressed only in the alb and stole. I say "only" because even to us who are in a measure used to it this seems a decidedly informal dress or undress. So it was regarded by the Greeks and Romans, who before appearing in public would have put on over their shirt a pallium or a toga—at a later period a chasuble or a dalmatic. But such is the custom now in the Church of Rome, and it has at least this much reason on its side, that a stiffly embroidered chasuble such as we now use would be awkward for an orator, especially in the pulpit. If the celebrant instead of mounting the pulpit stands at the front of the chancel to preach, he has not so much reason for taking off the chasuble.

But we have not yet exhausted the practical possibilities of the preacher's dress. How easily we forget that for a long time it was customary in the Church of England (and so also in America) for the preacher to wear a black gown. That was a pre-Reformation custom. Strange as it is to us now, it is still worth considering, for it would in some measure conciliate our Protestant brethren, and it is at least on a line with the Catholic custom which expects a monk to preach in the habit of his order. The preaching gown is not an academic gown and does not imply (God forbid it!) that no man can rightly divide the word of truth if he cannot boast an academic degree or has not been immured for three years in a seminary. For my part, I have never worn a gown in an Anglican church, yet here I would register my vote for it. A black gown covers a multitude of sins and would properly cover the unseemly undress of the alb. It has moreover the obvious advantage of distinguishing the teaching function of the minister (or the prophetic function if he prefers to say so) from his sacerdotal function, and of indicating plainly that he appears in the pulpit as a minister of the Word. With a view to the inclusion of laymen among the preachers it is important that the priest be not distinguished by his dress in the pulpit from every other teacher. I am glad that I have nothing more to say about the preacher's dress—but I would that I had license here to say something substantial about the sermons!

NOTICES AND EXHORTATIONS

Into the gap between the Creed and the Prayer for the Whole State of Christ's Church are thrown all the items which conclude the Mass of the Catechumens and prepare for the Mass of the Faithful: Notices, Exhortations, Bidding Prayer, Sermon, Offertory Sentences, Hymn or Anthem, Reception of the Offerings, Reception of the Oblations of Bread and Wine. There are eight items here with ten rubrics to define them, and yet all of them, except the sentences and the placing of the Bread and Wine upon the Holy Table, may commonly be omitted, and, since the Creed also may occasionally be omitted, the celebrant is at liberty to pass at once from the Gospel to the Prayer for the Whole State of Christ's Church. That, however, would be a very abrupt transition, and if a hymn or anthem cannot be sung, it might be well at this place to unite the people in a bidding prayer properly composed.

Although we are not instructed where the Exhortations are to be "said," it is obviously "convenient" to say them here, either before or after the Notices. The Exhortation "at the time of the Celebration of the Communion" we may omit except on the First Sunday in Lent, the First Sunday in Advent, and on Trinity Sunday; the second (or the third) Exhortation ("or so much thereof as, in his discretion, the Minister may think convenient") the priest "shall" say when he giveth warning of the celebration of the Holy Communion, "which he shall always do upon the Sunday or some Holy Day immediately preceding." So says the rubric—which is more honored in the breach than in the observance. For it is evident that this rubric dates from a time when the celebration of the Holy Communion was rare, perhaps not so frequent as once a month, and when parish notices were not printed. Today we find it very tiresome to hear the pastor recite a great variety of church notices which his parishioners hold in printed form in their hands. Sometimes it seems almost as if he gloated over every item of parochial activity, rolled it as a sweet morsel under his tongue, and was willing to curtail the time of the sermon for the sake of showing what an extraordinarily industrious parson he is. On the other hand, one seldom hears the Exhortations. To a certain degree they have been rendered obsolete by the change which has come about in our day, when it can be taken for granted that there will be a celebration of the Holy Communion at least once on every Sunday and Holy Day. But at the same time the practice of making frequent communion adds new urgency to these solemn Exhortations. They were evidently introduced into the Liturgy of the Reformed Church of England with the intent of supplying in some measure the lack of auricular confession, whereas the Lutheran Churches insisted upon attendance at a penitential service, a sort of public confession, before receiving the Holy Communion. Now when frequent communion is so common with us, and young people especially are so much urged to make their communions, while generally we lack the check which confession imposes upon an unwholesome increase of communions in the Church of Rome, the solemn warnings of the first two Exhortations ought surely to be heard in one form or another more than three times a year. I am far from wishing to revert to the practice of "fencing the table" which was characteristic of the Covenanters, but evidently something must be done to insure that the Holy Communion will not be taken in vain. This thing must be left to the "discretion" of the minister. But as things are now it is likely that the majority of our communicants never hear the warning that they "must try and examine themselves before they presume to eat of that Bread and drink of that Cup." What often is insisted upon is not a moral or religious preparation but a purely ritual prescription, that one must come to the Holy Communion "fasting." We have no such ritual law, but the fact that "fasting communion" is required in the Church of Rome certainly deserves attention. It may be called a Catholic custom, but it is not primitive, not Apostolic, inasmuch as in the early Church, perhaps for two centuries, the Sacrament was the conclusion of a hearty meal. We get, as I have said before, a hint of how "the Lord's Supper became an early breakfast" from the story in Acts 20:7-12 where it is related that when the disciples at Troas on the first day of the week (that is, the eve of Sunday, or Saturday evening as we would now call it) were gathered together to break bread, Paul prolonged his speech until midnight, so that, being delayed further by the accident to Eutychus, it was near dawn when they broke bread. We must remember that until Constantine made Sunday a day of rest, the Christians, whether they were living in a Jewish or a pagan environment, were not free to leave their daily occupations and gather together on the Lord's Day at any time except at night or in the early morning, and we must remember also that from the time the Roman Empire became "Christian" the people were more and more reluctant to communicate, so that the principal Eucharist, at which all the people were expected to be present, had to be regarded chiefly as a sacrifice, while the Sacrament was received by a few at an earlier hour, that is, before anyone would think of eating. But we must also take into account the fact that even to this day few of the inhabitants of the Mediterranean basin are accustomed to eat anything before noon. I was struck by this fact when I lived in Italy and Greece. I learned later that throughout the Middle Ages it was the same in northern Europe. This seems hardly credible to us. Yet we might rather wonder how they could have breakfasted without coffee, tea, chocolate, "breakfast-foods," or citrus fruits. At all events, this accounts for the fact that nobody ate before communicating. We make a virtue of what to them was a necessity, or rather a matter of course. It may be good for us to practice a little bit of asceticism in this easy-going age, but if this is insisted upon as a condition for worthily partaking of the Sacrament, we have to face the consequence that at the later celebrations, which always are the occasions for the congregation to gather together as a whole, only a few will communicate. You cannot have your cake and eat it too: if you desire a corporate communion of the parish, you must soft-pedal this little ascetic rule, which after all can be justified only by arguments which are so puerile that one would hardly advance them in the presence of adults who are in a measure acquainted with physiology and know what "this little city of sewers" is.

More important perhaps than the duty of reading general exhortations is the obligation laid upon the pastor to exercise personal discipline, to "advertise" a man whom he knows to be "an open and notorious evil liver or to have done any wrong to his neighbours by word or deed . . . that he presume not to come to the Lord's Table until, etc.," and to use the same order "with those between whom he perceiveth malice and hatred to reign." But this of course is not to be regarded as a feature of the celebration. If such discipline were not exercised before the culprits appeared in church, it would not be edifying either to them or to the congregation.

HYMNS

Our rubrics are for the most part so antiquated that they hardly take any account of the hymns, which since the Reformation have gradually assumed a very important place in common worship. Permission is given to sing a hymn or anthem "when the alms and oblations are being received and presented," and also to sing a hymn just before the Communion, and after the communion instead of the *Gloria in Excelsis.* Nothing else is said about hymns. If we were to be strict about the letter of the rubrics and conclude that what is not expressly permitted is implicitly excluded, we could have no processional hymn, no recessional, no gradual, and no hymn before the sermon, where we almost invariably have it, and where in fact it is permitted by Canon 25 of Title I of the Digest. Well, I could get along without seeing the choir sing a processional, except on solemn occasions, and I have already confessed that I would rather begin my sermon without a hymn, though of course if the preacher wants it, or the people do, there is as much justification for singing a hymn here as anywhere else.

It looks as though the Prayer Book and the Hymnal were not on the best of terms with one another. Yet they might well be, for the use of hymns at appropriate places will greatly enhance the beauty of the Liturgy and its popular appeal—if only the hymns are appropriate to the place and time. We have perhaps a hundred and fifty great hymns, the contribution of all sections of the Church through many generations. With as many hymns as that the ordinary church-goer might become familiar, and it is obvious that none but familiar hymns can be sung heartily and well by the congregation. Our Hymnal contains 739 hymns. While the beauty of the Liturgy may be enhanced by good hymns, it is also true that inferior hymns may detract from it; and to have this effect they need not be positively bad hymns, it is enough if in comparison with the sublimity of the Liturgy they are distinctly inferior, though in another place they might serve fairly well. It is not inconceivable that our Church might prescribe a limited number of hymns for use at the Eucharist, if it is thought necessary to include a greater number in the Hymnal, since it does not permit us to use in the Liturgy all of the prayers which are found in the Prayer Book. Of course as time goes on the number of hymns in existence naturally increases. So it may be regarded as a sign of progress that we have so many hymns in our Hymnal. When I was living in Peking I was struck by the fact that China is even more progressive than we are, for I was invited to contribute money for the publication of a new hymnal which was to contain one thousand hymns, so great a number being necessary to content all the denominations which were expected to use the book.

THE BIDDING PRAYER

Although it is evident that the notices, etc., ought to come before the sermon, it is by no means so clear that this is the place for the Bidding Prayer, if it is true, as I maintain, that the prayers ought to follow the sermon. I feel no diffidence about criticizing our liturgy with respect to this provision, which is not as old as I am, and therefore is not venerable. Moreover, I have never heard any one use the Bidding Prayer since it was introduced in the last revision of our Prayer Book, though I have used it myself (and it seemed to me with good effect) *after* the sermon. A bidding prayer seems to me a proper sequel to a sermon. Perhaps if our rubric had suggested the use of it in this place, it might not have been so generally ignored. For it deserves more appreciation than it has received; as an old custom in the Church of England it has a certain respectability, and our form of it is at least better than the old English form.

But it must be admitted that our Bidding Prayer makes a poor showing in comparison with the *synapte* of the Eastern Liturgies, which is its nearest equivalent. The *synapte* is not an adventitious addendum to the sermon but can be rationally construed as an essential component of the Liturgy. It is also one of the earliest components which we can trace historically to its origin. The early Church, sensible of the peculiar difficulty of common prayer, used due diligence to overcome it. One of the means it employed to this end is suggested by Justin Martyr in the brief description of the Sunday worship of the Church which we find in his *Apology*. He makes a distinction between the prayers made by the people immediately after the sermon ("then we all stand up together and make prayers") and the prayer which "the president of the brethren" (evidently the bishop) makes in their stead ("and the president offers petitions and thanksgivings, and the people respond with the Amen"). This ancient distinction is plainly reflected in the Greek Liturgies: the prayers of the people we find in the *synapte* pronounced by the deacon, which proposes the several subjects of petition in the form, "Let us pray for," etc., leaving time for the people to make each prayer their own; the prayer of the president, consisting as it did of two parts, petitions and thanksgivings, corresponds on the one hand to the *anamnesis,* in which the priest in the form of direct address to God repeats the same petitions which were proposed to the people by the deacon (roughly this is the Prayer for the Whole State of Christ's Church in our liturgy), and on the other hand to the Eucharistic prayer proper (our Preface and Canon). We see from this how precious an element in our liturgy the Bidding Prayer might be, if it were said in the right place and couched in a more appropriate form. The *synapte* is the most effective means of overcoming the difficulty of uniting in common prayer, for it states the subject of each petition severally and leaves time for the people not only to understand it but to appropriate it as their own prayer. When the priest recites substantially the same prayer but in the form of direct address to God, it is a repetition, but it is by no means a "vain repetition." The first prayer may be regarded as a preparation for the more solemn prayer which follows. We recognize generally that we need to prepare for the Holy Communion by prayer, to prepare even to hear the sermon devoutly, but we seldom reflect that we may need to prepare for prayer . . . by prayer.

The *synapte* differs from the litany in the fact that the several petitions are suggested to the people and are not in the form of direct address to God; it differs from our Bidding Prayer in the fact that it gives the people opportunity to respond. Our Bidding Prayer seems more like a lecture than a prayer. Alas, that was originally what it was meant to be—a lecture to instruct the "good Christian people" who lately had been delivered from Papistical superstition what they ought to pray for. This sort of prescribed instruction was prominent in both the Lutheran and the Reformed agenda; for a long while after the Reformation a bidding prayer was almost the only kind of prayer commonly used in the Lutheran Churches, and this sort of instruction is still too prominent in our Prayer Book. Our Bidding Prayer having this defect of intention was naturally enough brought into close relation with the sermon (although our rubric also associates it with the Creed), and probably because it too much resembles a lecture it has found no favor in the eyes of our people since it was reintroduced not many years ago. And yet precisely during this period a bidding prayer which follows the form of the *synapte* has come into vogue in Protestant ecumenical circles, especially at missionary gatherings. This suggests at least the possibility that a prayer in this form might be of use to us "on special occasions" (as the rubric suggests) and might greatly enrich our Liturgy. Curiously enough we are in this instance allowed complete liberty to rewrite the Bidding Prayer entirely, for the rubric permits the minister, "in his discretion," to "omit any of the clauses of this prayer" and "to add others as occasion may require." What an amazingly liberal law! We might rewrite this prayer in the form of the *synapte*—only we may not use it *after* the sermon. However, for this we need no special permission, if it is conceded that the preacher is free to conclude his sermon with whatever prayers he may, in his discretion, see fit to select or to compose. After the sermon is a tolerable place for such a bidding prayer as I have in mind. And yet it is not the ideal place, for not even such a prayer as this properly belongs to the Mass of the Catechumens. But I have already remarked that we can no longer draw a sharp line here. At this point our categories become hopelessly confounded. It would certainly be more ideal if such a prayer might be brought into closer connection with the Prayer for the Whole State of Christ's Church which substantially rehearses the same petitions, and perhaps our rubric may be tortured to give us this permission; for "to ask the secret intercessions of the people" is precisely what the *synapte* does.

Merely as an example to show how this Greek prayer may be adapted to our needs, I append here one of the forms I have often used. Of course one need not always, especially for use outside the Liturgy, adhere so closely to the Greek phrases. In war time one can easily add special petitions.

In peace let us make our supplications unto the Lord.

That we may know how to pray as we ought, with a sense of God's presence, faith in his love, and assurance of his power.

For the peace that is from above, for the love of God, and for the salvation of our souls: Let us make our supplications unto the Lord.

For the peace of the whole world and the unity of the holy Churches of God.

For the peace and prosperity of our own land, that justice may flourish and that true religion may prevail.

For the good temperature of the air, peaceful showers, pleasant dews, abundance of the fruits of the earth, the fulness of a plentiful season, the crown of the year of God's goodness.

Let us pray one for the other, all for each, for the illumination of our minds, that we may know the truth, and that we may have a right judgment in all things, that we may learn so to walk in this life that we fail not finally to attain unto life everlasting.

For all who are dear to us upon earth, who have done us good and are wont to pray for us, that blessing may be upon them and peace from God.

For every Christian soul in affliction and distress, for those especially who have asked our prayers or whom we are fain to remember before God; for the conversion of the erring, for the recovery of the sick, for the comfort of those who mourn: Let us make our supplications unto the Lord.

For those who have departed in the faith of Christ, who once were near to us and still are dear; that God may multiply unto them the manifold blessings of his love.

For the forgiveness of all that we have done amiss, and of all that we have neglected to do.

That our prayer may be heard and accepted before God, and that his rich mercies and pity may be sent down upon us.

THE OFFERTORY

The Offertory means a place for making an offering or sacrifice. Hence the rubric says expressly that "the Priest shall return to the Holy Table and begin the Offertory" *there* by saying "one or more of these Sentences following." This plainly implies that he is expected to make a considerate choice from among the sixteen sentences suggested in our book. Surely he might make a more thoughtful selection than priests commonly do. Seeing that a great part of the money offered in the parish is spent for the maintenance of the pastor and of others who serve it (including musicians and singers), it seems a pity that the sentences in our old book which were pertinent to this fact have in our last revision been omitted, only two being retained which are thought to be referable to missionaries rather than to the clergy of the parish. I confess that I liked to say them. It seemed to me realistic. But I know that most of the clergy were shamefaced about saying them—though St. Paul felt no such embarrassment. I still feel free to use them because they were once commended by the Book of Common Prayer. And I also feel free to use one which strangely enough was never included in our Prayer Book but is strongly commended to us by St. Paul and was used by him to stimulate the people to give abundantly: "For ye know the grace of our Lord Jesus Christ, that though he was rich, yet for your sakes he became poor, that ye through his poverty might become rich" (2 Cor. 8:10). Giving, whether it be in money or in kind, is expressly regarded in the New Testament as an act of "communion." For this reason the Offertory is essentially appropriate here. Money is spiritualized by this conception—as in general everything is spiritualized in view of the Incarnation. The Authorized Version correctly translates Heb. 13:16, "To do good and to communicate forget not, for with such sacrifices God is well pleased." But the compilers of our Prayer Book when they introduced this among the Offertory Sentences wrote "distribute" instead of communicate, doubtless because they feared that by a word of such lofty spiritual meaning the people could not be made to understand anything so grossly practical as the giving of money. But "distribute" is a heartless word, and there is no authority on earth that can persuade me to use it in an offertory sentence. Once (2 Cor. 9:13) even the A. V. slipped up and described the gift the Church at Corinth had sent to the poor brethren at Jerusalem as a "liberal distribution"—and the R. V. does not make the thing much better when it calls it a "contribution"—it is a communion.

This is an appropriate place to observe that in view of Christ's offering of himself everything we do at the Eucharist takes on the character of sacrifice. Our gifts are not simply given but "offered," our prayers are offered, our hymns are offered, we offer ourselves. This sacrificial language dates from the first century—indeed from the Apostles, for the gifts which St. Paul describes as "a communion" he also characterizes in one place (Phil. 4:18) as "an odor of a sweet smell, a sacrifice well pleasing to God." The *Didache* justifies the rule that such gifts were to be presented to the prophets by the consideration that "they are your high priests." This conception of the Eucharist as a sacrifice antedates by several centuries the first suggestion that it is a repetition of the sacrifice of Christ. This doctrine (popularly known as "the doctrine of the Mass") may be very important to the Church as a *botega* or business concern, but it has no other importance whatsoever—if it is true that Christ died for our sins once—and it is neither primitive nor early Catholic. Yet as a whole the Eucharist is a sacrifice—it is *our* sacrifice. Such is the language of the early Catholic Church. Nowhere was Luther so completely at fault as when he threw overboard the whole of the Roman Canon because he would not endure a trace of the sacrificial language and imagery which follows *Te igitur* and pervades the whole prayer.

The hymn or anthem which may be sung at this point is an offering, of course, but at the same time it fulfills the practical purpose of covering up the rather tedious process of collecting the alms. We are not required to make a collection at every Eucharist, but in our commercial age this is seldom omitted. It was not always so with us, for the old church in Newport of which I once was Rector preserves in the minutes of the vestry a record of a resolution of the congregation to inaugurate the custom of making a collection every Sunday to which each person was expected to contribute a penny; but it is reported also that this was found too onerous and soon was discontinued. Now it would be superfluous to urge that this be done and that it be done with due solemnity, since it is commonly the most pompous ceremony in our worship. There was a time when the gifts offered at the Eucharist were given in kind, and when Monica brought to Milan this simple African custom, good Bishop Ambrose had to explain to her kindly that in his great city this simply "was not done." Sporadically this custom has been maintained or introduced in primitive communities. Even *we* may resort to it on Thanksgiving Day. It is picturesque and satisfying to the imagination, but ordinarily this materiality is too cumbersome, and perhaps money, an exceedingly abstract symbol of everything we have to give, comports better with our "reasonable worship." In any case it is to be understood that the material elements which are to be consumed at the Eucharist, i. e. the bread and winc, are a part of the offering, which we distinguish as "the oblations"; they are in fact provided by the people, not by the priest, and it is just too bad if there is no server to act as representative of the people in presenting them to the priest. But if this is understood, there is no reason why we should adopt the suggestion recently made, that the wardens should carry the oblations up the aisle: it is enough if the server, as a vestige of the Greek chorus, carries them from the credence to the altar. The "decent basin" containing the alms (brass is not obligatory) is to be brought to the priest, "who shall humbly present and place it upon the Holy Table." The word "present" implies the gesture of lifting up the alms to God before placing them upon the Holy Table. With this mute gesture the offering of the alms is not complete, but it may be completed by an offertory sentence, if the priest finds it awkward to remove the alms from the altar during or after the prayers for the Church. The oblations are offered in the prayer for the Church, although according to the rubric they were mutely offered in the act of placing them upon the Holy Table. The rubrics require that both the alms and the oblations shall be offered to God by a gesture before they are verbally offered by prayer.

Unfortunately we are not in agreement as to *when* the bread and the wine are to be placed upon the Holy Table. The rubric says "then," and that may mean *after* everything prescribed in the preceding rubrics has been performed, that is, after the alms have been presented. But also it may mean *while* all this is being done. Taking up the collection necessarily involves a considerable time, perhaps a longer period that can be covered by the hymn or anthem which the following rubric permits us to sing "when the alms *and* oblations are being received and presented." It would be very inconvenient (in both senses of the word) if the priest with godly celerity might not employ this time by placing the bread and wine upon the Holy Table, for that also takes time, since it involves some deliberation about the amount required. Certainly nothing is more vexing to the congregation than to watch (as one cannot help doing) the priest pottering over such material employments.

There are many more things to be said at this point than the rubrics venture to say. Yet fortunately it is said distinctly enough that the elements which are presented must be bread and wine. In our day this creates a sharp distinction between us and every branch of Protestantism in America, except the Lutheran Churches. It is futile now to talk of union with the Protestant bodies in America who because of a zeal for Prohibition have given up the use of wine for the Communion, and because of a common squeamishness about hygiene have given up the common chalice. What sort of union would it be if we still cannot communicate with them in the sacrament of the Lord's Body and Blood? By the same token American Protestants are separated also from all Protestants in Europe, even from those who are of the same "denomination." When the Bible says "wine," they venture to think that it means grape juice, but no one is likely to take this liberty with our rubric. We must use wine, and wine is the fermented juice of the grape.

But our rubric also says "bread," and doubtless it means bread—not wafers. Bread is the leavened (fermented) flour of wheat baked in an oven. The use of individual wafers offends against the idea of communicating in "one loaf" in exactly the same degree that the use of individual communion cups (liqueur glasses) offends against the idea of communicating in "the cup," and "the breaking of the bread" has lost its original significance when there is no loaf nor even a part of a loaf. So Catholicism has on the one hand done as much to destroy the primitive symbolism of the Eucharist as modern American Protestantism has done on the other. Within a generation the wafer has made its way into our Church. I find myself constrained to use wafers. I do not know if bread is now anywhere used in our churches, but I have used it wherever I have been responsible as pastor of a congregation, finding it in no respect less convenient, except for the purpose of intinction, which is an advantage I am willing to forego.

The rubric does not say so, but it is generally understood that the wine is to be mixed with water. That is not only a Catholic custom, it is also primitive. The content of the chalice is described in some of the earliest references to the Eucharist, not as wine, but simply as "mixed." In Classical Greek *krasis* meant a cup of wine mixed with water, and a *krater* (whence the name of the hollow of a volcano) was the large Greek vase made for mixing wine. The symbolical significance of mixing wine with water—the association, that is, with "the water and the blood" which according to St. John's emphatic testimony flowed from our Lord's side—was secondary; it was first of all a practical requirement that the heavy wines commonly used in the Roman Empire should be mixed with water before they were drunk at meals. It required not a little water but much to make them palatable. For us too the mixed chalice has a practical value because the wine which is to be used for communion is made exceedingly strong with a view to its preservation from week to week. Unless it is diluted with an equal quantity of water it is not a tolerable beverage. If it is properly diluted with water, the priest will have no embarrassment about consuming what is left after the communion, and I reflect that if this custom had been generally observed (perhaps exaggerated for the sake of the weaker brethren), the outcry of the Prohibitionists would perhaps have had less effect upon the Protestant Churches of America.

When the priest has measured out so much bread and wine as he shall think sufficient he is to "offer" them, i. e. lift them up as a sacrifice to God, as he places them on the Holy Table. Then he is to cover the bread with a lap of the corporal and the chalice with the pall. But what am I saying! Our rubrics have nothing whatever to say about a corporal or pall or veil or bourse or purificators. They do not suggest that up to this time the sacred vessels have been covered, or even that they have been on the altar. We take all these adjuncts as a matter of course. Up to the Reformation they had been in use in the Church of England, but the Reformers preferred to ignore them. Was this because they thought all these items too fussy? Well, perhaps. One now can observe effeminate priests pottering fussily with these things; and to my mind it would be better to do away with them all rather than give the impression that the Holy Communion cannot be aptly (perhaps not even validly) celebrated without these trappings. But really we are not confined to this alternative. A manly man can deal manfully even with flummery. But are we then to conclude that the use of them is forbidden by the fact that the rubrics say nothing about them? That would be a rash conclusion, seeing that the rubrics also say nothing about a white linen cloth on the altar, and yet nothing is more certain than that this was expected and taken for granted. We cannot say, however, that in this instance the pall and veil and bourse were taken for granted, for when we read in a rubric after the communion that the consecrated elements which remain shall be covered with "a fair linen cloth" it is evident that by this new invention the traditional paraphernalia had been rendered superfluous. As no mention is made of covering the sacred vessels before this time, it may be assumed that they were not placed upon the Holy Table until the Offertory. Then, since the people were to be given the communion in both kinds, and since Calvin's ideal was cherished of making every communion as far as possible a corporate communion of the parish (which implied infrequent celebrations and justified the stern prohibition against celebrating unless a certain proportion of the people were ready to communicate), we can understand that besides the bread there would ordinarily be several chalices and flagons upon the altar which could not be covered by the traditional corporal and pall. Here we have one of the many ways in which Calvinism (rather than Lutheranism) influenced the Reformed Church of England. It was the custom of the Calvinistic Churches to cover with a large linen cloth the consecrated elements which remained after the Communion, to leave them thus covered upon the Holy Table until the people had been dismissed with the blessing—and then to treat them as if they were not consecrated. The English Reformers hesitated before this last step and ordained that even after the people had been dismissed the consecrated elements should be treated "as if" they were still the Body and Blood of the Lord, and that consequently the minister, instead of carrying them out of the church, should "reverently eat and drink the same," summoning other communicants to help him if necessary. Thus the "fair linen cloth," which still is a part of our equipment, though it has shrunk in size, is a vestige of the predominant Calvinistic influence upon the Church of England. But now we have gone back to the older custom and invariably are equipped with the pall and veil and bourse and corporal, which we are able to use in such a way that the fair linen cloth has become superfluous—unless the minister, having several chalices, etc., on the altar, is scrupulous in following the Calvinistic custom and will not cleanse them until the people have been dismissed with the blessing. (The blessing ought to be regarded as the dismissal of the people, for it takes the place of the *Ite, missa est.*) Among us this is still a controversial point. TARP I am told is an acrostic for: Take Ablutions Roman Place. It would serve quite as well for: Take Ablutions Reformed Place.

When the priest has received the alms and presented them, it is obviously seemly that he should take the ablutions (if there is anybody to give them to him), since he is about to begin the most solemn part of the Liturgy and to perform sacred acts in which his hands are necessarily employed. Surely no better words could be used at this point that the three verses from the twenty-sixth Psalm which the Roman rite prescribes:

> I will wash my hands in innocency, O Lord,
> And so will I go to thine altar,
> That I may show the voice of thanksgiving,
> And tell of all thy wondrous works.
> Lord, I have loved the habitation of thy house,
> And the place where thine honor dwelleth.

Only as a weak concession to our prevailing practice do I include the Offertory in the chapter which deals with the Mass of the Catechumens; for commonly the people who are not communicants leave the church *after* the Offertory. But though confessedly it is difficult now to know precisely where to draw the line, it is certain that Catholic feeling would prefer to include the Offertory in the Mass of the Faithful; and in the early Catholic Church it was required that *before* the people presumed to offer their gifts to God the deacon should announce: "Let the uninitiated depart." For he who cannot communicate in the Sacrament should not be allowed to communicate in the offering. This may seem to us very unbusinesslike, but it did not prove to be so in the early Church. The perception that only the gifts of the faithful are acceptable to God is obscured for us by the insistence with which the "every member canvass" is pressed upon us as the *articulus stantis cadentis ecclesiae;* for the aim of that economic measure is to constrain nominal "members" to pay down money as a dispensation from going to church.

5. MASS OF THE FAITHFUL

Again I admit that the line I draw here cannot be drawn clearly and consistently either in Anglican or in the Roman rite. In all the Eastern Liturgies the situation is far clearer, inasmuch as there the Creed is not said immediately after the Gospel.

There is room for the sermon before it, if a sermon is wanted. It is not said until the catechumens have been dismissed. With us it is different, and if we encourage outsiders to take part in the Offertory, it is only reasonable that they should be allowed to share the prayer in which their gifts are offered; and if there is any appropriate time for them to leave the church, it is after this prayer.

I have already remarked that the priest is not at liberty to introduce other prayers at this point. Even if in form or in content they were not discordant with the Liturgy, it would be inept to interject them between the Offertory and the prayer which expressly refers to the gifts, and moreover it would detract (alas, how often it does so) from the solemnity of the invitation, "Let us pray for the whole state of Christ's Church," which is the only expanded *Oremus* in our liturgy.

THE OREMUS

(Plate II)

In our Liturgy there are only two other occasions when the priest invites the people to pray: before the Collect of the Day, and before the thanksgiving after the Communion. On these two occasions he uses the simple formula, "Let us pray." In addressing this invitation to the people the priest of course turns towards them, extending and then joining his hands. He is standing then at the Epistle side, and he returns to his previous position facing the altar in the simplest way, without making a full turn, that is, having turned a half turn from left to right, he turns back from right to left. To the more formal *Oremus,* however, inviting the people to pray for the whole Church, there is added an appropriate solemnity when the priest, who now is standing before the middle of the altar, makes a full turn, as he should do also at the Benediction, and as the celebrant does in the Roman rite at the *Orate, fratres.* I can allege no compelling reason for doing this—but I can think of no reason for not doing it. Let us make the most of the one solemn *Oremus* we have in our Liturgy. In the Eastern Liturgies the deacon's exhortations to continue earnestly in prayer are frequent, and when we reflect upon the probability that many in the congregation may be at all times inattentive, and upon the dreadful possibility that at some moment no one in the church, not even the priest, may be really praying, such exhortations cannot seem superfluous.

Whenever the priest turns to the people and invites them to pray he is expected to raise and spread out his hands—*elevans et extendans manus* is the Roman phrase. What that means precisely some people may need to be told, for this is a gesture very observable to the people, and hence we ought to strive after some measure of uniformity. The direction that one is to lift up and spread out the hands is very indefinite. One may ask how high, how far, and not even an archaeologist can give a precise answer. Obviously we must avoid the characteristic Jewish gesture of deprecation, with hands spread out on either side of the head; but no less must we avoid the pagan attitude, with hands high upraised, as in the well-known bronze figure of the praying boy (Plate II, 3), one of the most beautiful creations of Classical art, a figure for which I feel a nostalgic love, for, alas, it is only children and pagans who can innocently pray in this fashion, with such exuberant *élan,* with such naive immediacy, calling Zeus *Pater* without any reflection, without the least suspicion that it might (as we now are reminded in our Liturgy) be an act of supreme boldness to address God as Father, and without a presentiment that certain of their own poets uttered a paradox when they said, "For we are also his offspring." I have often thought of referring to this statue as a perfect illustration of what Kierkegaard meant by "religion A." The adult Christian, though he too possesses immediacy ("the immediacy after reflection"), cannot forget that he is a sinner saved by grace, cannot even wish to forget the cross, to rid himself of its restraint and to ignore the fact that only as we are *praeceptis salutaribus moniti et divina institutione formati* dare we presume to say, Abba, Father. From the earliest days the Church has observed an attitude in prayer which is expressive of this sober restraint, and to this day it is preserved in the attitude or gesture of the celebrant at the Eucharist. The hands are not lifted high, the arms are not spread out broadly; with hands raised hardly higher than the shoulders the elbows touch the sides of the body.

Some of the earliest Christian writers (among them Tertullian, *De orat.* 14) remark upon the peculiarity of the Christian attitude in prayer, laying emphasis upon the fact that the hands are not merely lifted up but spread out, recalling the attitude in which Christ suffered. When St. Paul (1 Tim. 2:8) speaks of "lifting up holy hands" we are to understand him in the same sense. But what attitude exactly does this denote? The reference to the cross might readily suggest a broad extension of the arms—perhaps at a right angle with the body, as in Mexico a penitent may be seen to hold them as he kneels at confession. This subject, though it is anything but abstruse, is rather too complicated for tongue and pen, and therefore, to facilitate understanding, and perhaps to actuate consent more effectively than by a syllogism, I introduce a few little pictures—first of all the praying boy, and, as a contrast to that, an *orant* (Plate II, 4), the female figure in the attitude of prayer, which from the earliest times was a common symbol of the Church. I do not deny that the *orant* was frequently depicted with arms more broadly extended and hands more highly raised, for naturally the crude painters of the catacombs were in the earliest period very much influenced by pagan models, and it is possible that in the East this gesture was not used so soberly as in Rome; but there can be no doubt that the attitude here depicted faithfully reflects the prevailing Christian attitude in prayer. And to show how the analogy of the cross was understood I include here a picture of a fifth century carving on the wooden doors of Sta. Sabina in Rome (Plate II, 5), which is perhaps the earliest crucifix, though instead of depicting the crucifixion realistically it represents our Lord upon the cross in the attitude of prayer. "But if any man seemeth to be contentious" and would raise his hands higher or spread them out further, I can say as St. Paul said with regard to a matter of no more intrinsic importance, "we have no such custom, neither the Churches of God."

It goes without saying, one might think, that in addressing the people the priest must turn to *them*. But I have to put up with the sight of one Evangelical clergyman who turns to the people when he says, "Lord, have mercy," and turns away from them when he says, "Let us pray." Another more pronounced Evangelical will not fold his hands in prayer, but when he invites the people to pray raises his right hand on high, with a gesture which seems threatening because the fist is half clinched, but may be meant as a sort of benediction. Who can tell?

The priest folds his hands (i. e. places them palm to palm and holds them before his breast) as he turns to the altar, and of course everyone knows that it is the characteristic Christian custom (the only thing which distinguishes the Christian gesture from that of Buddhist monks) to place the thumbs in the form of the cross. He spreads his hands as he begins the prayer and folds them at the conclusion of each of the paragraphs into which the prayer is now divided. The most specific reason for dividing this prayer into paragraphs was to indicate the place for this gesture. Of course in praying God to accept the alms and oblations the priest is to indicate by an appropriate gesture that he is offering them.

But about so formal a matter as gesture I have perhaps said too much, and I shall not have much more to say at any other point. My bishop remarked to me lately that he was not zealous to tell his brethren what they ought to do in celebrating the Holy Communion. Neither am I (appearances to the contrary notwithstanding), but sometimes I am eager to tell them what they ought *not* to do. Many men are at a loss to know what to do with their hands, and it might be a kindness to tell them. For example I have seen "Evangelicals" who were ill at ease in Catholic vestments because they could not put their hands in their pockets—and therefore clapsed them behind their back, without reflecting how funny that must look when it rumples the chasuble. For people who are thus at a loss to know what to do with their hands it really might be a comfort to learn how they might occupy them by reading the instructions of the *Ritus servandus in celebratione Missae* which can be found in any missal. But far be it from me to advise this! I have an instinctive horror of meticulous scruple about ritual acts. And yet I cannot deny that parts of these instructions are excellent. The parts which strike me as most excellent are in the interest of godly celerity: *genuflectit et sine mora surgens;* and, "lest the priest by his prolixity should be annoying to the people" (*ne circum-*

stantibus sit morosus). I cannot even deny that as a whole these instructions are excellent, if it is an excellence to be as exact and complete and meticulous as the rules of a Buddhist monastery. But perhaps from a Christian point of view this is a defect. I could not wish to prescribe these rules, for I do not follow them meticulously, and though it is possible in the Church of Rome to exact such uniformity (since the rubrics simply register the customs which gradually have grown up), I am convinced that such petty precision cannot lead to uniformity among us but will only accentuate our differences.

As I am speaking here about ritual, I did not mean to introduce any criticism of the text of our Liturgy. I simply accept the prayers as they are prescribed. But when I note that the exponents of the "Liturgical Movement" in the Church of Rome feel free to criticize the Mass, with the hope that in time it may be improved, I am emboldened to mention here a couple of defects which must eventually be repaired. The first may seem hardly serious enough to mention, and yet to me it is an obstacle I cannot get over. It is the suffrage for "Christian" rulers. Why must I pray only for Christian Rulers? Peter and Paul exort us to pray for pagan rulers. And who are these Christian rulers? There are apparently very few of them today. Some of our rulers are Jews, and not many would profess themselves to be Christians. The illusion of "Christendom" is in our day pretty well exploded, at all events we cannot ignore the fact that in Europe as well as in Asia the fate of many many millions of people is in the hands of rulers who, if they are not openly hostile to Christianity, are frankly unwilling to practice it. The other defect is far more serious, because it seems to involve the common assumption that all the dear departed whom we remember lovingly in our prayers had been such exemplary Christians that we are bound to follow their examples. Alas, this is far from being the case. Kierkegaard remarks that in spite of the fact that all Protestant confessions of faith recognize various degrees of blessedness in heaven, one never hears a preacher refer to this fact—and yet there might be some young person ambitious of attaining a higher degree! Protestantism has been intent upon abolishing the distinction of the "counsels of perfection"—with the intent of leveling up, but with the consequence of leveling down and abolishing the invidious distinction implied in the word "saints." The last paragraph in the Prayer for the Whole State of Christ's Church is hardly prayable in its present form. At least it cannot be prayed without the disconcerting reflection that many whom we loved most, and of whom we may believe that they are saved by God's grace, did not leave us a conspicuous example of holy living. Doubtless many must feel instinctively impelled to insert almost unconsciously after "love and service" the clause which the Scottish Liturgy has expressly inserted: "And we yield thee most high praise and hearty thanks for the wonderful grace and virtue declared in all thy saints who have been the choice vessels of thy grace and the lights of the world in their several generations, beseeching thee," etc. And as for the modern American foible of stressing "service," rather than peace and rest, in the Kingdom of Heaven, does not this suggest a rather mistaken idea of heaven, one which certainly cannot be found in the New Testament, and perhaps was first suggested by Satan? For, according to Milton, it was Satan who affirmed, "Better to reign in hell than *serve* in heaven."

CONFESSION AND ABSOLUTION

It is notorious that in our Liturgy the Confession, being placed where it now is (or where it previously was), and being exacted expressly of "those who come to receive the Holy Communion," is an obstacle to non-communicating attendance, including the attendance of persons who already have made their communions at an earlier hour on the same day. This poses us with a dilemma. One horn of it is non-communicating attendance; the other is "non-communicating non-attendance." We are now pretty generally agreed which horn we must choose. For if the Eucharist is made the principal service on the Lord's Day, at which the congregation as a whole is expected to gather, there will be some who are not ready to communicate, and there will be others who have communicated earlier, perhaps because of a scruple about fasting communion. If we were realistic about it, we would require that no one should take part in this confession except those who are about to make their communions. The confession before the Mass is different, for in that place it is evidently a preparation for worship, as it is in our Morning and Evening Prayer. If the congregation were to join in the Confession at the beginning of the Mass, which now the priest seems to make alone with the server, there would be no need of another at this place.

I have not much to say here about how the priest is to comport himself. But mindful of what he ought not to do and often does, I would exhort him not to rise from his knees before he has quite finished the Confession—as if confession of sin were not altogether appropriate to him. And I would remark that to make a sweeping gesture such as is appropriate for a benediction is not appropriate when one is declaring an absolution. At all events it is not Catholic. The Roman priest contents himself with making an almost imperceptible sign of the cross, as though to intimate that the absolution applies to those who (unostentatiously) sign themselves.

Strangely enough, the Anglican absolution is distinctly sacerdotal, whereas the Roman absolution before the Mass is not. The authoritative character of the Anglican absolution is clearly evidenced by its form, which is more like a declaration than a prayer, and is so interpreted by the direction that the Bishop if he is present is to say it, whereas in the Roman rite, even if the Pope is present, the celebrant says it, and prays that the Pope may be absolved. Indeed the same prayer for absolution is made by the server in behalf of the priest, and the prayer which the priest alone utters begs for the absolution not of *your* sins but of "our sins." This is clearly more Evangelical than our formula. It is evident that the Reformed Church of England felt that a more authoritative absolution was required here because the priestly absolution following upon auricular confession had fallen into disuse. And yet obviously a more definite and consoling (i. e. an unhypothetical) absolution (like *Ego te absolvo*) could not be used except where there was a particular and personal confession of sins. But however authoritative our formula of absolution is, it is not appropriately accompanied by a laying on of hands, i. e. a gesture which imposes it like a benediction.

Lately I have often been obliged to assist, very unwillingly, at a celebration where a bishop, who knows better than the Prayer Book what ought to be done, is so doubtful of his authority as a minister of Christ that he will not pronounce the Absolution. By suppressing the "you," which is prescribed, and saying instead of it "us" ("pardon and deliver us") he makes it simply a prayer to God—but at the same time, very incongruously, he faces the people and makes a gesture (not prescribed by the Prayer Book) which clearly implies absolution.

The Comfortable Words which aptly follow the Absolution are of course Scriptural, in part they are the words of our Lord, and hence they are so comforting. Yet some may find additional comfort in the reflection that, though they are not taken from the Roman Mass, they are Catholic nevertheless, inasmuch as we owe them to the suggestion of Herrmann, Archbishop of Cologne.

THE EUCHARISTIC PRAYER

Preface and Canon

How the celebrant will comport himself in the performance of the most sacred part of the Liturgy depends upon how he has understood it, whether he understands that essentially it is a prayer he is uttering, not something he is accomplishing by his own human or sacerdotal power, that essentially it is nothing but a prayer, that essentially it is one prayer, although we can distinguish in it several parts, and that essentially, even though several petitions are interjected, it is a prayer of thanksgiving (*eucharistia*).

There is no place in the Liturgy where uniformity is more desirable, and no place, alas, where it is less likely to be achieved. It certainly will not be achieved by following the directions of the Roman rubrics, for by introducing an invocation (*Epiclesis*) after the manner of the Eastern Liturgies we have implicitly altered the conception of how and when the consecration is brought about, and thus have shifted the emphasis, shifted the place where the accent falls, so that even if we cannot be sure that it falls upon the Invocation, it certainly does not fall upon the Words of Institution. But not for this reason only are we restrained from following closely the Roman rubrics; for the great majority of us, and with us very many Roman Catholics, have in the course of a historical evolution come to feel that the great Eucharistic Prayer would be far more solemn and more numinous if the ritual acts of the celebrant were more simple and more restrained by awe, if he were really to behave as if God were doing all while he was doing nothing but pray. I shall remark subsequently upon other reasons for discarding the Roman rubrics as inapplicable to our Liturgy.

In view of the importance of a general agreement upon this subject, and mindful of the difficulty of attaining it, I make here a few observations which cannot be thought too serious and profound for a book like this, unless it be accounted a light and trivial matter "to know how men ought to behave in the house of God."

About the first point I have to urge, that is, about the wholeness of the Eucharistic Prayer, there is no controversy, there is no room for controversy, but unfortunately there is room for a great deal of misunderstanding. From the *Sursum corda* to the *Amen* we have *one* prayer, the Eucharistic Prayer *par excellence,* and as a *whole* it is the Prayer of Consecration. This is the Anaphora of the Eastern Liturgies. There the wholeness is perfectly plain, whereas in the Western rite it is obscured by the Proper Prefaces. Roman liturgists, however, are agreed that the introduction of the Proper Prefaces does not imply a break in the continuity of the prayer, although it interrupts the sequence in manuscripts or printed books and obliges one to distinguish sharply between the Canon (the invariable part of the prayer) and the Preface (which is in part variable). It is important to recognize that the Preface, though it may be regarded as a preface to the Canon, is not a preface to the great Eucharistic Prayer but is the beginning of it. It is not superfluous to call attention to this fact, seeing that the English Reformers were led so far astray by the way the missals were printed that they had no sense of the continuity of Preface and Canon, imagining that between them there was a great gap into which they might throw any new matter they cared to introduce—the Prayer of

Humble Access and so forth. We have only recently been delivered from the effects of this misunderstanding, and even now the misunderstanding still remains in the minds of many. Roman liturgists have taken more pains to clarify it than have we.

So far as concerns the mode of celebrating the Eucharist, the first inference to be drawn from the wholeness of the prayer is this, that the celebrant should pass from the Preface to the Canon without delay, without even the delay of fumbling to find the place. This again is not a superfluous admonition, since before the Canon we still have an antiquated rubric which suggests that the priest might for some time be appropriately employed at this point in arranging ("ordering") the bread and wine. Another implication is that the priest should not begin the so-called Canon in an inaudible voice (*secreto,* as late medieval custom prescribed) but should make evident the wholeness of the prayer by uttering it at this point in a voice not totally different from that which was used in the Preface, if the Preface was said. Certainly, if it were not for the interjection of the Proper Prefaces, which makes it seem as if the Canon were a completely separate entity, it could not occur to anyone that the thanksgiving for the salvation of the world ought to be less hearty than the thanksgiving for creation and providence—least of all in our Liturgy where the Canon, instead of beginning with *Te igitur,* begins (in spirit of the Greek liturgies) with "All glory be to thee, Almighty God," that is, with words which recall the conclusion of the Cherubic Hymn and the *Benedictus.*

About the Proper Prefaces I would say, by the way, that, though they are a peculiarity of the Western rite, Rome cannot be held responsible for them. On the contrary, the Church in Rome did all it could to restrain the exuberance of the Gallican practices which were fashionable in Merovingian times, preferred not only a special preface but a special liturgy for every Sunday and Holy Day. Rome ultimately succeeded in reducing the number of Proper Prefaces and in keeping the latter part of the prayer (the Canon) inalterable and sacrosanct. I cannot be altogether grateful for this triumph of sobriety, seeing that the fact of having one inalterable formula too readily suggests the notion of magic, and seeing also that the Greek

Church enjoys a certain advantage in using more than one liturgy.

The second theme I have in mind I approach with some diffidence; for of this I can by no means assert that it is pacific, although, were the discussion of it to conciliate some measure of agreement, this result would be irenical in the highest degree.

It has long been the Roman view that the consecration of the bread and wine is wrought by the recital of the Words of Institution. It hardly can be denied that this notion is close to magic. It is evident that it was not entertained at the time when the liturgies were formulated, for the use of the *ipsissima verba* is essential to magic, and it is a striking fact that the liturgies are very far from being meticulous in modeling the commemoration of the Last Supper in literal conformity to the accounts given by the Evangelists or by St. Paul. But this view was held by the English Reformers—in so far as they believed that any consecration was effected—and it has been held generally in the Anglican Church. At the time of the Reformation there was no other theory to compete with it. The Calvinistic Churches insisted, as they do to this day, upon the recitation of the Words of Institution, not perhaps as a means of consecration but as a form of legitimation, and not in the course of a prayer but as a Scripture lesson. Hence there was a superficial plausibility in the hope lately entertained that the Protestant Churches might unite with us on the basis of the Chicago-Lambeth Quadrilateral, which insisted upon "the unfailing use of the Words of Institution." Yet in the East no such emphasis was ever placed upon these words, notwithstanding that they were always commemorated in the course of the Eucharistic Prayer; and although all the Eastern Churches can boast of having an invocation of the Holy Spirit upon the gifts of bread and wine, they have not been commonly inclined to ascribe the consecration to this alone but rather to the prayer as a whole. At least this much can be said for the necessity of reciting the Words of Institution, that if the event of "the night in which he was betrayed" is not expressly commemorated in the Eucharistic Prayer, then the passion is not duly commemorated ("the passion," as Cyprian says, "is the sacrifice"), and the thanksgiving prayer has no pertinence to the Holy Communion.

After we had adopted the Invocation from the Scottish rite some were petty enough to argue that because the Roman rite (like the Reformed English rite) did not have so express an invocation, *ergo* the bread and wine were not duly consecrated. Strange contention! Strange misapprehension! Evidently it can be traced to the ambiguity of the Jewish and early Christian use of the word "blessing," whether it was the blessing of the bread at every common meal, or the blessing of the bread and wine at the Holy Communion. At the common meal God was thanked (blessed), and *thereby* the meal was blessed. The formula was not, "Bless, O God, this food," but "Blessed be thou, O God, who givest us this food." It is notorious that in the various accounts of the feeding of the multitude and of the Last Supper the words "bless" (*eulogein*) and "give thanks" (*eucharistein*) are used interchangeably, the choice of one or the other being determined by the desire to emphasize either the effect or the form. In effect the physical objects were blessed, in form it was God who was blest, that is, thanked. Whether in the little eucharist for our daily bread or in the great Eucharist for our supersubstantial bread (to use the translation of the Vulgate in Matt. 6:11), the form is thanksgiving, the effect is blessing. Hence the word *eucharistein,* which in the passive mood can properly be applied only to the person who is thanked, is occasionally applied to the object for which thanks are given to God. Thus in John 6:23 the bread miraculously multiplied is spoken of as "the eucharisticized bread," and in his greater *Apology* (c. 66) Justin Martyr speaks of the bread and wine as "eucharisticized" so as to become the Body and Blood of our Lord. If for us it requires a certain mental agility to straddle both these conceptions, or rather to pack them both in each of these words, *eulogein* and *eucharistein,* yet for the early Church this process of thought was so familiar that without fear of misunderstanding St. Paul could affirm (in 1 Tim. 4:3-5) that even food ceremonially unclean was "sanctified by the word of God and by prayer," that is, by the thanksgiving (blessing, grace) before meals.

Seeing that we have not commonly understood what the "blessing" at meals is (that in form and intent it is a thanksgiving to God for giving us the daily bread for which we constantly pray) and therefore are rarely gracious enough to give thanks for our food, but only pray God to bless it or to sanctify it and us, it is no wonder that we have misunderstood the greater Eucharist and imagine that besides giving God thanks for His inestimable benefit we must ask Him expressly to sanctify the holy meal. But according to the early Christian writers, and according to the earliest liturgies, the prayer of thanksgiving, the great Eucharistic Prayer, is the prayer of consecration, which properly contains (in the Preface) a remembrance (*anamnesis*) of God's goodness as Creator (who gives us the bread), and also of course a remembrance of the work of redemption he wrought for us through Jesus Christ our Lord, not omitting, of course, a remembrance of Christ's institution of the Sacrament.

Thus the Eucharistic Prayer contains a double memorial (*anamnesis*) of God as Creator and God as Redeemer—though for us unfortunately this distinction has been obscured by the Proper Prefaces, which dwell appropriately upon the Church seasons to which they are proper, but inappropriately introduce into the first part of the prayer an *anamnesis* of God's acts of redemption. The first part of the prayer, which in the Eastern Liturgies deals only with the thankful remembrance of God's works of creation and providence, including perhaps His signal acts of grace under the Old Covenant, culminates fitly in the exultant *Tersanctus*. The *Benedictus qui venit* affords a triumphant transition to the second part, which essentially is a thanksgiving for man's redemption through Christ, a grateful memorial, remembrance or commemoration (*anamnesis*) of his great works; but also an *anamnesis* of all the faithful in Christ, the living and the dead, which in the nature of the case must take the form of petition, and may properly include a petition (invocation) for the effectual reception of the Sacrament.

If this brief exposition of the intention of the Eucharistic Prayer is true in any measure, how is the celebrant to comport himself? All will agree in saying, With austere solemnity; for he acts in Christ's stead. Cyprian (*Epist.* 63, *de sacramento Dominici calicis*) earnestly insists upon the necessity of following the tradition of the Lord who was "the author and teacher of this sacrifice." "For you know," he says, "that we are admonished that in offering the chalice the Lord's tradition is to be followed, nor may anything be done by us but what for us the Lord first did. . . . For if our Lord and God is himself the High Priest of God the Father and first offered himself to the Father as a sacrifice and ordained that we should do this in remembrance of him, then that priest truly acts in Christ's stead (*vice Christi vere fungitur*) who imitates what Christ did, and he then offers a full and true sacrifice to God the Father when he so undertakes to offer as he sees that Christ offered. . . . And since we make mention of his passion in every sacrifice (for the passion of the Lord is the sacrifice), we ought to do nothing else but what he did."

What our Lord did was to look up to heaven (as all the early liturgies reasonably assume in analogy with the account of the feeding of the multitude), to take the bread into his hands (and after that the cup), to give thanks, and then to break the bread and distribute it, and after that the cup. We may be sure that in giving thanks at the Last Supper our Lord uttered the customary blessing at meals, regarding the material food, the bread and wine, as an instance of God's fatherly goodness. This too we must do, and we do it in the Preface; but in doing as Christ did we cannot be unmindful of what he did, and that we remember in the second part of the prayer. For the rest, the priest may well be fearful of doing more than Christ did.

I have said something already about kissing—or rather *not* kissing the altar. This Christ did not do. Now I would say—and I say it diffidently because perhaps it expresses only my idiosyncrasy—that to make the sign of the cross upon the host or upon the chalice, or to make this sign with them, is to me abhorrent. Is it only I who shrink from gilding the lily? Can it be imagined that any of the Apostles felt so insecure about the effectual consecration of the bread and wine that they had to stretch out a finger . . . as it were to support the Ark? Can this be what Christ did? There is no hint in the early Christian writers that such a thing was done in their time. Is not this essentially Baroque, even if it can be ascribed to the Middle Ages? At all events, far be it from me to prescribe it. Neither do I prescribe that when he begins the Canon the priest should lift up his eyes to heaven. This heavenly glance is so natural to priests that they may rather need to be admonished by the Roman rubric to cast their glance down again "at once." Our own rubrics prescribe what must be done, and though they need not perhaps be understood to exclude every other act, it is certain that the more closely we adhere to them, the more hope there is of attaining uniformity. The priest is told that in uttering the words, "he took the bread," he too is to take the paten into his hands (with the implication, of course, that the bread is on it); that in uttering the words, "he brake it," he too is to break it (and this he must do, although we all know someone has blundered, since the Lord did not break the bread till he had finished the blessing); in uttering the words, "this is my Body," he is to lay his hands on all the bread (very properly, for even though this be not necessary for consecration, it is important as indicating the priest's intention); in uttering the words, "he took the cup," he is to take the cup into his hands; and at the words, "this is my blood," he is to lay his hands upon every vessel in which there is any wine to be consecrated. I have repeated exactly the words of our rubrics, and this is all we are expressly told to do with our hands. Yet it may be understood as a matter of course that if the priest is ever to spread out his hands and again join them as he prays, he is to do so here. And I think that there can be no controversy that here he is to hold his hands spread out during the whole of the prayer, except when they are employed in the manual acts above described, with the understanding that at the end of each paragraph into which the prayer is divided by the printer, and of the three paragraphs of the last section, which are logically distinct but not distinguished by the printer, he is to join his hands. Also that at the end when the people respond with the Amen which appropriates this as their prayer, the solemn Amen which is emphasized by Justin Martyr, the priest is to break the bread (this being the place where the *fractio panis* comes in all the other liturgies), and, if he will, make a genuflection.

I know very well that many priests will wish to do more—and will do it. I may as well confess that I do too. Yet I cannot recommend that others should do as I do—so long as it seems to me illogical to do it. For it seems to me illogical to follow the Roman practice of making a genuflection at the Words of Institution and of elevating the host *then* for the veneration of the people, seeing that the presence of the Invocation in our Liturgy implies that the bread and wine were not consecrated before it was uttered. According to my view as exposed above, the only logical place to demonstrate reverence for the Sacrament is at the conclusion of the whole prayer. Nevertheless I do as the Romans do, because when I ministered for many years in Rome I was unwilling to seem to differ upon a point which I could not regard as essential, and because I do not now like to differ on mere questions of attitude and gesture from the priests with whom I commonly worship. For all that, and in spite of the immense prestige of the Church of Rome, I cannot believe it possible that all could be brought to unite in this practice, and I cannot wish that a practice so illogical and so contrary to the practice of the Eastern Churches should become more common among us. And that all the more because the liturgical reformers in the Church of Rome are disquieted by this emphasis upon the Words of Institution, recognizing as they do that the prayer of thanksgiving as a whole is the act of consecration. We ought to remember that the Elevation was not heard of before the last years of the twelfth century and did not become common until the thirteenth—and this of course involved the genuflections and the ringing of a bell at this point. It was evidently a polemical accent upon the doctrine of transubstantiation at the moment when it was most hotly contested. A practice which for more than a millennium was unknown in the West and is still not practiced in the East cannot be called Catholic in the broader sense. We must rethink our practice in this respect, must reflect whether it is reasonable for the sake of conformity with Rome to place the emphasis (whether by elevation or by genuflection) at a point where in our Liturgy it obviously does not belong. And we have the more reason to hesitate in view of the fact that in the Church of Rome, in spite of serious efforts to stem the tide, the Elevation, not the Communion, has come to be regarded popularly as the culmination of the Mass, and the mere sight of the Host as an efficacious sacrament.

Another thing which the Roman rubrics prescribe, and which many of our priests do, I do not do. In reciting the commemoration of the Last Supper and pronouncing the Words of Institution I do not lean over the Table and rest my elbows upon it. I was taught as a child that such an attitude is unseemly at table, and as a man I have learned to feel abhorrence for all hocus-pocus or even the appearance of it. Even those who in spite of the existence of our Invocation persist in regarding the repetition of the Words of Institution as the moment of consecration might well be fearful of giving the people an impression that the consecration is effected magically, by an incantation. They might well remember that it was not scoffing Protestants but offended Catholics who long before the Reformation tellingly satirized the performance of the priest and his magical pronunciation of HOC EST CORPUS by calling it hocus-pocus. If the priest is addressing God, and if this part of the prayer is essentially a commemoration (*anamnesis*) of God's work in the redemption of the world through Jesus Christ, in exactly the same way that the Preface is a commemoration of his goodness in creation and providence, then this part of the prayer of thanksgiving is not to be uttered in a tone totally different from the rest, although the commemoration of Christ's passion is not a lyrical theme, and therefore is not composed "with pomp of words" (as Justin Martyr expresses it) nor concluded with an exultant hymn.

In this book I say next to nothing about pronunciation and rhetorical stress—not because little need be said, but because I am fearful of saying too much. At this point, however, I am prompted to remark that the celebrant who desires to "do as the Lord did" will not recite the words of institution with an emphasis which Christ certainly did not use. There are but four words in each phrase, and it is certain that when they were uttered for the first time the emphasis must have been upon the last words, "body" and "blood," and that, if there was any subordinate stress, it must have fallen upon the word "this." No one had yet exclaimed incredulously, "How can this man give us his flesh to eat?" the dogma of transubstantiation had not yet been defined . . . nor denied, and therefore it would have been inappropriate to lay stress upon the substantive verb and say, as some now do, "This *is* my body." And although now we have behind us a long history of controversy, it is not edifying to be reminded of it when we come together in faith to partake of the Sacrament. The "*is*," positive as it sounds, implies a negation, and the more emphatically it is stressed, the more unpleasantly it reminds us of the miracle of Bolsena.

I am not unaware that the Church of Rome requires the "minister" to ring a little bell, and that many think it a pretty custom. To me it seems rather pretty, especially if it is not a clangorous or a jangling bell, and more especially if it is a bell rung in the belfry which can be heard outside the church, perhaps throughout the whole parish; and the fact that it is a late custom and one which might perhaps be called Baroque is not even to my antiquarian mind a sufficient reason for rejecting it. It is a serious consideration, however, that it lays a strong accent upon a point which we cannot in our Liturgy emphasize so strongly, if we attach any importance to the Invocation. There can be no doubt that the sacring-bell is commonly supposed to intimate to the people the moment of the miracle, the miracle of transubstantiation. But if we take seriously the Invocation of the Holy Spirit, if we conceive that what is wrought upon the bread and wine is not in the strictest sense a miracle, but has the effect of spiritualizing (pneumatizing) these "eucharisticized" elements, i.e. of making them spiritually potent, so that those who duly receive them are made partakers of Christ's most blessed Body and Blood (I use the words of our Liturgy, which are satisfactory to me), then we must be prepared to conceive that, like the kingdom of heaven, the Spirit of God "cometh not with observation." But this bell is also called the sanctus-bell, and is rightly so called, for the Roman ritual prescribes that it shall be rung also at the Sanctus. In fact it is commonly used at several other points, where it is not prescribed. Therefore it need not be regarded simply as an intimation that the sacring had taken place. Hence it might not be inconsistent for us to use it as a pretty embellishment. But is it in fact used because it is pretty, and not rather because it is done by Rome? But really it is not very prettily done by Rome, for it serves chiefly to notify a congregation unacquainted with the language of the Roman Liturgy what point in the Mass the priest has reached. Indeed in the Eternal City the most practical use of it seems to be to notify the people who are standing (as most of them are) at what moments they ought to kneel. It can be of no such use to us.

At this point I may say incidentally something about the use of incense in the church. I may say that I like it, because it is really pretty, and because the sense of smell more vividly than any other recalls associations. It is well that we should have in connection with the church building potent associations, reminding us that *there* it is we hear proclaimed the mysteries of the Gospel, that although these truths are true outside the church and in the whole world, yet it is there they belong, there they came to us by revelation. I have often wondered that the Calvinistic branch of Protestantism did not yield to the temptation of using incense, the symbol of the prayers of the Church, as it was used in the Temple at Jerusalem. And indeed the Irvingites, a sect from the Scottish Church, did succumb to this temptation. For the Reformed theologians were diligent in proving that their common worship was modelled after the worship of the Synagogue, and just because they had no sacrificial cult they fairly revelled in the sacrificial symbolism of Old Testament ritual. They alone have made a serious study of it. The early Catholic Church was clearly exposed to this temptation, for the worship in heaven as it is depicted in the book of Revelation furnished the favorite themes for the apsidal decoration of the early churches and colored the language of the liturgies. But the early Catholic Church resisted this temptation. Incense was too closely associated with paganism. It therefore did not creep into the liturgical use of the Church until the Middle Ages. Literally it "crept in," and it is interesting to recall how. In fig. 8, which is a fresco dating from the very last years of the eleventh century, we see censers swung, and one might suppose that they accompanied the Mass. But no, this picture represents the translation of St. Clement, and the clergy are censing his body. Incense was commonly used by the Romans in funeral processions, for very practical reasons, and the Church had less scruple about adopting this custom because it was primarily not religious but hygienic. When the bodies of the saints were buried under the altars, the altar was censed as any tomb would be. But this was not till the Middle Ages; and in view of this history the use of incense in the church is perhaps not so pretty a custom after all, at all events it is far from being a compelling precedent.

Incense and the sacring-bell have drawn me so deep into the Middle Ages that, although I had no intention of speaking specifically about the inventions of that period, I may as well say something in passing about the bishop's mitre and the priest's biretta. It is notorious that in Classical times Greek and Roman men wore no hats, any more than the Japanese do, unless as fishermen, etc., they were much exposed to the sun. Hence hats were not a part of the ecclesiastical dress before the Middle Ages. For inclement weather everybody had the protection of the hood attached to the *paenula* and the cope. The biretta, as the name implies, was originally a small cape, the *birrus*. Something like the mitre is still worn by old women in some parts of the Alps. I would speak indulgently of the use of the mitre, for without it a bishop who wears Eucharistic vestments has nothing to distinguish him—and certainly he ought to be distinguished. For the biretta I can think of nothing good to say. It is only worn by us to ape the Roman priesthood, and for the Roman priests it is a solecism and an anachronism in a place and in an age when the churches are well heated in the coldest weather. In many parts of Europe there is still no provision for heating the churches, and there it may be useful as a protection against the cold, as it was everywhere in the Middle Ages. When Anglican priests wear the biretta, it may be taken as an almost infallible sign, not of a genuine sympathy for the sober traditions of the Church of Rome, but of a hankering after the Baroque Catholicism which characterized the Counter Reformation, of which the Jesuits were the principal exponents. But to call this kind of churchmanship Baroque is a euphemism, for it is notorious that what it produced was the Rococo, both in thought and expression. In clerical heads covered by the biretta a fantastic way of thinking was hatched which found an apt expression in Rococo art. In the late sixteenth century, the age of the Baroque, the biretta in its modern shape, the *tricorno,* was not yet worn.

The use of the biretta, though it does not always indicate a "spike," may be taken as an infallible indication that the man who wears it would like you to address him as Father. This filial mode of address seemed so natural in the Greek Church that every priest is there called Papa or Pope; but in the West this title has been limited traditionally to the Holy Father, the Papa or Pope of Rome, and only monks are addressed as Padre or Father. In Italy the secular priests, though of course they are celibates, as not many of our so-called "fathers" are, are addressed as Don (short for *Dominus*) or as *Reverendo* Rossi, for example —corresponding exactly to the term Reverend Jones which is common among us, and which to every finely fibered soul seems vulgar. Having lived for twenty-five years in Rome, I cannot easily accommodate myself to the endearing Irish practice of addressing every parish priest as Father. The fact that this was never an Anglican practice, not even before the Reformation, does not recommend it to me; and the invidious implication that it is a proud distinction which not every minister of Christ can boast, at least not Protestant pastors, raises a serious objection against it, both from the moral side and from the ecumenical.

With this I have said all I am disposed to say about the Canon, but much remains to be said about the Preface.

Our Preface begins with the *Sursum corda.* It would obviously be much more graceful if this were introduced by the reciprocal greeting: The Lord be with you. *And with thy spirit.* Some such transition is evidently needed after the Comfortable Words. The fact that our revisers timidly introduced in *one* place this greeting which is so frequently exchanged by priest and people in all the liturgies may be taken as an encouragement to use it more often, and no place is more appropriate than here.

At this point, as I hinted before, the Roman rubrics are clearly inapplicable to our Liturgy. But at this point they are also inconsistent with themselves. Contrary to the general rule that the priest is to turn to the people when he greets them with, "The Lord be with you," he is here expected to face the altar and remain in this position when he says the *Sursum corda,* etc. The fact that the Preface is commonly sung and that the music for it can be seen on the altar is hardly a sufficient reason for addressing the people without turning to them. At all events this position is impossible for us, even if it were desirable; for as the priest is expressly instructed to turn to the people when he pronounces the absolution, he must obviously remain in this position when he repeats the Comfortable Words, and after that, as the rubric directs, he "shall proceed, saying, 'Lift up your hearts.'" That he is expected to face the people until he is about to say, "It is meet and right," is made abundantly plain by the rubric which enjoins that he "shall *then* turn to the Holy Table." Any one therefore who follows the Roman rubrics at this point must know that he acts in defiance of our rubrics, and hence that he is not following a maxim which could or should be universal in our Church. Moreover our version, "Lift up your hearts," is more unequivocally a direct address to the people than is *Sursum corda,* and gives us therefore no pretext for turning away from the people. But the circumstance that the priest faces the people instead of the altar does not in the least diminish the pertinence of the gesture prescribed at this point by the *Ordo Romanus,* which differs from that used for the more common salutations for the fact that the hands are not spread out but are held parallel to one another, as though to lift something up, and are finally raised higher, even higher than the shoulders. It is appropriate that a special gesture should emphasize the unique character of this invitation. The hands are to be held thus until the priest joins them in turning to the altar with a profound reverence to begin the *Tersanctus.*

Universally we are accustomed to sing the *Tersanctus* when there is a choir or a group that can sing this most ancient hymn of the Church. More rarely is the Preface sung—perhaps because many priests can't sing. And yet that the Preface be sung, or at least the *Sursum corda,* is hardly less important, though it is of course unseemly for the choir to sing the responses when the priest can only manage to *say* his part.

I have remarked that in the Roman rite the priest says before the *Sursum corda* "The Lord be with you," and the people make the customary response, and that inasmuch as our revisers have lately permitted us to use this traditional greeting before the Collect of the Day, that is to say, at the beginning of the Mass of the Catechumens, we may perhaps regard this as a general commendation which would justify us in using it here where it is equally in place at the beginning of the Mass of the Faithful. I cannot but reflect that the Greek Liturgies have a more solemn blessing at this place: "The grace of our Lord Jesus Christ, the love of God the Father, and the communion of the Holy Ghost, be with you all," to which the people respond with, "And with thy spirit." The fact that the brief Roman blessing was (almost by an inadvertence) not prescribed here may perhaps leave us free to use the more solemn form of the Greek Liturgies.

There can hardly be any question that after the *Tersanctus* we are permitted to sing or say the *Benedictus qui venit* which is found in all the liturgies except the early Egyptian. For when it was not adopted by the House of Bishops, though there was a majority in favor of it, it was perfectly well understood that the use of it was not prohibited. At the time of that discussion I reflected that there would have been less opposition to this hymn, which is common to all Christian liturgies, if friends and enemies had not stressed the point that this hymn indicates the moment when Christ is about to come to the altar. That is in a sense true enough; but, as I pointed out above, the chief reason for singing this hymn here is to herald the prayer of thanksgiving for God's redemptive work in Christ Jesus. At an earlier time when this hymn was first sung it expressed the glad expectation of Christ's second coming, as did the *Maranatha* in the *Didache*. Except for this hymn the only trace left in our Liturgy of the eschatological expectation is in the words, "until his coming again," which like an erratic boulder is deposited in the Canon.

The eschatological significance of this sacrament (and of the Last Supper, and of the feeding of the multitude) is definitely emphasized, in the sixth chapter of St. John's Gospel, by the repeated affirmation, "and I will raise him up at the last day"—and this by an author who was inclined to supplant the eschatological term "kingdom of God" by "eternal life," and who prompted St. Ignatius to describe this sacrament as "the drug of immortality, the antidote of death." The eschatological implication of the Holy Communion cannot be entirely ignored without leaving the faith in immortality hanging in the air, either as the "good wager" of an idealistic philosophy, or as a superstition. For this reason it is important to retain the *Benedictus qui venit,* which is so evidently Messianic and eschatological in the reports of all four Gospels and is so pointedly insisted upon in our Lord's own word, "I say unto you, Ye shall not see me henceforth till ye shall say, Blessed is he that cometh in the name of the Lord."

From the fact that this hymn is permitted but not prescribed we might perhaps suck some advantage, the advantage of being free to sing it as the Greeks do, in a way which corresponds more closely with the accounts in all the Gospels:

Hosanna in the highest!
Blessed is he that cometh in the name of the Lord.
Hosanna in the highest!

The first hosanna knits it closely to the last words of the *Tersanctus.*

Before the *Benedictus qui venit,* although it comes immediately after the *Sanctus,* in the sense that no *words* intervene, there ought nevertheless to be a pause, for the *Sanctus* concludes the first part of the Eucharistic prayer, and the *Benedictus* begins the second part. If it is said by the priest or sung by the choir in one breath with the *Sanctus* (as if it were a part of it, which it clearly is not), the appropriateness of this hymn will not be appreciated, and therefore it hardly will commend itself to the people generally. This last is an important consideration when with us the *Benedictus* is as it were still on trial and probation.

THE LORD'S PRAYER

I notice that lately Roman liturgical authorities are inclined to regard the Lord's Prayer as a part of the preparation for communion—in spite of the fact that in the Roman rite (as in ours) it seems to be inseparably attached to the Canon and, except for the last petition, is said by the priest alone (which is a peculiarity of the Roman rite). Roman liturgical authorities are doubtless impressed by the fact that in the Eastern Liturgies the Lord's Prayer is distinctly separated from the Canon and exalted as a substantial component of the Eucharist by the long prayer which introduces it and by the embolismos which follows it and embroiders not inelegantly the last two petitions. But though this clearly separates it from the Canon, it does not clearly bring it into relation with the preparation; it presents it rather as a separate entity, and so I regard it here.

It is generally believed that the old Roman Liturgy, like the Clementine, made no use of the Lord's Prayer until the time of Gregory the Great, who, being impressed by the fact that the Greek Liturgies had it, and understanding a well-known affirmation of Justin Martyr's ("the food is eucharisticized by the word which comes from Him and by prayer") to mean that the "Lord's Prayer" was essential to the consecration, introduced it as the conclusion of the Canon and quite consistently ascribed it to the celebrant. Thus to the same Gregory who sent St. Augustine to convert England we owe it that in the Anglican Liturgy the Lord's Prayer now comes at this place, though with us it is said by the people and so cannot be regarded as the conclusion of the consecration. This at all events is a more appropriate place than where we used to have it, after the Communion, where no other Catholic Church says it. The analogy of the Greek Liturgies shows that it is independent of the Canon, but we cannot now separate it—nor do we need to. We cannot even make a noticeable pause after the great *Amen,* for we must say, "And *now,* as our Saviour Christ etc." But we should say this "now" and the rest of the sentence with an emphasis which solemnly introduces the Prayer which our Lord taught us, when he encouraged us to say "Our Father" ("my Father and your Father"), not as a trivial commonplace but as the incredibly bold claim of the "spirit of adoption." Thus introduced, the Lord's Prayer is introduced with sufficient solemnity. I could wish that we had also the embolismos to round it off, as every liturgy but the Byzantine has. But at least in place of that we have a pause while the priest is about to kneel down at the Lord's Table to say the Prayer of Humble

Access, which is the beginning of the Preparation for Communion.

The recitation of the Lord's Prayer will appear the more significant in this place when it is known that it was first rounded into a prayer by liturgical use. For it seems pretty certain that the brief instruction *how* to pray which we have in St. Luke's Gospel is what our Lord taught his disciples. St. Matthew's text expands "Father" into "Our Father who art in heaven," rounds out the first two petitions by adding a third, "Thy will be done," creates several rhythmic parallelisms which are not observable in English, and as a pendant to "Bring us not into temptation" has "But deliver us from the evil one." It is evident from this that our Lord's laconic instruction was gradually rounded into a liturgical form by use in the Liturgy, until the doxology which is so familiar to us was finally formulated, but formulated too late to affect the original text of St. Matthew's Gospel. It is noteworthy that the last petition is still treated in all the ancient liturgies as if it were an addendum, being recited by the priest alone in the Eastern Churches and by the people alone in the Roman Church, and in both cases artfully embroidered, as I have said, by the priest.

I have nothing to say about *how* the Lord's Prayer is to be said, except that the priest is here to join his hands, and might well be more careful than priests ordinarily are to divide the clauses precisely where the capitalization suggests, so that the people may repeat the prayer with him in unison—as also he ought to do, and seldom does, when he leads the people in the Confession.

PREPARATION

The only preparation immediately before the Communion which our book prescribes is the Prayer of Humble Access. The rubric requires that it must "then" be said, that is, immediately after the Lord's Prayer. There is thus no place for the *Agnus Dei* before this prayer. The only reason why we might prefer to put it before is the fact that in the Roman Mass it comes before the *Domine, non sum dignus*. But this is far from being a compelling reason, and on the other hand we are not only permitted but graciously invited to say or sing the *Agnus Dei* after the Prayer of Humble Access, where the rubric says, "Here may be sung a hymn." It is not "inconvenient" (in either sense of the word) that the priest, who has been kneeling to say the Prayer of Humble Access, should continue to kneel for the *Agnus Dei,* or at least for so long as it may take him to *say* it for his own account. On the other hand there is a great convenience in singing it at this place, so that while it is being sung the priest may make his own communion and communicate those about the altar. When I urge "godly celerity" I am very far from advocating haste in uttering the prayers of the Liturgy. I would utter them more deliberately than most men do, but I would save time where others waste it.

The *Agnus Dei* cannot be so highly recommended as the *Benedictus qui venit,* either on the score of antiquity or catholicity; for it is not used at this place in the Eastern Liturgies and was introduced into the Roman at the end of the seventh century by Pope Sergius I, who decreed that it should be sung by choir and people during the *Fractio panis.* Pope Sergius was involved in a hot controversy with the Eastern bishops, who, among other iconoclastic decrees, prohibited the symbolical representation of the Saviour under the form of a lamb, the symbol which from the earliest times had been dear to the Romans. Pope Sergius responded not only by introducing the new hymn into the Mass but more strikingly by depicting on the façade of the Basilica of St. Peter the Lamb of God, in place of the figure of Christ, the work of Leo the Great, which had been destroyed by time. This is in part a digression to which I was tempted by the interest of an archaeological discovery due to Padre Grisar, which he has registered in his *Analecta Romana,* XI.

THE COMMUNION

In the Eastern Liturgies the Elevation of the Sacrament is made at the moment of inviting the people to partake of the Holy Communion. It is done solemnly, both by word and gesture. While the deacon bids them "draw near," the priest, holding up before their eyes the chalice and the paten, encourages them by saying, "Holy things to holy persons," and the people respond, "One Holy, one Lord, Jesus Christ." In the Roman rite the priest announces: "Behold the Lamb of God who taketh away the sins of the world." We surely are not forbidden to say something at this place or to make at least a mute elevation.

This elevation is appropriately made after the priest has made his communion and has communicated those about the altar. At least that is the moment when the people are invited to come. Although the people are instructed to kneel when they receive the communion, the priest is by Catholic custom not permitted to kneel. He may make a genuflection or a profound reverence after receiving the Sacrament in each kind, but to kneel he is not permitted; that would destroy his witness to an ancient practice which the celebrant at the altar alone maintains. The Roman Missal, like the English Missals before the Reformation, makes provision only for what the priest is to say when he makes his own communion: "The Body of our Lord Jesus Christ preserve my soul unto everlasting life," and likewise for the cup. It is a matter of course that in addressing himself the priest should say "my"—but how often I have heard a celebrant say "thy," having no other formula offered to him by our book but the one he is to use for the people.

Immediately after the Reformation, in 1549, the formula the priest was instructed to use in communicating the people was: "The Body of our Lord Jesus Christ which was given for thee preserve thy body and soul unto everlasting life," and for the cup, "the Blood of our Lord Jesus Christ which was shed for thee, etc." It is notorious that this formula was soon rejected because it was thought to imply that Christ was "in or under" the Bread and Wine, and in its place was put the unobjectionable formula: "Take and eat this in remembrance that Christ died for thee, and feed on him with thy heart [*not* thine 'art, as I hear some Virginia priests say it] by faith with thanksgiving," and the same formula which we have today for the cup. It was good statecraft on the part of Queen Elizabeth that in 1559 she united both formulas. But who can estimate how much time has been spent in the course of nearly four hundred years in pronouncing this long formula to every communicant! It is small comfort to us when the learned Dr. Blunt suggests that this difficulty can be remedied by having fewer communicants. It is for the sake of the communicants when they are many that the priest desires to abbreviate the formula. It is not to save his own breath. The tempo of our life in this generation prohibits such deliberateness as was tolerable a generation ago. Unquestionably we are obliged to use both formulas, although there is no longer any objection to the first. But surely we are not obliged to recite them both, or even the whole of every one of them, to every communicant. That every communicant should feel that the gift is given personally and individually to him, is most true, but this is sufficiently provided for when we say "thee" and "thy"—and all the more because the pronoun of the second person is now so rarely used that it is exceedingly emphatic. Alas, in most of our churches there is only one priest—and, thank God, the communicants are multiplying. The single pastor must do what he can. The shortest formula ("the Body of our Lord Jesus Christ," "The Blood of our Lord Jesus Christ") is the most effective—or would be if we might use it. But I suspect that many of these men of God are inclined to magnify their office, are disposed to think that the Sacrament is made effectual to the communicants by what the priest says or does. The people are much in need of instruction, but they do not need to be instructed at this moment as to what the Sacrament is or what it may be expected to do for them—they come simply to receive it. And some priests seem to imply that the bread is not duly consecrated until they wave it with the sign of the cross before the eyes of each communicant. I am meek enough not to be angered by this, but I experience no additional edification, nor am I more truly fed.

It is an ancient custom and a good one, when the Communion lasts a long time, to encourage the people who are sitting in the church to rise and sing hymns. Only if the choir is in the chancel, it had better not be asked to lead them, since that would disturb the peace at the altar.

It is a practical observation, almost too practical, to say that the communicants had better be instructed to leave the altar and make room for others soon after they have received—to be more precise, as soon as the person next beyond them has received. I should think it unnecessary to say this if I had not heard the people instructed that the whole "rail-full" (hideous expression!) ought to leave at once.

In giving the communion to the people, the priest is instructed to give it "into their hands," that is, both the bread and the cup. The people are generally instructed to receive the bread in the open right hand and to support this, "like a throne," with the left. But what then about intinction? There are several ways of administering the Sacrament by intinction. There is no use considering the Greek way of putting both the wine and the bread in a spoon and thrusting it into each person's mouth—for that does not relieve our hygienic scruples. A few years ago when I returned to Rome for the winter it was a great sorrow to me that I could not communicate in the church where I had ministered for twenty-three years, because my successor had taken it into his head to use intinction. He carried precariously the chalice and the paten in one hand and intincted the wafers as he placed them on the tongue of each communicant. It is true that he offered to administer the Sacrament "in the old way" at the end of the service. If he had said in the "legal" way, I might perhaps have been meek enough to come up among the last, who evidently were regarded as "the weaker brethren." That has now been stopped in Rome, though not by the Bishop. Probably it is not done anywhere in the diocese where I now live, and certainly it is illegal: it is not giving the bread or the cup "into their hands." I am not squeamish about matters of hygiene, and yet I am in excellent health. I know, however, how sensitive Americans are on this subject, and I notice that not a few pious people find various ways of avoiding unobtrusively the danger of putting their lips to the common chalice. Probably something has to be done to relieve them. I can make no objection (it is not properly the priest's responsibility) if instead of consuming the host at once when it is given to them they hold it till the chalice is passed and then dip it in the wine. If such a custom should become very common in a parish, the Bishop must be asked to define what is to be done about it.

AFTER THE COMMUNION

Undeniably our liturgy culminates in the Communion, as do all the liturgies of the Eastern Church, and as the Roman Mass does not in its present form, since it has definitely placed the accent upon the consecration which is thought to be effected by the Words of Institution. The Roman Mass therefore is not glaringly inconsistent with itself when it goes on rather indefinitely and peters out slowly after the dismissal, the *Ite, missa est*—although this is emphatic enough to give the name to the Mass, and though to make it more emphatic it is sung, albeit nothing could be less lyrical than a dismissal expressed in these dry words, which does not even invite the people to "go in peace," as do the Greek Liturgies. One would think that this *must* be the end. But not at all; there is no definite end. One thing after another has been added, and yet there is no real ending. It was not always so with the Roman Mass; it once *ended* with the dismissal, and everything after the Communion hastened towards that end. Therefore even now the Roman priest, as soon as he has made his own communion, or it may be has communicated the people, hastens to consume what is left of the consecrated elements and to purify the sacred vessels. That is one of the things I would imitate. I am accustomed to "tarp," i.e. take the ablutions at the Roman place. For that is the natural place for it—in spite of the third of our General Rubrics, which bears evidence on the face of it that it was designed to put a stop to a disorder, or rather a sacrilege, with which we are not now seriously threatened. It is said quite justly that the second rubric after the Communion does not expect the priest to take the ablutions immediately, but it might rather be said that it does not expect him to take them at all, nor does it expect him at any time to purify the vessels. As late as 1887 the Privy Council in its judgment of the case of the Bishop of Lincoln decreed that it was unlawful to purify the chalice by pouring water and wine and consuming it. Because at the Reformation no provision was made for the ablutions immediately after the Communion it was natural for the disorders to occur which were dealt with later by the rubric referred to above.

But after "the fair linen cloth" and the Calvinistic rubric which enjoins it I have already said enough.

I must leave it to St. Vincent's Guild to instruct the server how he is to assist the priest at this point. It is very desirable that a uniform practice should be established. For my part, I cannot see the reason for the Roman rule that the server is to offer wine instead of water to purify the chalice and the two fingers of the priest which in the Jewish sense have become "defiled." To the priest I am fain to say, "My dear friend, this is the place where by pottering over the vessels and their appurtenances you can annoy the people more than by any of your other performances. Pray remember that you are not expected to polish the vessels or even to cleanse them, but only to 'purify' them ritually, and in doing this a certain degree of dexterity can be acquired by practice." This is a place where a hymn can often be used to distract the attention of the people from the manual acts of the priest. As the people are kneeling at this time, not every hymn is appropriate. The most appropriate is the *Nunc dimittis. O Saving Victim* is obviously not appropriate if the Sacrament is not reserved.

When the people have come to receive the Holy Communion and after making many prayers have received it, there is obviously nothing left to do but to give thanks and go. Nothing much can be added without detracting from the effect. The benediction by the priest (or by the bishop) is a misunderstanding, if it is not rather an impertinence, after the Holy Communion. The Eastern Liturgies have no such thing after the Communion, and it was introduced very tardily into the Roman Mass. After the Communion anything more than a prayer of thanksgiving (such as we have) and a word of dismissal (as our rubric understands the blessing of the priest to be) is superfluous, and in this place anything that is superfluous is bad.

Yet we have one thing more—the *Gloria in excelsis.* We can well understand that the Reformers were moved to place this hymn here (instead of at the beginning of the Mass, where it had previously been used) by the consideration that the Last Supper ended with a hymn—and this hymn is in fact so ancient that it might perhaps have been sung by the Apostles. Because of my veneration for this hymn I am sorry it was placed here, where perhaps because of an obscure feeling that it is inappropriate so many are prompted to omit it that it is in danger of falling into disuse. It is a hardship that it cannot ordinarily be sung where there is no choir, and it was not written to be *said.* The rubric permits us to omit it, or rather to use instead of it some "proper" hymn. But there's the rub, for really there is no proper hymn for this place. The most improper hymns are those which hail Christ upon the altar at a moment when no particle of the consecrated bread and wine remains there (in case the priest has tarped), and of course these are the hymns usually chosen. Perhaps the most innocent choice is the doxology of Bishop Ken's morning hymn.

But what seems to me too much, most of my brethren count too little. They would tuck in one or more or many "Post-Communion" collects before the Blessing. But this they do in part because, the people being on their feet during the *Gloria* or the hymn which is substituted for it, they must be invited to kneel for the Blessing, and the priest often can think of no other way of inviting them but to say, "Let us pray"—and then of course he has to make a little prayer. Some say more appropriately, "The Lord be with you," expecting the customary response; but at this place it would be still more appropriate to say, "Peace be with you." This salutation would put to no embarrassment even the people who are not familiar with it, for the response is the same as that they commonly use, and it would rescue from oblivion the ancient formula which is common enough in the Latin Church and universal in the Greek. Thereupon the priest (or the bishop) "shall let them depart" with the Benediction, looking at the cross while he gives the "Peace," and turning towards the people when he gives the "Blessing." In the gesture of benediction the priest not only raises his right hand but extends it towards the people, making the sign of the cross once only. The position of the fingers is different in East and West. Originally the gestures of benediction were the common gestures of oratory among peoples who then as now were voluble even with their hands. The position with thumb and first two fingers outstretched was preferred in the Western Church because it suggested the Trinity. There is surely no good reason why we might not use it today after it has been in use for more than fifteen hundred years. But in this gesture the essential thing (if there can be anything essential about a gesture) is that the right hand should be *extended over* the people. For the benediction is an instance of "the laying on of hands." In confirmation and ordination this is a tactual imposition, and so it should be also when a single person is blessed. Although the priest cannot touch each member of the congregation when he pronounces the benediction, his gesture should indicate the intention of imposing a blessing upon them. Alas, only too commonly we thoughtlessly follow a modern Roman abuse and, instead of calling down a blessing *upon* the people, many merely make the sign of the cross *at* them. One might do that just as effectively with the left hand. The Christian apprehension that with the right hand a fuller blessing is bestowed derives from a very early conception in Israel, and this makes it superfluous to raise both hands in benediction, as some Protestant ministers do.

With this the priest leaves the altar, everything is over, and the people too are free to leave, unless they prefer to stay until the server has expeditiously extinguished the altar lights. So one might think. But, no! The priest goes to the Gospel side and reads part of the first chapter of St. John's Gospel in an inaudible voice. Thereupon, in the Roman Church, the priest divests himself of the chasuble, perhaps puts on a cope or something, kneels below the altar and begins a litany—in which the people join with the more fervor because they have for a long while been perfectly passive, hearing little and understanding less. And the Anglican priest, what does he do? He has not gone far from the altar, not far enough to be out of earshot, when he says in a loud voice, evidently meant for the congregation, a prayer which perhaps might be appropriate in the sacristy or in the choirroom. Then he hurries out to shake hands with everybody.

Everything the priest does in the church after the people have been dismissed with the Blessing is too much. Having described other practices as Baroque (without meaning to disparage them greatly), I would stigmatize all these things as Rococo. The Rococo in art is characterized by the fact that it knows not where to stop. It adds one gaud to another, all of them perhaps pretty in themselves, but having no relevance to the whole. It is like the *chinoiserie* made in Europe without an inkling of the golden mean of Mencius. A Louis-Quinze ornament may be quite pretty on the mantelpiece, but Louis-Quinze behavior at the altar . . . is another thing.

With this then I have said all I would say about the celebration of the Eucharist? By no means! I have said only what I can say. For who can say what most needs to be said about the way of celebrating the Holy Communion?—with what profound reverence it must be done, with what fear and trembling before God, and therefore without any awe of men, with a voice which comes evidently from the heart, not from the lungs, devout but not unctuous, audible without effort, without haste and without delay, with just emphasis and correct diction, using diligently every art to enhance the power of speech, but without artificiality, without a trace in speech or action of cowed subservience to human training, like one who is fearful of forgetting his part. But who is sufficient for these things? Who even can be sure of reaching the ears of all without bellowing—when the church is large and the altar against the wall at the end of a deep chancel? Yet something can be done nevertheless. And I might perhaps venture to say to a very young priest, "My dear friend, know this, that if you hope to save souls, with God's help you may be able to do it . . . by worthily reciting the Liturgy, rather than by your most eloquent sermon."

EPILOGUE

What have we been doing here? Tithing mint, anise and cummin? Well, surely our Lord expected us to do that—and not to leave the weightier matters of the law undone. But, after all, is the proper performance of the Liturgy such a trivial matter? No, it is surely of the utmost importance, if Christians who now are divided are ever to be able to pray together, and, insofar as they are not divided, are to be able to unite, with a right comprehension of what they are doing, in the loftiest act of worship.

The leaders of "Liturgical Reform" in the Church of Rome are keenly aware that this name is an unfortunate one because of the petty meaning long associated with the word "liturgical." They mean, and I mean, reform in worship—and from no point of view can the worship of God be regarded as a trivial matter. Perhaps even the "technique of worship" (a phrase which is now much used by the Protestants) may have some claim to attention—but that is not a phrase I would be willing to use, and nothing of the sort can be found here. I am intent upon making our way of worship more profoundly real, as a bond of union, as an inspiration to good living, and as an incentive to work.

Father Gerald Eller, S.J., in his sprightly and well documented book on *Men at Work at Worship,* takes pains to point out how fine was the sense attached to the classical Greek word *liturgia* (work for the people) from which we derive our word liturgy, and how lofty a meaning it attained in the New Testament. Originally it signified a work or gift magnanimously contributed in the interest of public welfare. In the Septuagint, the Greek translation of the Old Testament, it was used of the sacrificial service in the Temple, where we translate it as "ministry"—as we do also when St. Paul uses it for the gifts made by the churches for the poor saints at Jerusalem, or for his own needs, and even when he uses it in a definitely priestly sense in Acts 13:2 and Rom. 15:16. But in the most exalted sense it was applied to Christ by the Epistle to the Hebrews (8:2, 6), where Christ is called a "liturgist of the true tabernacle, which the Lord pitched, not man. . . . Now He hath attained a liturgical office the more excellent, inasmuch, etc."

But it is not easy to rescue this word from its trivial connotations. At a gathering of clergymen who had come together to talk about liturgical matters (not under my leadership) one of the brethren threw a coldness over the meeting by a warm effusion of vague Evangelicanism which haltingly raised the question whether there might not perhaps be some incongruity between the picture of our Lord which the Gospels present to us (meaning the picture he had derived from the Gospels) and the discussion of liturgical details, especially in a time so earnest as the present (meaning this time of war when all serious people are thinking only how to kill and to destroy).

Well, yes . . . and no, emphatically, no. Such interests may be incongruous with the vague figure of Jesus which Modern Liberal Theology constructed, and which, after it had been sugar-coated by religious piety, Modern Evangelicanism ardently embraced. The worst thing about this Liberal Jesus is not what Albert Schweitzer affirmed of it, that such a figure never existed, but that, alas, it *does* exist in the imagination of multitudes of pious people, and now, when the Liberal Theology which created it is no more, this figure is still the object of sentimental devotion. How unlike is this figure ("His talk sweet toned and blessing all the time") to the majestic Christ depicted in the apsidal mosaics of the fourth century, enthroned in the midst of his Apostles and delivering to the world the New Law! How unlike the Pantocrator of the Byzantine mosaics, who holds the whole earth in the hollow of his hand! How unlike the tremendous figure of Michelangelo's Last Judgment! And how unlike the *Christus Rex*, reigning from the cross, which has again been brought to honor by Pope Pius XI!

Not only are these great symbols more worthy of Christ, but they reflect the Gospels more faithfully. And perhaps it may not be so incongruous with the Christ of the Gospels if we talk sometimes about the Divine Liturgy. For not only is he the great High Priest and Liturg of the heavenly Tabernacle, as the Epistle to the Hebrews represents him, but "in the days of His flesh," according to the Gospels, he showed as great an interest as did St. Paul in "how men ought to behave in the house of God, which is the Church of the living God"—though it is true that he spoke more trenchantly about how people ought *not* to behave, just as I have been doing here. No, Jesus was not "sweet toned and blessing all the time." In Jerusalem he made a whip of small cords and carried out in the Temple the most drastic liturgical reform. For that reason he was put to death. For already he had directed the most scathing satire against the piety of the Pharisees, and now, when he had dealt so rudely with the priests, he had made a clean sweep of all the official religion there was in Israel. Everybody was now against him. Hence he was promptly put to death—and therewith he inaugurated a new conception of sacrifice, both living sacrifices and dead sacrifices, and it hardly can be supposed that he is altogether indifferent how the memorial of his sacrifice is celebrated in the Church.

But, according to the Gospels, Jesus showed an interest in the most refined points of ritual—as, for example, when he said, "When thou bringest thy gift to the altar and there remembrest that thy brother hath aught against thee, leave there thy gift before the altar and go thy way: first be reconciled with thy brother, and then come and offer thy gift." Or when he depicted the heavenly glance of the Pharisee in the Temple—did it with such subtlety that it was merely implied in the statement that the publican "did *not* dare to lift up *his* eyes unto heaven." This heavenly glance, alas, is so natural to religious people. Jesus too "lifted up his eyes unto heaven" when he blessed the bread in the wilderness, and the Roman Canon assumes plausibly enough that he did so again when he blessed the bread at the Last Supper. Therefore, as the celebrant at the Eucharist is expected to do what the Lord did, it is prescribed that the priest too shall lift up his eyes. That is a liturgical refinement, but not an unreasonable one. Even more refined and more evidently reasonable is the rubrical instruction that he shall "at once" cast them down. That perhaps is the only instance where the priest, for a moment, is permitted to indulge in the heavenly glance. But, alas, as a preacher he does it only too often.

I might go on at some length to illustrate our Lord's interest in ritual and liturgical reform. But I will conclude here with the remark that the Christian minister, regarded simply in his capacity as a preacher, might be expected to devote all his time to the preparation of his sermons. Indeed he would be well employed in that. But he must not forget that he is also a pastor and perhaps must devote very much time to the personal care of his flock. And surely he must not forget that he is a priest. I do not lay special emphasis upon the sacerdotal implication of that title; I am thinking in this instance of the minister as the liturg, the leader of the people in worship. It is in this capacity preeminently he is formally distinguished from the flock. This is what a presbyter essentially is. It cannot therefore be thought incongruous with his office that he should be seriously employed, sometimes together with other presbyters, in considering how he may best lead the people in worship. In teaching them how to pray and leading them together in common prayer he will edify them more than by his sermons, or even his pastoral calls. The people perhaps need not engage in such studies; but they need to be instructed, and in my opinion the pastors have not been diligent enough in this matter; they often are uninstructed themselves, and it is very observable that the ministers who think liturgical questions unworthy of their attention make a mess of the Divine Liturgy, and are so far from helping the people to pray that they hinder them.

A SELECTED LIST OF BOOKS

1. Yngve Brilioth: *Eucharistic Faith and Practice, Evangelical and Catholic,* 1930. Swedish Lutheran.

2. Romano Guardini: *The Spirit of the Liturgy,* 1940. Roman Catholic.

3. D. H. Hislop: *Our Heritage in Christian Worship,* 1935. Scottish Presbyterian.

4. Gerald Ellard, S.J.: *Christian Life and Worship,* 1933. Roman Catholic.

5. The same author: *Men at Work at Worship,* 1940.

6. Scott F. Brenner: *The Way of Worship,* 1944. German Reformed (U.S.A.).

7. A. G. Hebert: *Liturgy and Society,* 1935. Anglican.

8. The same, as Editor: *The Parish Communion,* 1937.

9. N. Micklem, Editor: *Christian Worship,* 1936. Free Church.

10. R. F. Webber: *Studies in the Liturgy,* 1938. American Lutheran.

11. Henry de Candole: *The Sacraments of the Church,* chapters IX and X, 1935. Anglican.

12. The same author: *The Church's Offering.*

13. F. C. Burkitt: *Christian Worship.* Anglican.

14. F. C. Hicks: *The Fulness of Sacrifice,* part III, chapters II and III, 1930. Anglican.

15. F. Heiler: *The Spirit of Worship,* 1926. High Church Lutheran.

16. Rudolf Otto: *Religious Essays,* 1931. Lutheran.

17. Evelyn Underhill: *Worship,* 1936. Anglican.

18. W. P. Ladd: *Prayer Book Interleaves,* 1941. Anglican.

ABOUT VESTMENTS

J. Wilpert: *Die Gewandung der Christen in den ersten Jahrhunderten,* Cologne, 1898.

The same author: *Un capitolo di storia del vestiario,* in 2 parts, folio, Rome, 1909.

F. Braun: *Liturgische Gewandung,* Freiberg in B., 1907.

The same author: *Die Liturgische Paramenten,* Freiberg in B., 1924.

Articles by Dom H. Leclercq in Cabrol's *Dictionaire d'archéologie et de liturgie,* Paris, 1907-38.

A BIBLIOGRAPHICAL NOTE

I assented to the suggestion that it would be well to print here a select list of books which those who would pursue this subject might profitably read. But this meant that I must read some sixty recent books recommended by scholars whose counsel I had asked. Without reading them I could neither recommend nor discard them. It happens that my learning was limited to earlier authors. The result of this labor is a short list; for I mention only books which are available in English and discard works of major importance which deal only with the text of the early liturgies or with the doctrine of the Sacrament. Only because on the subject of ecclesiastical vestments there are no English works that have any importance, I mention the best that have been written in French, Italian and German.

For myself, of course, I got a good deal of instruction from reading so many books, many of them issued within the last decade; but all this learning was acquired too late to enhance the value of this volume. Perhaps my book would have been too ponderous, if I had known so much before I wrote it.

I single out the first nine works as the most important, and I call attention to the fact that, so far as concerns questions of liturgical form, they are practically unanimous, in spite of the fact that the authors are Lutherans, Scottish Presbyterians, German Reformed, Free Churchmen, Anglicans, and Roman Catholics. This demonstrates very clearly that the Liturgy, if only it is studied seriously by men of good will, is not now a subject for sectarian strife.

Because (for reasons beyond the author's control) this book is published six years after it was written, I have had to insert at the end of the list three books which deserve a higher place but which came out too late to furnish me with instruction. *The Shape of the Liturgy* by Dom Gregory Dix has been generally admired, and my only criticism is that, like this little book of mine, it has no shape. Professor Shepherd's book *The Living Liturgy,* along with the companion volume I have listed, is so much like mine, even with respect to shapelessness, that the Oxford Press which was publishing the one could not publish the other. This remark, coming from me, cannot be misunderstood as faint praise. Both Shepherd and I were embarrassed by the fact that we were dealing with occasional discourses which could not be welded into a harmonious whole without sacrificing something of the vigor they derived from being addressed to a particular audience on a special occasion. Alas E. Dix has died!

GLOSSARY

ABLUTION: of the priest's hands after the Offertory and after the Communion—when he also purifies the chalice.

AGNUS DEI: O Lamb of God, who takest away the sins of the world, etc., which is said or sung before the Communion.

ALB: a long tunic of wool or linen reaching to the feet and having long sleeves tightly fitted. It was commonly worn with a girdle. Although in the early years of the Empire it was accounted effeminate as used by males, it came to be regarded as more dignified than the short tunic. It was adorned by the *clavus*, a narrow stripe of a different color woven into the fabric with woolen thread and running from top to bottom over each shoulder. This was omitted when it became customary to wear a dalmatic or a pallium over the tunic, and it was transferred to the dalmatic.

AMICE: a medieval adjunct to the classical dress, i. e. a linen band which served somewhat like a collar to cover the neck, which was left bare by the other vestments. Except as it was preserved in ecclesiastical use, it degenerated into the stock and the white tie.

AMPHIBALUS: see CHASUBLE.

ANAMNESIS: "in *remembrance* of me" is our translation of this word in St. Paul's account of the Last Supper. In the great Eucharistic prayer it is used also for other commemorations, which make petition for the living and for the dead in Christ.

BASILICA: literally, royal (house). It was used for imperial halls of judgment, and the Christians preferred it as the name for the house of God. It is applied more particularly to churches which have the form which was established in the 4th cent., with aisles divided by columns supporting a clerestory with timber roof and flat ceiling.

BENEDICTUS QUI VENIT: the chant, "Hosanna in the highest! Blessed is he that cometh in the name of the Lord. Hosanna in the highest!" which is invariably sung after the TERSANCTUS.

CANON: a distinction of the Western rite, indicating the invariable part of the Eucharistic prayer which follows the PREFACE.

CASULA: see CHASUBLE.

CHASUBLE: the modern name for an ecclesiastical vestment derived from a woolen overcoat or rain-coat (a sort of poncho) called in Greek *Phenoles, phainoles, phainolion,* and in Latin *paenula, casula, planeta.* It is distinctively the Eucharistic vestment.

CIBORIUM: the *baldacchino* erected over the altar to give this small table due prominence in a large church.

CLAVUS: a narrow strip in color woven into the tunic and dalmatic for its adornment. It passed over each shoulder from one end of the garment to the other.

CONFITEOR: the confession of sin made by the priest and server at the beginning of the Liturgy.

CONTABULATIO: a system of pleating which transformed a garment into a ceremonial scarf. Wilpert discovers it in the Consular toga and traces it further in the sacred pallium and in "stoles" of the priest and deacon.

COTTA: a meager surplice, used by choristers, etc.

DALMATIC: an ample tunic, ungirdled, worn as an outer garment over the tunic, decorated with *clavus* and fringe. It was usually of wool but might be of heavy linen. It became the distinctive dress of the deacon.

DISCIPLINA ARCANA: A temporary aberration of the Christian cult, aping the secrecy of the Greek mysteries. It has left clear traces in the Eastern Liturgies.

EPICLESIS: prayer invoking the descent of the Holy Spirit upon the bread and wine of the Eucharist to sanctify them.

EUCHARIST: celebration of the Holy Communion—so called for the fact that this was essentially a prayer of thanksgiving, a *eucharistia,* which in view of the Hebrew form of thanksgiving (which "blessed" God for the gift) was called also a "blessing" (*eulogia*).

FRACTIO PANIS: Latin for "the breaking of bread," which was the characteristic name for the Holy Communion, and was used in no other connection.

GRADUAL: the hymn sung before the reading of the Gospel, while the deacon was ascending the steps (*gradus*) of the high pulpit or ambone from which for many centuries the Gospel was read.

INTINCTION: any method of administering the Bread of the Holy Communion by first dipping it in the Wine.

KYRIE: the Greek word for Lord—indicating here the "Lord have mercy," which is repeated responsively in the Liturgy, and is the only vestige of Greek which remains in the Roman Mass.

LITURGY: may be used of divine service in general but is more appropriately used of the Holy Communion, with reference especially to the performance of the rite and the texts which prescribe it.

MAPPULA: a napkin or handkerchief from which was derived the "stole" of the deacon and badge (now of silk) worn by the priest on his left wrist when he is celebrating the Eucharist.

MARANATHA: a combination of two Aramaic words which mean, "The Lord cometh," used in the Greek-speaking Church to express a lively and glad expectation of the second coming of the Lord (1 Cor. 16:22), and (like the BENEDICTUS) associated especially with the celebration of the Holy Communion (*Didache*).

OBLATIONS: the bread and wine offered at the altar, which our rubrics distinguish expressly from the other gifts made in the OFFERTORY.

OFFERTORY: the place in divine service when the offerings and oblations are made, with the appropriate prayers and hymns.

ORARIUM: literally mouth-cloth, a name applied appropriately to the linen towel or napkin which the deacon needed for his serviceable ministry at the altar, where he had to furnish water to the priest for purifying his hands and the sacred vessels. The deacon wore it over his left shoulder or on his forearm, as a servant might when waiting on table. It ultimately became a ceremonial scarf of silk, indistinguishable from the stole of the priest which had a very different origin, being a scarf to protect the neck.

ORPHREYS: gold embroidery, especially as applied in a conventional form to the CHASUBLE.

PAENULA: see CHASUBLE.

PALLIUM: an oblong rectangular garment of wool used as a cloak by the Greeks and eventually adopted throughout the Roman Empire by all persons of culture who did not need to emphasize their standing as Roman citizens by wearing the toga, which probably had the same origin but acquired a very complicated form. One end of the pallium was thrown forward over the left shoulder, reaching to the knee, while the rest was drawn around the back and under the right arm, then thrown backward over the left shoulder, where it was fastened by a pin (*fibula*).

PALLIUM, the sacred: the *pallio sacra* is a white woolen scarf, derived by CONTABULATIO from the garment of this name, once the exclusive distinction of the Bishop of Rome, now bestowed by him upon archbishops.

PHENOLES, PHAINOLES, PHAINOLION: Greek terms used for the CHASUBLE.

PREFACE: the beginning of the Eucharistic Prayer, beginning with the Sursum corda and ending with the TERSANCTUS and the BENEDICTUS.

STOLE: see ORARIUM.

SURPLICE: a very loose linen shirt with flaring sleeves worn incongruously over the ordinary garments of a clergyman when he is officiating in church. A smaller sort, used by choristers etc., is called a COTTA.

SURSUM CORDA: "Lift up your hearts" etc., with which the PREFACE begins.

SYNAPTE: a prayer consisting of a number of separate petitions "linked together"—especially of the deacon's exhortation which in the Greek liturgies recounts the subjects for which the people are asked to join in silent prayer.

TERSANCTUS: the Angelic Hymn, "Holy, Holy, Holy," etc. at the end of the PREFACE.

TUNIC, TUNICA: the indispensable outer-garment of wool or linen worn over an undershirt and loin-cloth. Even in the house it was not seemly to wear it without a girdle, and out of doors a cloak (toga, pallium, dalmatic, or *paenula*) would commonly be worn over it. It had short sleeves or none at all, and in its common form reached hardly below the knees, but had to be of greater length to allow for the tuck which must be taken in it by the girdle. Very properly, it was a little longer in the back.

TUNICA ALBA or TALARIS: see ALB.

TUNICA EXOMIS: the scanty tunic affected by philosophers, sleeveless and fastened only over the left shoulder, leaving the right arm free and part of the breast.

WORDS OF INSTITUTION: the words with which Christ explained and enjoined the sacrament of the Holy Communion. In the ancient liturgies these words are used without any anxious effort to repeat exactly the reports of the Evangelists or of St. Paul.

INDEX

Parallel passages and others where some importance is attached to a word are registered first. This index is not cluttered up with references to pages where a word is used without emphasis.

APPENDIX

The Christian Sacrifice, a recent book by Professor W. Norman Pittenger, deserves attention, and, as I remarked in the Preface, I have contrived to find here a place where I can give it all the attention it deserves. It is an attractive book because many things which ought to be said are said exceedingly well; but it is repellent because some things which ought not to be said are said too persuasively. For this reason it requires close and cautious attention. And, fearing that it may seduce ingenuous laymen who have not yet learned to discriminate, I cry: Stop! Look! and Listen!

My sympathetic antipathy for this book can be expressed only paradoxically: it is, with regard to its main contention, so clear and so misleading; so persuasive and so unreasonable; so sprightly and so tedious; so suave and so insolent; so radically liberal and so narrowly dogmatic; so portentious and yet so trite. These paradoxes are not invented, they are plainly discernible under the sleek surface of Pittenger's artful composition.

To take the last of them first, it is portentous that the book is written by a professor in our largest seminary, which also is the only one directly subject to the control of the General Convention of the Protestant Episcopal Church. An incautious man might therefore regard this book as an authoritative exposition of the doctrine of this Church. And all the more because Professor Pittenger was lately chosen to collaborate with Dean Pike in producing a book called *The Faith of the Church,* which (after a very meticulous revision) was published with the *imprimatur* and recommendation of our highest ecclesiastical authority, the National Council. And yet this portentous book is trite because it repeats, with some embellishments, the arguments formulated in the thirteenth century in support of the Roman doctrine of the Sacrifice of the Mass, a doctrine which was vehemently repudiated by the Reformed Church of England. For essentially this is what Pittenger means by "the Christian Sacrifice," with only one modification ("pleaded," or "re-presented," or "recalled," instead of "repeated," p. 42, 44, 59) which most Roman theologians would be glad to accept if they could.

Pittenger says on p. 99 that the title of his book "was chosen with no controversial thought." I have no doubt that he says sooth. For, though it is obviously the most controversial title that could have been used, it was not, in any proper sense of the word, "chosen," it was imposed by a psychic "compulsion" or fixation or obsession with the theme of sacrifice. No other title, it may be said, would be appropriate here, for the theme of sacrifice pervades the whole book from beginning to end. Therefore the title announces candidly what the book is about. I could praise such candor, were it not that every reference to sacrifice, in the broad sense in which the word is used in the Christian tradition, is artfully distorted to coincide with the specific and narrow sense of a propiatory sacrifice for sin.

Pittenger says on pp. viii and 4 that the understanding of the Church "as the living Body of Christ is basic to our whole enterprise." Therefore he properly begins his book with a long chapter on "The Mystical Body of Christ." It is not surprising that in this chapter the phrase "Body of Christ" occurs 45 times, but it seems exorbitant that in six succeeding chapters it occurs 67 times—a total of 112 times in a book of only 200 pages. This is not "according to the proportion of faith"; for in the New Testament it is used only 9 times, only by St. Paul, and only in four of his epistles—4 times as a metaphor in Romans and 1 Corinthians, and 5 times in a realistic sense (which Pittenger calls "mystical") in Ephesians and Colossians, which are more doubtfully attributed to the Apostle.

Unfortunately, we have to put up only too often with the tiresome reiteration of the phrase "Body of Christ." It is the watermark, or, among other shibboleths, the countersign by which Anglo-Catholics recognize one another. It is not so often used by unhyphenated Catholics, nor by them is it often abused. Not long ago a group of distinguished Anglo-Catholics was selected by the Archbishop of Canterbury to consider how the tension between militant parties in the Church might be reduced. They reported that, alas, there was scant hope of assuaging these tensions, but they made an important contribution to this pacific end by admitting that High Anglicans, beginning with so great a leader as Charles Gore, had abused the definition of the Church as "the Body of Christ" by interpreting it in a Hegelian sense, under the influence of the eminent philosopher T. H. Green. This report was entitled *Catholicism,* and I remember that two of the members of the group were men who are highly admired by Pittenger: T. S. Eliot and Gregory Dix. I hoped that this report would have a salutory effect. But upon Pittenger it had no effect. The Hegelian interpretation was evolutionary in a general way, but Pittenger, as I shall show presently, understands irreverently that the "living" and "growing" Body of Christ is subjected to the laws of biological evolution as interpreted by Darwin (pp. 25 f., 29 f., 32, and 71).

Seeing that the medieval argument in support of the doctrine of the

Sacrifice of the Mass is no longer very effective, now that we are better informed about the Bible and patristic literature, Pittenger comes to its aid with theories which are thoroughly up to date and in the eyes even of Protestants are radically liberal. No Roman theologian would feel free to use them because by his Church they are condemned as damnable heresies. Pittenger concedes in the Preface (pp. ix f.) that it may seem hazardous for him to use them.

First of all there is the kenotic theory, once popular among German Liberals, which emboldens Professor Pittenger to say (pp. 39 f.), "The human mind of Jesus was necessarily limited. . . . We are thus justified in saying that the full intention of God in the actions that the historic Jesus performed at the Last Supper included more than the human mind of Jesus may have foreseen"; and (on p. 95) "It is necessary to remark that even though we may not find this full sense of the Christian Eucharist in the human mind of Jesus, so far as we are able to read that mind, it is obvious that, once the orthodox understanding of the Incarnation and the reality of the Church's guidance by the Holy Spirit are accepted, the record of what transpired in the upper room and the Church's developing insight into the eucharistic action fit into a pattern which is perfectly plain and comprehensible. . . . The historic Lord, with his historic limitations, did that which was *required* to be done, if the purpose of the eternal Word to provide for men the true sacrificial action and the true 'supersubstantial' food was to be effected." These are awkward sentences, not written so clearly as Pittenger commonly writes. Perhaps he felt some embarrassment at saying such things. On page x he repudiates "mythological kenoticism." But what does he give us here? It is a kenoticism far worse than the mythological variety because it is more disparaging to Jesus.

Whatever may be meant by the phrase "emptied himself" in Phil. 2:7, we are compelled to make the admission, whether it agrees with the doctrine of Incarnation or no, that Jesus was not omniscient, either when he was a babe in the manger, or when he was active as a prophet. The doctrine of the Incarnation, if rationalistically conceived (as it is by Johannes Climacus according to Kierkegaard), is consistent with the haphazard selection of *any* man to exemplify the union of the divine and the human; it may even seem that God's condescension in becoming man would be better illustrated by a very ordinary man. But actually the choice was made on a very different principle: the Christ had to be of the seed of Abraham, of the tribe of Benjamin, of the house of David, and Jesus, according to all accounts, was a very remarkable man, in spite of the humble occupation of his father. As an autodidact he won fame in Galilee as a rabbi, and at Jerusalem he was acclaimed as a prophet. This means even more than being a professor! He "spoke with authority not like scribes" or professors. Hardly will a professor venture to say, "I am the truth. Verily, verily, say I unto you." If Jesus had not succeeded in gaining a perilous distinction, the civil rulers of his own nation and of the Roman Empire would not have joined hands to put him to death. They would simply have scourged him and let him go. The Church has always regarded Jesus as "the perfect man" (*teleios anthropos*), and outside the Church men have commonly agreed to regard him as an extraordinary man—"so extraordinary," said Renan, "that I have no quarrel with those who take him to be God." But Pittenger thinks him so exceedingly ordinary that he may not have known fully what was meant when at the Last Supper he took the loaf and broke it and distributed it to his disciples, saying, "This is my body for you." He did not know so much as Pittenger now knows about the significance of this sacrament! Such disparagement of Jesus does not sound sweet in a believer's ear. But it does not sound shocking to the sectaries whom Pittenger desires to please. For they feel no need of exalting the historical Jesus whose mind was deplorably limited by the ignorant environment in which he lived, in a little corner of Galilee and at a time far anterior to the great discoveries which have enlarged the compass of the human mind, since instead of him they have now in his mystical Body the Church (which they fondly regard as an "extension of the Incarnation") a fuller revelation which is constantly growing into correspondence with the free and infinite development of philosophic reason. But with this they renounce the Christian idea of the objective authority of revelation and reject the Catholic alternative: either "the faith once delivered"—or the autonomy of human reason. According to Kierkegaard in his "Book on Adler" (VII B, pp. 175 ff.) it is blasphemous even to raise the question whether Christ, the God-Man, was intellectually "profound," for this is an impudent way of slinking out of the obligation to obey him. One may admit that the Rabbi of Nazareth was in some respects not so erudite as a modern professor; but surely it is not extravagant of us to believe that with respect to God and to eternal life he knew as much as any professor in the General Theological Seminary. If he had been "empty" even of such knowledge as this, no one would have thought of calling him Lord.

So far as Pittenger's purpose is concerned the theory of "emptiness" is superfluous, since the Professor has up his sleeve the "form-criticism" of Rudolph Bultmann by which he is able to discount the Gospels, so that we are left without any reliable record of what Jesus knew and what he actually taught. He goes far beyond Bultmann when his disparages even the account of the Last Supper which St. Paul solemnly affirmed he had "received of the Lord."

What is the purpose of all this negative criticism? What bearing can it have upon "The Christian Sacrifice?" Its only purpose is to create a vacuum. Where we thought we could rely upon something stable in the Scriptural record—we find only a vacuum! Who can fail to see that this is perilous to Christianity as an historical religion? The vacuum, of course, proves nothing, but it leaves the Professor free to believe anything he wants to believe about the Lord's Supper—and he wants to believe in the doctrine of the Sacrifice of the Mass as it was formulated by the Schoolmen of the thirteenth century. So he makes one prodigious leap to the Middle Ages. Finding no reliable information in the New Testament, he might, in conformity with the Anglican position, have sought light upon the meaning of the Eucharist in the writings of the early Fathers. But he leaps over all this, not because he is unacquainted with the patristic literature, but because he cannot find there what he wanted. He makes only the lame excuse that Cirlot, Dix and others have thoroughly covered this ground.

But he claims that he is justified in making this long leap, or even a longer one, by the doctrine of biological evolution, which declares that the primitive form of an organism is never the most perfect form. A long period of development is needed before it becomes what it *is*. This is what Pittenger has in mind when he derides "geneticism" and the "genetic fallacy": "The genetic fallacy has never been more plainly manifested than in much of the discussion that has been centered in the Christian Eucharist. . . . This fallacy is found especially in the treatment of religious questions, and among those who have investigated the origins of Christianity it is a peculiarly tempting point of view" (p. 27). "When we turn to the central Christian rite, the tendency to fall back into 'geneticism' is present in many scholars" (p. 29). Many will ask with wonder, What is this "genetic fallacy" upon which Pittenger heaps so much scorn? It is the fond belief that in the words of Christ and the Apostles we have an adequate expression of the Christian faith, "the faith once delivered." He says, "The development of the primitive action into the full-orbed Christian Eucharist is the intention and purpose of the eternal Word of God . . . meaning a deeper penetration into the significance of the early witness" (pp. 81 and 53). I would not deny that, as Baxter said, "There is still more light to break out of God's Holy Word," but I wonder what the eternal Word and the Holy Spirit have to do with biological evolution, and I remark that the doctrinal forms developed in the thirteenth century can hardly be regarded as the biological ultimate. The doctrines of the Protestant Reformation in the sixteenth century have the advantage of being later, and therefore *ex hypothesi* more perfect—not to speak of the "deeper penetration" of this twentieth century. Can any one fail to see that all this is destructive of Christianity as an historical religion, as well as a repudiation of the

Protestant position as expressed in the Sixth Article of the Church of England? This article never seemed so important as it does today in view of recent *developments* in Roman doctrine. Pittenger's doctrine of "The Christian Sacrifice" is thoroughly reactionary, but it is at the same time rebellious; and the rebellion of individual priests (or laymen) unchecked by the Pope or the Bible would soon lead us . . . God knows where!

It is an example of suave insolence on Pittenger's part when he says (p. 93) "the Anglican liturgy is heavily weighted on the sacrificial side." He must have said this with his tongue in the cheek. For he is painfully aware, like others of his ilk, that our liturgy is heavily weighted on the side of communion and regards this as the culmination of the Eucharist. And he knows as well as any man how heavily it is weighted *against* the sort of sacrifice he has in mind, a dead sacrifice immolated as an expiation for sin, and weighted on the side of "a reasonable, holy, and living sacrifice," representing that, as disciples, it is "our bounden duty and service to offer unto God ourselves, our souls and bodies." I am quoting here from the American Liturgy. But Professor Pittenger knows as well as I that Archbishop Cranmer, suspicious of any references to sacrifice of any sort, such as are found in the latter part of the Roman canon, ended his canon abruptly, as Luther did, with the words of institution, and inserted in this truncated canon words which were meant to exclude expressly the notion that the Eucharist is a sacrifice: "for that thou of thy tender mercy, didst give thine own Son Jesus Christ to suffer death upon the cross for our redemption; who made there (by his one oblation of himself, once offered), a full, perfect, and sufficient sacrifice, absolution, and satisfaction, for the sins of the whole world." Although I do not share Cranmer's suspicion of every association of sacrifice with the Eucharist, I recite these solemn words gladly because they are true and because they are Scriptural; but I wonder with what mental reservation Pittenger pronounces them.

Pittenger goes far beyond Rome when he talks of "*the* Christian Sacrifice," as though it were the chief, if not the only, sacrifice Christians are expected to make. A Roman theologian would hardly be so indiscreet as to use this expression, knowing that the professors of ascetic theology would remind him of the ancient tradition which regards the following of Jesus, even if it be to martyrdom, as the preeminent sacrifice of Christians. Even the Jews had attained the lofty apprehension that a broken spirit and a contrite heart is a sacrifice dearer to God than any ritual act—even than the repetition or re-petition of Christ's sacrifice on Calvary.

Professor Pittenger is so intent upon proving that the Lord's Supper ("in the intent of the eternal Word") means the Sacrifice of the Mass that he grasps at a reed which pierces his hand. He affirms on

p. 90 that "the breaking of bread," which was a common name for the Eucharist, was a symbolical indication that the Lord's body was broken on the Cross, in spite of St. John's solemn declaration that not a bone of him was broken, and in spite of his own recognition on the opposite page that the breaking of the loaf was a memorable gesture of Jesus at every common meal with his disciples and signified fellowship or sharing. Some may suspect that this is another example of insolence—an attempt to put something over on the uninformed. "Written for laymen," says the blurb, but "thought-provoking" for clergy. "It is indeed provoking." But more likely it was only ignorance. For, if Professor Pittenger had known that the concordant tradition of the East and the West associates the *fractio panis* with the Communion and not with the Sacrifice, he would not have laid himself open to the retort which many a man could have made as sharply as I.

Owing to an unfortunate misunderstanding on the part of the English Reformers, we have a rubric which requires the celebrant to break the bread at the moment when he recites the words of institution which declare that Jesus broke it. But Jesus broke the bread *after* he had given thanks, and every other Catholic liturgy, expecting the priest to "do as Jesus did," puts the *fractio panis* at the end of the eucharistic prayer, and regards it not as an immolation of the host but as the invitation to communion. Our rubric reflects a Calvinistic misunderstanding, which becomes serious only when Anglo-Catholic priests begin to break the host with a clamorous sound to make known to the people that they are then breaking the body of the Lord. This is false pathos, for they are only breaking *bread,* since the consecration is not accomplished till the prayer is completed, by "the total eucharistic action," as Pittenger says on p. 63. But perhaps no theological professor except Pittenger has ever encouraged the action I have referred to. Although he recognizes the difference in our situation, he is so thoroughly committed to the Roman doctrine of the Mass that he insists illogically that we should ape the Roman ceremonial. He argues lamely on p. 89 that "there is no time or moment more climactically significant than the time or moment when Christ's words and actions, together, are dramatically repeated in the Eucharist," and that therefore at this moment (in spite of the fact that in our liturgy the epiclesis follows it) the celebrant should genuflect and elevate the host and cause the sacring bell to be rung to make known to the people that the miracle has been accomplished. This may be logical enough in the Roman Mass, but romanizers who will not become Romanists must have a logic of their own. It is a matter of course that Pittenger defends (pp. 139, 159) all sorts of eucharistic devotions which were repudiated by the Reformed Church of England. I will not dwell upon these matters here. But incidentally

I would call attention to a fact more curious than important, that we always translate *venerare* by venerate (p. 98) when we use the prayer St. Thomas composed for the festival of *Corpus Domini* to glorify the miracle of Bolsena for which he had a special devotion—whereas the Roman Church, which may be supposed to know some Latin, always translates it by "reverance." Is it possible that in eucharistic adoration we go further than Rome? And I would remark upon the curious fact which has no importance at all, that Pittenger on p. 163 derides the notion that "ritual" has anything to do with action or ceremonial: "For ritual means, of course, the words used, and not the actions performed, despite a prevalent misunderstanding of the term during the past hundred years." I blushed at my ignorance, till I learned that the Oxford Dictionary is as ignorant as I. For it defines ritual as "the performance of religious acts."

Pittenger grasps at a frail support for his notion that "the breaking of bread" means the sacrifice of Christ. It is strange that one who is so sceptical about the tradition of Jesus' words seems to entertain no doubt that the Lord said at the Last Supper, "This is my body which is broken for you." Yet none of the Evangelists report this word. Matthew and Mark report that Jesus said simply, "This is my body." St. Luke adds, "given for you." This is evidently a gloss, echoing the word "gave" in the preceding phrase. It is notorious that St. John does not associate the eucharistic sacrament with the supper in the upper room, but with the supper in the wilderness, where Jesus blessed and broke the bread—in no connection whatever with the idea of sacrifice. In St. Paul's account of the Last Supper (1 Cor. 11:24), which Pittenger is inclined to disparage, we find in some important texts, including the *Codex Vaticanus,* "broken for you." This phrase is familiar to us and sacred because it was used in the King James' Version. The R.V. omitted it, but now the R.S.V. has restored it, in spite of the fact that no modern Greek text presents it. Moffatt calls it "a good gloss," meaning that it was a gloss added by St. Paul. But the weight of authority favors the simpler phrase, "for you"; and, if it is properly attributed to St. Paul, he likely had in mind the bread, not the body. Instead of *klomenon* (broken) Codex Beza originally had the more striking word *thruptomenon* (broken in bits), which is appropriate only to the loaf and not to the body. We find this word also in the liturgy of the Eighth Book of the *Apostolic Constitutions.* At all events, in the Christian tradition "breaking" always meant sharing, not immolation. Pittenger knows this as well as I do, for he is an erudite professor, one of the most scholarly of our theological professors; but he was not able to resist the temptation of using, as an *argumentum ad hominem* addressed to the unlearned, a phrase we have all heard from our youth and few have been taught to call in question.

Pittenger might defend himself by appealing to the liturgies. The facts are these: the liturgies which are attributed to James, Mark, Basil and Chrysostom, as well as the Jacobite, Armenian, Coptic and Abyssinian liturgies, have in the Canon "my body broken for you for the remission of sins." The Liturgy of St. James has in addition the Lucan gloss, "given." But the Byzantine liturgy now in use has dropped both these glosses, and it seems likely that neither of them had crept into the Eastern liturgies before the seventh century. The Roman canon is earlier than that, and therefore it has simply the formula, *Hoc est enim corpus meum.* After the Reformation the Church of England added the Lucan gloss, "given for you," both in the Canon and in the first sentence addressed to communicants. The second sentence, containing an implication of sacrifice, "in remembrance that Christ died for thee," was added by Elizabeth to satisfy the extremer Protestants. But now the English Calvinistic denominations prefer for the Lord's Supper the Pauline gloss, "broken for you," as in the Presbyterian *Book of Common Worship,* because they cling to the Anselmian doctrine of the Atonement, and, like Pittenger, associate the sacrament almost exclusively with Christ's death as an atoning sacrifice—though, unlike Pittenger, they regard it as communion in the sacrifice, which is very far from being the same thing as a repetition or a re-petition, or re-calling or pleading of the sacrifice. Pittenger wonders (p. 110) that such Evangelicals and John and Charles Wesley emphasize this association. But all Evangelicals do so, because in this respect they are under the influence of the Western Tradition.

On p. 99 Pittenger deals unfairly with our Catechism, trying to make out that it means to subordinate "the benefits which we receive in the Sacrament of the Lord's Supper," viz. "the strengthening and refreshing of our souls by the body and blood of Christ"—to subordinate this to "the continual remembrance of the sacrifice and death of Christ," which Pittenger insists upon understanding as equivalent to the sacrifice of the Mass. In view of the text of the Black-Letter Prayer book, this is a disingenuous argument. It may also be said that the Lord's Supper, so far as it is regarded as a sacrifice, is not a sacrament at all, in the sense of "an outward and visible sign of an inward and spiritual grace." But we have no need of turning to the Catechism to know what the Liturgy means, for in the Canon it defines itself as "our sacrifice of praise and thanksgiving." A sacrifice of praise is not what is meant in the Bible by a "sin offering" or expiatory sacrifice. Again in the thanksgiving after communion our liturgy speaks *only* of "the benefits which we receive." "We most heartily thank thee, for that thou dost vouchsafe to feed us who have duly received these holy mysteries, with the spiritual food of the most precious Body and Blood of thy Son our Saviour Jesus Christ."

It is almost incredible that Pittenger, dealing with the Anglican liturgy, can make so much of sacrifice and so little of communion. "Sacrifice seems to have been the primary and all-over interpretation of the action, but communion in the sacrificial action was normal and regular" (p. 64). What an understatement! "No offering of the Christian Sacrifice has ever been recognized as right unless at least some communions are made . . . At least the celebrant must make his communion so that the action of the Eucharist may be complete" (p. 93). "Sacrifice once accomplished but also accomplished again and again" (p. 118). "Accomplished" must mean even more than "recalled," "pleaded," or "shown forth"; it seems to mean more than "repeated."

One may wonder why Pittenger takes such prodigious pains to explain away the manifest meaning of the Lord's Supper, why he magnifies the aspect of sacrifice and reduces to a vanishing minimum the sacramental aspect of communion or fellowship with God and man, which is plainly implied in the supper and aptly expressed by the word *koinonia.* He had to do this for the sake of salvaging the conception of the Mass which was forced upon the Church of Rome by the refusal of the people to communicate. When the priest alone communicated, there was no communion in the sense of fellowship; and when *normally* he recited the Liturgy alone, without a congregation to hear or see what he was doing, he could only be supposed to be doing something *for* the people—and what could that be but a sacrifice? This raised the prestige of the presbyters (*priester,* priests) to an eminence above the people of God which they did not enjoy in early times. The people of God (*plebs Dei*) lost their priestly privilege, not by the machinations of the ambitious clergy, but because of their cowardly rejection of their birthright. Making a virtue of necessity, the Medieval Church made this abnormal practice the pivot of Catholic piety, and in this path many Anglo-Catholics are fain to follow them.

From this one can see how much depends upon Pittenger's success in denaturizing the Lord's Supper. But even the Roman Missal bears witness against the custom which now prevails in the Church of Rome, first by its use of plural pronouns and verbs, then by frequent exhortation to the people to join in prayer (*Oremus*), and most strikingly by the invitation, *Orate fratres*: "Pray, brethren, that my sacrifice and yours may be acceptable to God the Father Almighty." We have nothing so explicit in our Prayer Book! For the Roman Missal is older than the present Roman practice. And even though it may seem to some that the forms of modern Roman Catholic piety, most of which date from the Counter Reformation, are preferable to such forms of devotion as are still preserved in Protestantism, it must be admitted that they are far remote from the spirit of piety which was exhibited by the Apostles and the Fathers.

I often ask whether any practice can properly be called Catholic which is not also Apostolic. To judge from Pittenger's faltering remarks on pages 16 to 26, his reply would be that the Church, as the living, changing and growing Body of Christ, though it has "developed" far beyond the doctrine and the practice of the Apostles, can still be called apostolic because its identity is preserved by the articulated structure of its "ministry" (he hesitates to say the hierarchy) which owes its *initiation* to the Apostles. This would all be very nice, if all these apostolic ministers, who possess separately or *in solidum* a *charisma veritatis,* were in perfect agreement about doctrine and practice. But, alas, they differ, and their differences obscure the "identity" of the Church. It would be far simpler to ascribe infallibility to only one bishop—as a check to the infallibility which every bishop, priest and professor is inclined to claim for himself. The infallibility of the Pope is perhaps the only practical alternative to the infallible Bible.

The interpretation of the Eucharist as a sacrifice is not forced upon us as it was upon the Church of Rome in the Middle Ages when the few people who communicated received the sacrament outside the Mass, so that sacrifice was the only meaning it could have. On page 131 Pittenger recognizes that in the East the sacrificial death of Christ was never prominently associated with the Eucharist. There the host is immolated on the table of prothesis (one might say in the sacristy) as a preliminary to the public rite, which was associated rather with the Incarnation. On the other hand, in the Church of Rome, because the Mass contains no express *anamnesis* of the Incarnation, this has to be remembered outside the Mass by reading the Prologue to St. John's Gospel. This indicates a fundamental difference between the East and the West. In the East today, as in the whole patristic tradition, the words of Jesus, "in remembrance of me," were interpreted much more broadly than they are with us, whether we be Protestants or Catholics. The remembrance was not limited to the sacrificial death of Christ upon Calvary, but it included the Incarnation, "the days of his flesh," the Resurrection and the Ascension—especially the Resurrection, for the Eucharist was the sacrament of life. This marks a difference in what Professor Pittenger calls soteriology, when he says on p. 5, "we are not particularly interested in the various kinds of soteriology which have been taught by theologians." It would have been more correct to say that he was interested only in Anselm's theory of the Atonement, which dominates the West and provides the basis for the Roman doctrine of the Sacrifice of the Mass, and that he had no interest in what Professor (now Bishop) Gustav Aulén calls the "classic" theory of Redemption, which was dominant in the New Testament and predominant, in various forms, throughout the whole patristic period.

Here, because I would speak briefly, I need refer only to Col. 2:15: "He disarmed the principalities and powers and made a public example of them, triumphing over them in the Cross." This strikes the key note of the Scriptural and patristic notion of the Redemption Christ wrought for men upon the Cross. It meant deliverance from the powers of evil, of sin and of death. The prime difference between the East and the West is that the one regards Christ as Victor upon the Cross, the other as Victim. Pittenger prefers to regard him as victim. Otherwise he would have no basis for the sacrifice of the Mass. For, though it is difficult to conceive that God needs to be reminded of the sacrifice of Christ, it is impossible to imagine that he might need to be reminded that Christ is Victor, or that there could be any sense in saying that Christ's definitive conquest of the powers of evil needs to be pleaded before God, or recalled to him, or shown forth* to him, or "placarded in his sight."

I think I can discern why Pittenger sacrifices to Bultmann on p. 9 what I, following Albert Schweitzer, regard as a "pillar passage" in the Gospel of St. Mark (10:45): "The Son of Man came . . . to give his life a ransom for many." Pittenger is fain to attribute this thought to St. Paul—because the word "ransom" is distasteful to him, for ransom evidently does *not* mean a propitiatory sacrifice. It points to the "classical" theory of redemption by Christ the Victor, not to Anselm's theory that Christ died as Victim upon the Cross to satisfy the righteousness of God. This was Anselm's answer to the question *Cur Deus homo?* (Why did God become man?). How different was the answer of St. Athanasius: "Christ became man in order that men might become gods." Nothing could indicate more strikingly the difference between the theologies of the East and of the West. But this difference is indicated conspicuously in Christian art, by the immense popularity in the West of the crucifix, the image of an excruciated victim, which has no vogue in the East, and indeed was not known in the West until the Middle Ages. It is indicated also by the figure of the Lamb of God, which in Rome was a popular theme of Christian art, whether in the form suggested by John the Baptist, as "the Lamb of God which taketh away the sins of the world," or with a reference to the picture

* These extravagant expressions of which Pittenger is so fond that he repeats them often prompt me to remark that "show forth" with which King James' Version has made us familiar in 1 Cor. 11:26 has in all modern versions been changed to "proclaim," as a translation of *kataggelein,* which occurs 17 times in Acts and in several of the Pauline Epistles, and has always the sense of a proclamation made to man—not to God. The King James's Version commonly translated it by "preached" and not many men are bold enough to preach to God. Pittenger, knowing this as well as I do, uses the obsolete translation "show forth" disingenuously to support his argument.

presented by John the Divine of "a lamb slain from the foundation of the world." The Greek Church had no liking for this picture, and when the *Agnus Dei* was introduced into the Roman liturgy (to be sung "at the *fractio panis,*" i.e. during the communion) there was a strong protest against this innovation. We may wonder at this unless we reflect that the seemingly harmless addition weighted the Mass more heavily on the side of sacrifice and widened the distance between the East and the West.

During the Middle Ages and in the climate of Western Scholasticism there were born after long gestation two doctrines exhibiting the characteristic traits of Roman theology and so closely related to one another that they may be regarded as twins, in spite of the fact that nearly two centuries separated their reputed parents: St. Anselm, who formulated the doctrine of the Atonement, and St. Thomas, who gave final expression to the doctrine of the Sacrifice of the Mass. It should be remembered that St. Anselm, whom we associate with Canterbury, was an Italian like St. Thomas Aquinas, and like him was a Schoolman.

It is astonishing to observe how differently these two Roman doctrines fared at the hands of the Protestant Reformers. While the doctrine of the Sacrifice of the Mass was vehemently rejected (chiefly because it was responsible for grave practical abuses), Anselm's doctrine of the Atonement was regarded as sacrosanct and (in spite of the fact that time and again it has caused disruptive explosions) it is retained unto this day—simply because the Protestants suppose that it is the only way of understanding the divine redemption of mankind. They cling to it with a cramplike grasp, having never heard of the "classical" doctrine of salvation, and never reflected that in reciting the one creed which is universal they affirm *first of all* that "for us men and for our salvation" the Son of God "came down from heaven . . . and was made man."

Because these twin doctrines naturally hang together, the Protestant Churches, having embraced the one, are not able to shake off entirely the other which they denounce. And we, so long as we suffer from the fixation that the Anselmian theory is the only adequate expression of faith in God our Saviour, may expect to be plagued by the reaction it will exert upon the doctrine of the Lord's Supper. Commonly, Western Christendom has been too much preoccupied with the sacrificial death of Christ. We emphasize it to a degree which is not "according to the proportion of faith" and which tends to obscure the importance of the Incarnation, the Resurrection, and the hope of eternal life. For all this, it may be said for the Anglican Church that our understanding of the Eucharist is not nearly so narrow as that of the Protestant Churches around us—which may account for the fact that this sacrament is not so dear to them and is too often neglected.

Here I have been drawn, almost inadvertently, into the deep waters of Systematic Theology, where I have reason to fear that I shall find myself far beyond my depth. For this is not my element, and I do not like it. Perhaps I may claim to have some proficiency in Polemical Theology. But, as I said in the Preface, "I am only infinitely polemical." I wish I could attack this book of Pittenger's without involving the author in my criticism; for I love this author, though I do not like his faults. Yet I must say of this book frankly, as I have said implicitly, that, though it is evidently sincere, it is not perfectly honest. I like sincerity, but I want honesty too. If Professor Pittenger did not sincerely believe that the Sacrifice of the Mass is an *articulum stantis cadentis ecclesiae,* he could not have defended it so warmly and so persuasively, nor perhaps would he have felt justified in adducing so many disingenuous arguments in behalf of it.

Perhaps I have devoted to this small book more attention than it deserves. I admit that it would not deserve so much attention were it not symptomatic of a wide-spread disorder; for presumably it registers correctly the views of an arrogant party in our Church. Thus it fulfills an ardent wish expressed by Job: "Oh that mine adversary had written a book," collecting all the allegations he and his colleagues commonly advance, and presenting them in a form which leaves them evidently open to attack. Or the ardent wish of Caligula, that the heads of his enemies (which meant all mankind) grew upon only one neck.

For this reason Pittenger's book deserves the closest attention. And perhaps it is appropriate that *I* should answer it—rather than one of our theological professors who might reply to it more ably. For inevitably the professor would involve his own seminary in what would seem then a partisan dispute, pitting one seminary against another. But I am not a professor of any sort, to no seminary in our Church do I owe such theological instruction as I have, and I do not clearly belong to any party. If I were to call myself a Protestant, I would not be believed, seeing that recently I attacked and, as I hope, demolished the favorite Protestant slogan, "Justification by faith alone." It has always seemed to me that the claim to be an Evangelical is an invidious presumption. There is nothing presumptuous in calling oneself a Catholic when so many millions use that name—or abuse it. But I fear that the Anglo-Catholic ranks may be closed against me because of my pronounced preference for Apostolic Catholicity, which makes me more sympathetic towards the Church of Rome than are many of the priests who ape its ways—who romanize without becoming Romanists.

It is my advantage that I am *nothing*. I am nothing but an old man appropriately employed in preparing to meet my God. I can see some sense now in the refrain of a hymn which as a youth I often heard at prayer meetings: "O to be nothing, nothing!" I am nothing but "a voice crying" . . . and crying only for more honesty. If on all sides we had simple honesty (even though it were without much love), most of our theological dissensions, if they were not quickly relieved, would be assuaged.

Today heresy hunting is fortunately no longer in fashion; but it may not be so fortunate that the frank repudiation of false doctrine is now so generally frowned upon that theological professors are afraid to stick out their necks by engaging in any serious controversy. For in the absence of honest debate what have we now? Not more peace and good will among men, but the grim opposition of partisan prejudice, which is the more poisonous because it is uninformed and inarticulate —too much heat and too little light. When trenchant criticism is discouraged in the Church, every Christian miscreant is encouraged to say whatever happens to come into his head, being assured that he can say it with impunity, if only he has the knack of saying it plausibly and not too precisely.

PLATE I

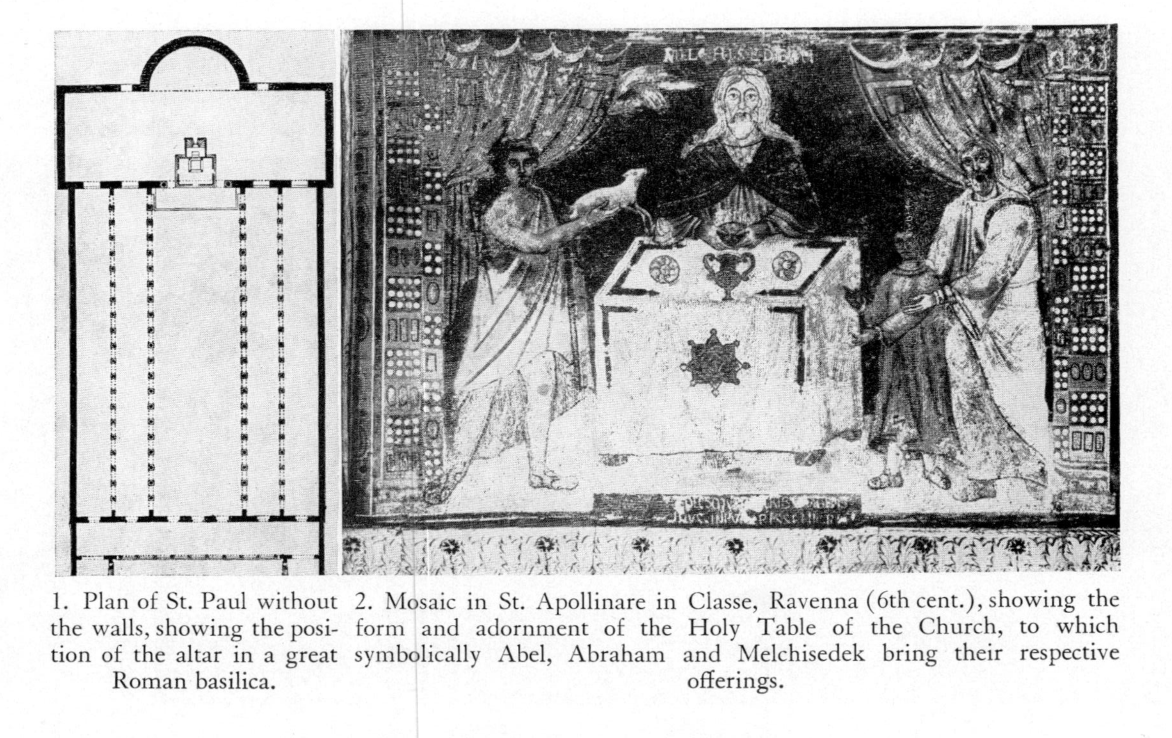

1. Plan of St. Paul without the walls, showing the position of the altar in a great Roman basilica.

2. Mosaic in St. Apollinare in Classe, Ravenna (6th cent.), showing the form and adornment of the Holy Table of the Church, to which symbolically Abel, Abraham and Melchisedek bring their respective offerings.

PLATE II

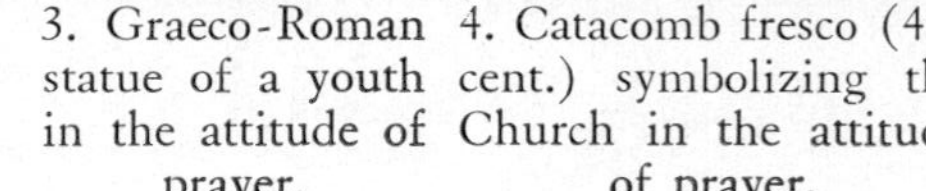

3. Graeco-Roman statue of a youth in the attitude of prayer.

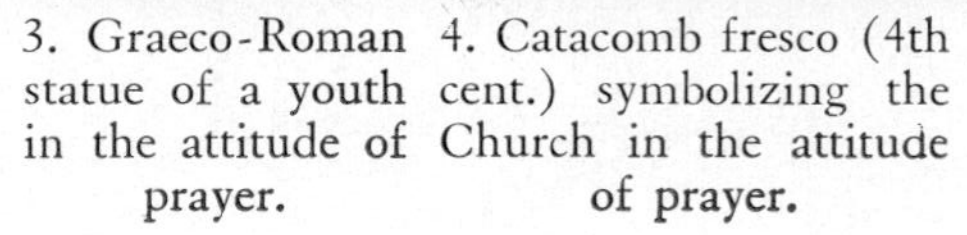

4. Catacomb fresco (4th cent.) symbolizing the Church in the attitude of prayer.

5. Panel of wooden doors of Sta. Sabina in Rome (5th cent.) showing Christ crucified in the attitude of prayer.

6. Mosaic in the Oratory of St. Venantius (about 642 A.D.) attached to the Baptistery of St. John Lateran, illustrating ecclesiastical vestments.

Above: The donor, Pope John IV, wearing tunic, dalmatic, chasuble and sacred pallium (scarf); St. Peter, with long tunic and pallium; St. Maurus, bishop, dressed like the Pope.

Below: St. Antiachiochianus, soldier, wearing the paludamentum, the dress common to military officers and court officials; St. Septimius, deacon, wearing tunic and dalmatic; St. Austerius, presbyter, wearing tunic and chasuble, St. Anastasius, layman (?) in long tunic and pallium.

7. Deacon carrying linen maniple. From an illuminated manuscript of the 12th century.

8. Fresco in lower church of St. Clement, Rome, near the end of the 11th century. Translation of the body of St. Cyril from the Vatican to this church — Pope Nicholas II in the procession and at the altar.

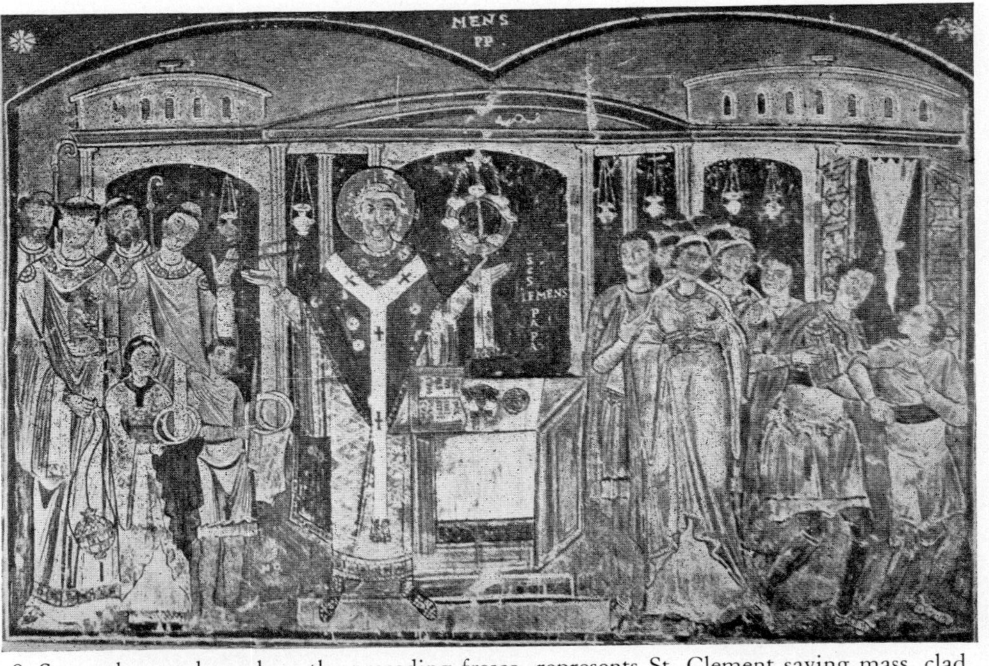

9. Same place and epoch as the preceding fresco, represents St. Clement saying mass, clad in the long tunic (alb) and what Wilpert calls a "baroque" chasuble. The sacred pallium has assumed the later form.

PLATE VI

10. At the right, dignified surplice of early Renaissance, by Fra Angelico. Vatican, Chapel of Nicholas V.

11. St. John Nepomuk, barely revealing his Rococo surplice.